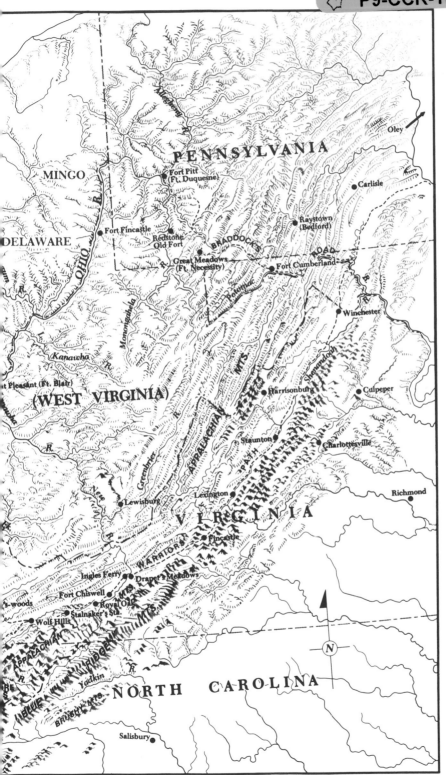

PENNSYLVANIA

MINGO

Fort Pitt
(Ft. Duquesne)

Carlisle

Raystown
(Bedford)

DELAWARE

Fort Fincastle

Redstone
Old Fort

BRADDOCK'S

ROAD

Great Meadows
(Ft. Necessity)

Fort Cumberland

Oley

Winchester

Kanawha

t Pleasant (Ft. Blair)

(WEST VIRGINIA)

Harrisonburg

Culpeper

APPALACHIAN MTS.

Staunton

Charlottesville

Shenandoah

PATH

Lewisburg

Lexington

Richmond

V I R G I N I A

Fincastle

WARRIORS

Ingles Ferry

Draper's Meadows

woods

Fort Chiswell

Royal Oak

Stalnaker's Sta.

Wolf Hills

BLUE RIDGE MTS.

APPALACHIAN

Yadkin

NORTH   CAROLINA

BLUE RIDGE MTS.

Salisbury

N

Daniel Boone

Daniel Boone

AN AMERICAN LIFE

MICHAEL A. LOFARO

THE UNIVERSITY PRESS OF KENTUCKY

Scholarly publisher for the Commonwealth,
serving Bellarmine University, Berea College, Centre
College of Kentucky, Eastern Kentucky University,
The Filson Historical Society, Georgetown College,
Kentucky Historical Society, Kentucky State University,
Morehead State University, Murray State University,
Northern Kentucky University, Transylvania University,
University of Kentucky, University of Louisville,
and Western Kentucky University.
All rights reserved.

Editorial and Sales Offices: The University Press of Kentucky
663 South Limestone Street, Lexington, Kentucky 40508-4008
www.kentuckypress.com

08 09 10 11 12   8 7 6 5 4

Frontispiece: Daniel Boone. Oil on canvas by Chester Harding, 1820.
MHS image number 386. Courtesy of the Massachusetts Historical Society.

Library of Congress Cataloging-in-Publication Data

Lofaro, Michael A., 1948–
Daniel Boone : an American life / Michael A. Lofaro.
p. cm.
Includes bibliographical references (p.) and index.
ISBN 0-8131-2278-3 (alk. paper)
1. Boone, Daniel, 1734–1820. 2. Pioneers—Kentucky—Biography.
3. Frontier and pioneer life—Kentucky. 4. Kentucky—Biography. I. Title.
F454.B66L628 2003
976.9'02'092—dc21
2003008805

This book is printed on acid-free recycled paper
meeting the requirements of the American National Standard
for Permanence of Paper for Printed Library Materials.

Manufactured in the United States of America.

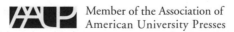 Member of the Association of
American University Presses

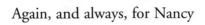

Again, and always, for Nancy

CONTENTS

Illustrations follow page 112

PREFACE

Daniel Boone! The very name evokes and echoes the epic exploration of the American West. Just as the existence of a changing frontier has always exerted a great influence upon the American people, no one, from the time of Capt. John Smith to the present day, is more central to the frontier experience than Daniel Boone. He is commonly regarded as the prototype and epitome of the American frontiersman, a near ideal representative of the westward movement of the nation.

The facts are impressive. Nearly seventy of his eighty-six years involved the exploration and settlement of the frontier. In 1734 he was born on the western perimeter of civilization in Berks County, Pennsylvania. At the age of thirty-one he ventured as far south as Pensacola, Florida, in search of a new home. And when he died in 1820 he was living on the western boundary of civilization in St. Charles County, Missouri, one of the outposts for outfitting expeditions to explore the Rocky Mountains. Boone seemed constantly to place himself upon the cutting edge of civilization's advance and did so with relish.

Boone also typifies the inner conflict between civilization and the wilderness of many of the early hunter-explorers. He was both the pioneer who paved the way for civilized life and the natural man who preferred the simplicity and rugged vitality of wilderness life as an end in itself. To Boone, the frontier was simultaneously a challenge and an inspiration, something to subdue and improve and to preserve and enjoy.

His paradoxical relationship to the wilderness often accurately reflects a basic and perhaps even stereotypical American attitude toward the frontier. If for Europeans the frontier was a boundary that indicated territorial limits, for Americans of Boone's day and their descendants, a frontier was more an area that invited and even demanded exploration. The real and continuing desire to penetrate the unknown in quest of new land and wealth motivated discoverers from many nations, but took on renewed meaning for those facing the vast wilderness of America. This same desire provides both a tangible and a spiritual link between the first walk into the forests surrounding Jamestown in the seventeenth century and the first walk on the moon, the zenith of exploration of President Kennedy's "New Frontier" of the twentieth century. Daniel Boone's life was permeated by this same frontier spirit and as such provided and still provides one extraordinarily popular model of national self-definition for his countrymen and women.

Regrettably Boone's unique relationship to his own historical period—the significant events in his life and their consequent bearing upon the development of America—is often a blur in the popular mind. Chronologically, few place him as Washington's contemporary or the one who encouraged Abraham Lincoln's grandfather to move to Kentucky. Fewer still remember that the march of civilization into the trans-Appalachian West and beyond, areas opened by Boone and his fellow "Long Hunters," also brought with it the legal mechanisms used so dexterously to strip Boone of the nearly one hundred thousand acres of land he had acquired under what he thought was just claim. And yet he was never long defeated or discouraged. If the lawyers took his land or if the settlers who followed the trails he had blazed ruined the hunting, there was always more land and better hunting to be found farther west.

It quickly becomes evident in examining the life of Daniel Boone that he was the continual victim of a restlessness that occurred whenever the population around him grew too dense. As his uneasiness with civilization increased, he remedied the situation by plunging farther into the wilderness. But in so doing he blazed a trail for others to follow. His example and fame unintentionally encouraged rapid settlement, which only renewed his restless spirit and forced him to move deeper into the forest. This outline of the general progression of events in Boone's life is far too simplistic to reflect accurately the total picture of his motives for exploration. It does show, however, the historical pattern that serves as the basis for the ambivalent attitude toward the frontier that marks Boone's image in biographies from 1784 to the present day, and provides an overview of the ironic cycle that at times seems to have dominated the frontiersman's life.

Irony and ambiguity permeate Boone's life story. Although remembered and enshrined for his role as a pioneer, he often was happiest following the same wilderness life as Native Americans. With them Daniel was comfortable and familiar, coexisting far more in mutual respect than in warfare. As someone who bridged and understood both native and pioneer cultures, Boone sought to avoid bloodshed, to negotiate solutions to conflicts, and literally to hold on to a shrinking geographical and cultural middle ground as the violence of native-settler conflict and of the Revolutionary War in the West escalated around him in Kentucky. His move to Missouri in 1799 resonates with the same dualities. In addition to renewed economic opportunities in this next Promised Land, Boone found a new borderland, a land that, like Kentucky decades earlier, struck a tenuous balance between civilization and the wilderness; Daniel found as well some of the same Shawnees and Delawares who, like him, although by different means, had been displaced by the pressures of land speculators and waves of new settlers.

Boone's story is further complicated because he has not been well served by most of his early biographers. John Filson's "The Adventures of Col. *Daniel Boon* . . ." was published in 1784 as part of his *The Discovery, Settlement And present State of Kentucke.* The first printed account of Boone's life, it made him a celebrity on both sides of the Atlantic in less than a year. Unfortunately Filson's bombastic, ghost-written retelling of the pioneer's "autobiographical" adventures represents Daniel as more a philosopher than a frontiersman and contains a number of historical inaccuracies.

It is also clear that Filson saw and portrayed Daniel Boone as one integral part in the working out of what would become known as "Manifest Destiny," a doctrine and a singular driving force envisioning the United States as a continental empire ordained by God to stretch from the Atlantic to the Pacific Ocean. The thirteen united colonies that existed when he wrote *Kentucke* were merely the starting point of what Filson and many others believed was a grand providential plan designed to civilize the West.

Yet the basic factual information gleaned from Filson's personal interviews with Boone and his companions still managed to emerge from the rhetoric of early nationalism. Since the "Adventures" consist of Boone's life from 1769 to 1782 and chronicle one of the most vibrant and exciting eras in American history, a number of quotations from Filson's Boone are incorporated in the sections of this book that deal with this period. The statements are usually described as coming from the "autobiography" or from Filson to warn the reader that Filson modified Daniel's recounting of his life and that these are not Boone's actual phrases.

These fourteen years are generally well documented in regard to Boone. His boyhood and to a lesser extent his later years, however, are times for which the full scope of events may never be known. Twice the aged Boone attempted to dictate his life's story to a relative, and twice the resulting manuscript was lost. Such disasters, of course, only enhance the value of Filson's work. But his narrative is neither the sole nor the main source of material for this biography. Recently published manuscript accounts of Boone's early life as written by Lyman C. Draper and of the firsthand reminiscences of Daniel's son Nathan and his wife, Olive, and of a young friend of Daniel's, Peter Houston, do much to flesh out the present portrait of the pioneer even though they, like Filson, tend at the very least to polish the speech of the pioneer somewhat. Together with the earlier firsthand reports and records of William Calk, Richard Henderson, Felix Walker, and others involved in the exploration and settlement of Kentucky, and with the wealth of new critical material that investigates Boone's life and its significance, these accounts provide a way of documenting far more of the pioneer's life than was previously possible.

The matter of tone and approach presents a major problem in writing a biography of a figure whose name evokes almost instantaneous recognition and then confusion as to dates, events, and places (other than Kentucky). It is perhaps as impossible as it is undesirable to write a biography of Daniel Boone that does not tend in some ways toward the romantic. His life often explodes with drama and color, the stuff romance is made of. In trying to give an accurate, orderly exposition of the actual occurrences in the pioneer's life, I attempt to stress the distinction between legend and popular belief on the one hand and documented fact on the other. In Boone's case, myth and man usually can be separated to their mutual advantage. Stories, tales, and events that persistently crop up in his life, but whose authenticity or degree of truth cannot be verified, are labeled as traditional materials. Those that are in between and interweave history with folk and family lore so artfully that truth cannot be discriminated from fiction are identified as such a combination.

My intent throughout this volume whenever possible has been to let Boone and those who knew him speak for themselves and thus directly to the reader through personal recollections, letters, surveys, records, and other documents that yield firsthand information about the pioneer, his family and companions, and the history he helped to make. To this end, the works produced by John Filson, Lyman C. Draper, Nathan Boone, Peter Houston, William Calk, Richard Henderson, Felix Walker, and others are used as primary sources and, together with a wide variety of appropriate critical materials, are extensively quoted, paraphrased, and interpreted in the text in the specific areas of Boone's life for which they provide the best information. While Draper's *Life of Boone* is not strictly speaking a primary source, it is essentially treated as such because of the wealth of firsthand information collected and incorporated into it. Although it covers only the first half of Daniel Boone's life, Draper's biography has been the mainstay of every serious writer who has dealt with Boone for more than a century.

I also attempt to maintain the flavor of these materials throughout this book because I believe that the value of such intimate views thus presented overcomes the slight awkwardness of language, the passage of centuries, imperfect recollections, and even the overt agendas of some of those who wrote and spoke about Boone, to produce a compelling narrative that both shows him as he was in his own age and yields a greater understanding of the significance of his life in its original context.

And beyond who he was, these views also reveal the ongoing creation of other Boones, ones constructed from the foundation of his life—but modified intentionally or unintentionally to mirror the changing views of Americans—and projected onto the frontier and its first premier hero.

Such an approach demands that the reader too be aware that present-day standards, particularly in the treatment of race, gender, and nationalism, are often at odds with the norms of the eighteenth and early nineteenth centuries. Even though Boone is surprisingly more "modern" in his beliefs in these areas than his companions, he is a man of his age, not ours. However, as I trust you will discover, he is ultimately best seen as his own man. The power of his life's story shines through the language, the centuries, and even through the tinted lenses of authors, to tell an extraordinary tale of an individual so involved with the creation of a new and unique country that he remains a national symbol for multiple generations of Americans who defined themselves and their character at least in part in terms of the frontier.

I should like to express my sincere appreciation to all those who have offered assistance and encouragement in the preparation of the first versions of this volume. For the 1978 and 1986 editions, I again offer my sincere thanks to all those who helped with those texts by now noting my original acknowledgments. These include Ms. Katherine Bartlett of the Museum of Northern Arizona; Mr. John D. Cushing of the Massachusetts

Historical Society; Dr. Thomas Field of the Department of Geography at the University of Kentucky; Dr. F. Gerald Ham and Dr. Josephine L. Harper of the State Historical Society of Wisconsin; Mrs. Eugenia Y. Jacobs of the Washington County Historical Society, Washington, Pennsylvania; Ms. Lou Delle McIntosh of the Department of Parks, Frankfort, Kentucky; and Ms. Lucy Ude of the Washington University Gallery of Art, St. Louis, Missouri. I extend my special thanks to Mr. Nelson L. Dawson, then editor of *The Filson Club Historical Quarterly,* for his help with my Boone projects, and to the Filson Club of Louisville, Kentucky, for its willingness to share its many unique resources and materials.

My colleagues and friends, particularly Drs. Richard Beale Davis, John Hurt Fisher, James C. Klotter, Martin P. Rice, Mr. Howell P. Boone, and Mr. Louis R. Boone, have given me words of advice and cheer at times when they were most welcome. I am grateful for grants from the Better English Fund, established by Dr. John C. Hodges for the Department of English of the University of Tennessee, which supported the travel and research expenses necessary to complete this book.

Both my parents, Mr. and Mrs. Anthony L. Lofaro, and my wife's, Mr. and Mrs. Stephen J. Durish, have provided the aid and understanding that only parents can supply. And finally, I thank my wife, Nancy, for her insightful comments, keen-eyed proofreading, and indexing. Without her dedicated help, the writing of this biography would have been neither possible nor pleasurable.

While there are many more institutions and people to thank for their help in the preparation of the present, far more comprehensive treatment of Boone's life, I wish to express my gratitude to the Kentucky Historical Society, the Henry H. Huntington and Newberry Libraries, the libraries of the University of Tennessee and the University of North Carolina at Chapel Hill, Houghton Library of Harvard University, Washington University in St. Louis, the St. Louis Mercantile Library Association, Stackpole Books, The University Press of Kentucky, the Natural History Museum of Los Angeles County, and all those who have generously allowed me to use and quote from their materials.

The John C. Hodges Better English Fund of the University of Tennessee has continued its generous support of my work on Daniel Boone. The Faculty Senate Research Council and the Office of Research at the University of Tennessee kindly provided funding for a summer research assistant.

My special thanks are also due to Dr. Paul Andrew Hutton, Mr. Gary Foreman, Mr. Steven P. Harthorn, Mr. Kenneth Cherry, and Ms. Joycalyn Ann B. Skinner. Their support and interest, along with that of my children, Ellen and Christopher, and as always, my wife, Nancy, have encouraged my continued investigation of a man whose life is a subject that always repays determined effort.

1

❧〰❧

"LET THE GIRLS DO THE SPELLING"
The Boyhood of Daniel Boone

In 1717 Daniel Boone's grandfather, George Boone, took the courageous step of uprooting his large family from the sleepy village of Bradninch in England and sailing to America. A weaver by trade, fifty-one-year-old George Boone was well past the age when one would normally determine to start a new life. But he was driven by the same two desires that would later encourage the zest for adventure and historic actions of his famous grandson: freedom and land.

As a religious dissenter, a Quaker, George Boone had heard remarkable tales of a sanctuary for Quakers in the New World, a colony founded by William Penn, where no one was persecuted for religious beliefs, with particular interest. Sects such as the Quakers, Mennonites, and Dunkers, the German Baptist Brethren, peacefully coexisted with the native tribes. And cheap land was available in the 28-million-acre land grant that came to be known as Pennsylvania. All this news must have seemed an answer to George Boone's prayers. Yet he was not an impetuous man. He refused to base a journey across the Atlantic upon rumor and supposition; he demanded direct knowledge and facts. Sometime before 1713, probably in 1712, he sent three of his children—George, Sarah, and Squire—to investigate the land of promise. Squire, the future father of the famous woodsman, shipped out as a cabin boy.

The prospects they anticipated and the land they explored impressed the threesome quite favorably. Sarah and Squire remained in America, and George returned to Devonshire with a glowing report. His father, however, delayed four years more before committing himself, his wife, Mary, and their children to the rigors of the voyage and resettlement. The younger George returned immediately and was wed by May 1713. Eventually the Boones embarked on their journey, traveling eighty miles by land to Bristol, where they took passage for America on or about August 17, 1717. By October 10, and perhaps as early as September 29, they landed in Philadelphia, a small but growing city.

The town of Abington (now Montgomery County), approximately thirteen miles north of Philadelphia, was a community composed nearly exclusively of Friends and was where the Boones first settled. But they soon moved on. As John Bakeless, Boone's first definitive biographer, aptly put it: "They did not stay. There was always a branch of the Boone family that never stayed. The Boones were wanderers born. They had the itching foot. Something called. Something beyond the mountains always whispered. They heard of distant lands and knew that they must go there."

Their first remove was only a few miles away to Gwynedd Township, and they made their home in the village of North Wales. George Boone was accepted into the Gwynedd Meeting after producing "a Certificate of his Good Life from the Monthly att Callumpton In Great Britain." His daughter Sarah married Jacob Stover and settled in Oley Township (now Berks County), a setting so pleasing to George Boone that on one of his visits in 1718 he obtained a warrant for four hundred acres of land on September 4. He likely moved the family to Oley within two years. Although a large community of Quakers had settled in this region, Huguenot and Moravian families were also present, a mix that testified to the widespread drawing power of William Penn's dream of a colony where all were free to practice their religions as they chose.

Squire Boone married Sarah Morgan, a descendant of the early Welsh inhabitants of Gwynedd, on July 23, 1720. He was a small man of fair complexion with red hair and gray eyes, she a large woman of dark complexion with black hair and eyes. Squire followed both his father's trade as a weaver and his propensity for acquiring land. He was also a good hand as a blacksmith and gunsmith, abilities he later passed on to Daniel. Squire's industry and frugality allowed him to purchase 147 acres in New Britain Township in Bucks County on December 3, 1728, and he soon erected his first home. At the close of 1730 he obtained 250 more acres from one Ralph Asheton. He, Sarah, and their growing family of four children moved to this site in Oley, which adjoined his father's land, sometime in early 1731. Squire soon rose in the esteem of his neighbors and his church.

Records indicate that he was a member in good standing of the Oley Meeting and was named a trustee in 1736 and an overseer in 1739.

A sixth child was born to Squire and Sarah Boone on this Berks County farm on November 2, 1734. He was called Daniel. His parents may have named him for Sarah's brother, the Reverend Daniel Morgan, or for a notable Dutch painter, Daniel Boone, who had died in England in 1698 and was perhaps a distant relative. If Daniel was indeed named for this artist, the boy, although truly appreciative of nature's beauties, exhibited little inclination toward static endeavors such as painting.

Although it survives for the most part in legend and anecdote, the story of Boone's early youth is nevertheless a keenly attuned preview of his future exploits. He loved his freedom and was irked by anything that restrained it. He easily forgot his duties as the family's herdsman and wandered delightedly in a wilderness yet unchanged by civilization. He was a hunter, a fighter, a stout comrade. And he was a boy. He possessed a boy's sense of humor and commanded respect as an adept prankster. Young Daniel was all this and much more. He and his family sensed that he was different, somehow unsuited to the more domestic aspects of their lifestyle. He naturally helped with the farm, learned rudimentary blacksmithing, and perhaps helped his father in the family trade of weaving. Still, it was only when hunting or trapping that he seemed to feel truly and fully alive.

Perhaps the earliest information about Daniel concerns a smallpox epidemic that broke out in Oley when he was a small boy. To prevent her children from exposure to the dread disease, Mrs. Boone kept them at home. Daniel and Elizabeth, his next older sister, soon decided, with the direct and irrefutable logic of children, that the way to eliminate the restrictions they regarded as punishment was simply to contract the disease, for once over it they could resume their normal activities. The plan formed, they sneaked out of bed one evening, stole away to a neighbor's farm, and lay down beside a victim of the disease, probably one of their stricken playmates. Then they jubilantly made their way home and slipped back undiscovered into their beds, gleefully awaiting the red blotches that would eventually set them free. Mother Boone all too soon recognized the symptoms that she had vigorously tried to prevent, and riveting her eyes upon Daniel, she quietly asked him to tell her "the whole truth." He made a full confession of his solution to his problem. Too concerned to scold him overmuch, she told him how badly he had behaved and fretfully added: "Why did thee not tell me before so that I could have had thee better prepared?" Daniel, as did Elizabeth and the other Boone children, recovered with no complications. His confinement was at an end and, as far as he was concerned, the pox had been a great success.

Squire Boone purchased twenty-five acres of grazing land in Oley about five miles north of his present home in October 1744. From the age of ten until he was sixteen Daniel regularly accompanied his mother, who always took charge of the dairy, on the annual migration to the site. During the grazing season, from spring to late fall, they lived in a small rustic cabin built under some shady trees by a swift-flowing brook. Daniel's job as herdsman tantalized him with many opportunities to neglect the cattle. Often he would slip away into the woods for days at a time. One of his relatives remarked that Daniel was "ever unpracticed in the business of farming, but grew up a woodsman & a hunter." His only weapon was what he called his "herdsman's club," a staff so shaved from a small sapling as to create a lethal point from the knob at the end of its root. During his wanderings through the woods and fields, Daniel became expert in killing small game with a single toss of the spearlike club. When Daniel was twelve or thirteen his father yielded to his pleas and presented him with a short-barreled rifle. Overjoyed, he took it upon himself to keep the family larder filled with fresh game. He became a crack shot for his age and began to take extended winter journeys to the Flying Hills and the Oley Hills, and to the Neversink Mountains "to the north and west of the Monockasy Valley." Daniel was never to stop his explorations; he would continue to range farther and farther in his hunts to the south and west.

The education of Daniel Boone is a much disputed matter. He insisted to his children that he never had a day of formal education. His older brother Samuel's wife, Sarah Day, is said to have taught him the basics of the three Rs, but a glance at any of his letters reveals that he never completely mastered spelling and grammar. One legend has it that his uncle John Boone, a schoolteacher, gave up trying to improve Daniel's composition as a lost cause. Squire Boone was said to have responded to John's despair with the now famous remark, "it's all right, John, let the girls do the spelling and Dan will do the shooting, and between you and me that is what we most need." No worse a grammarian than many a frontier hero such as Simon Kenton and George Rogers Clark, Daniel was, however, the only "creative" speller of George Boone's forty-five surviving grandchildren.

A whimsical tale surviving about the young boy's education concerns the tiny country school that Daniel supposedly attended. The teacher was a hard-drinking Irishman whose mood fluctuated violently. He would grow despondent with his charges, excuse himself from the room, and return minutes later with a wide grin on his face to deliver an enlivened, animated lecture. One day when chasing a squirrel in the woods nearby, Daniel stumbled upon the source of his teacher's inspiration—a bottle of whiskey hidden in the underbrush. After a quick conference, Daniel and the older boys hit upon what they thought would be a just compensation for the Irishman's all-too-generous use of the hickory switch; they mixed a potent tartar emetic with the whiskey. Needless to say, the next journey out to the thicket resulted in the return of a less-than-cheerful instructor, whose usually reddened face was blanched and strained. He called upon Daniel to solve a mathematical problem. Young Boone blurted out the wrong answer and was whipped with heavy strokes for his error. The blows kept coming. The other children screamed and shouted. The somewhat bewildered Daniel knocked the teacher down and ran for the woods. The Irishman, not Daniel, was dismissed, but Boone was said never again to have ventured into any formal institution of learning. In many ways, nature became his sole teacher, experience and observation his guides.

A typical boy, Daniel Boone had a best friend. Henry Miller, a cousin a few years older than Daniel, worked in Squire Boone's smithy repairing guns and farm implements. Daniel, as his pupil, became competent at metal work, at least as it related to the rifle. Boone and Miller were a congenial, lively pair who were truly fond of mischief. Any farmer they thought offensive might well find his wagon disassembled and its wheels handsomely displayed on top of his barn or perched in a tree.

One time, the prankish duo learned that George Wilcoxen, a neighbor of Squire Boone who had no training in the use of firearms, wished to borrow a long musket to try his hand at deer hunting. He asked Squire to load the gun for him so it would be ready "for early morning use." Unnoticed, the boys took the gun, withdrew the ball, and added six additional charges of powder. They then reloaded the ball and secretly returned the musket. Wilcoxen set out at sunrise, no doubt reciting to himself the various instructions given him by his friends. Boone and Miller had begun to doubt the wisdom of their deed; they knew the overloaded musket might explode and seriously harm the unsuspecting hunter. Their thoughts were interrupted by a noise that sounded like the report of a cannon. They ran toward the sound and, much to their relief, met Wilcoxen returning. His bruised face was bloodied from a gash in his forehead. The kick of that "darned gun," he said, had knocked him to the ground. Squire Boone saw Wilcoxen and earnestly inquired how all this mayhem came about. When Wilcoxen related the story and laid the blame for his wounds on the musket, Squire Boone vigorously told him that the load was so light he could have rested the breech of the gun on his nose and fired it without the least danger. The boys interrupted to ask Wilcoxen if he had killed a deer. He replied that he had a fair shot, but was so dazed by the force of the blast that he did not notice if he had hit the animal. His humor still intact, he wryly added that he thought "it was a pretty *dear* shot." Daniel and Henry found the dead deer and brought it in for the novice woodsman, who ever after loaded his musket himself.

Sometimes their escapades did not end nearly as well. They had learned of a dance in a distant settlement and decided to attend without asking Squire Boone's permission, for they knew that he would categorically refuse because of his Quaker beliefs. Hoping to make a grand entrance, they appropriated Squire Boone's finest horse and set off double-mounted for an evening's entertainment. On their return they tried to jump the horse over one of Squire's cows lying quietly in the path to the stable. The cow bolted up just as the horse was in the midst of its leap. The horse fell with a sickening crunch, breaking its neck. Daniel and Henry, bruised but uninjured, resolved to keep the incident secret. They put the saddle and bridle back in their proper places in the barn and stole stealthily into bed. Poor Squire never was able to figure out how a horse could break its neck in an open field.

Young Daniel was also involved in a boy's normal share of disputes, and his notions of frontier gallantry, at least at this age, depended upon actions rather than gender. Once, two needy neighbor girls, who were going to Mrs. Boone's to bring home the remainder of a plentiful catch of shad for their mother, emptied a pail of fish entrails upon the sleeping Daniel's face as a joke. They went home with the shad, bloodied noses, and swollen faces. Their mother soon presented herself to Mrs. Boone to demand that the young ruffian be punished. Sarah Boone, the most devout Quaker of the family, gave a reply that bristled with the Boone family spirit: "If thee has not brought up thy daughters to better behavior, it is high time they were taught good manners. And if Daniel has given them a lesson, I hope, for my part, that it will, in the end, do them no harm; and I have only to add, that I bid thee good day."

Clearly, the Boones were not typical Quakers. They were peaceful people, but people ready to defend their possessions and rights with their lives. When there was great fear of an Indian uprising, Daniel's grandfather George wrote to the governor on March 12, 1728, that though the general populace had fled there remained "about 20 men with me to guard my mill, . . . and we are resolved to defend ourselves to ye last Extremity."

Similarly, the records of the Exeter Quaker Meeting, the new name given to the Oley Meeting, further testify to the Boones' independence and reveal that they were not always in accord with the doctrines of the Friends. In 1742 Sarah, Daniel's oldest sister, married a "worldling," someone outside the order, and subsequently was disowned by the Society when they discovered that she was with child before the wedding. Called to account for both these matters, Squire Boone confessed "himself in a Fault in keeping them in his House after he knew of their keeping company, but that he was in a great streight in not knowing what to do, seeing he was somewhat sensible that they had been too conversant before." Five years later, Squire's son Israel married a non-Quaker, and although no scandal was involved, he too was disowned. On this occasion Squire expressed no contrition and in fact insisted on Israel's right to marry whomever he pleased. Still not recanting his position after a few months, Squire Boone was judged unfit for membership in the meeting and was expelled.

This accumulation of censure left Squire Boone in a quandary. He had fallen from grace with the Society of Friends and forfeited his leading position in the meeting. His businesses were doing well, but social pressures mounted to such a degree that he resolved to leave Berks County. The desire to see each of his children with good land, now too costly to obtain in Pennsylvania, and the rapidly decreasing fertility of his own fields due to contemporary agricultural methods undoubtedly contributed to the decision as well. On May 1, 1750, a little more than two years after his expulsion, having disposed of all nonessentials and having sold his home and farm for three hundred pounds to his cousin William Maugridge (or Mogridge), Squire Boone led his family out of Pennsylvania. Their destination was uncertain. His wife, Sarah, still a Friend in good standing, requested and received letters attesting to her good character addressed to meetings in Virginia, Maryland, and North Carolina.

Daniel may well have served as the guide for the family band that was comprised of Squire's three married children and their families, his eight as yet unmarried offspring, Henry Miller, and possibly some other relatives. The little caravan wended its way west to Carlisle and then down the Cumberland Valley and into the Shenandoah Valley. The Boones perhaps remained for two years on Linville Creek, a half dozen miles north of Harrisonburg, Virginia. Here, Henry Miller decided to leave the pioneers and make his home south of Harrisonburg, near the residence of Squire's good friend from Berks County, John Lincoln, whose great-grandson would one day be the sixteenth president. Daniel did not see his friend again for thirty years. When they did meet, one was a well-to-do businessman and the other a living legend of the American frontier.

Between the fall of 1751 and the spring of 1752 the Boones eventually reached the Yadkin Valley of North Carolina. In the present Davie County, Squire built his new home on Dutchman's Creek, a tributary of the Yadkin River, at a place called the Buffalo Lick. William Byrd II, who had explored the region in 1728 as he headed the Virginia Commission to determine the boundary line between Virginia and North Carolina, described the area in terms that left no doubt as to why Squire Boone settled there: "The Soil is exceedingly rich on both sides [of] the Yadkin, abounding in rank Grass and prodigiously large Trees; and for plenty of Fish, Fowel, and Venison, is inferior to No Part of the Northern Continent. There the Traders commonly lie Still for some days, to recruit their Horses' Flesh as well as to recover their own Spirits."

On December 29, 1753, Squire purchased 640 acres of choice land in Davie County on Bear Creek from the Earl of Granville and was issued a license to operate a "Publick House [a tavern or inn] at his own Plantation" in the following year according to the minutes of the county court. The rates for this bit of civilization were set at six shillings for a gallon of spirits, one shilling for a meal of boiled or roasted meat, and two pence per night for a good bed.

Surrounded by a wilderness abundant in deer, turkey, otter, beaver, muskrat, and some buffalo, Daniel, nearly twenty years old, evinced even less interest in farming than he had as a boy in Pennsylvania. The Yadkin region was the extreme western frontier and had very little of civilization about it. A mediocre hunter could bring down four or five deer in a day; Daniel Boone could kill thirty. He helped the family by transporting pelts, furs, and produce to Salisbury during the summer, but took advantage of every opportunity to indulge the hunter's roving life.

As his extraordinary marksmanship became common knowledge, his fame almost led to his first encounter with a hostile Indian. Daniel was an expert student of Indian habits and hunting techniques and until now he had only friendly relationships with his forest brethren. His sharpshooting, however, soon excited the jealousy of Saucy Jack, a Catawba warrior who felt his abilities with a rifle were the equal of Boone's. Despondent that his claim was supported only by himself, Jack, after bolstering his courage with whiskey, announced his plan to kill his rival. Daniel was away hunting. When Squire Boone heard of the threat against his son, he could not control his fury. He grabbed a hatchet and rushed out after Saucy Jack yelling, "if it has come to this, I'll kill first!" Fortunately for the Catawba, someone warned him, and he fled toward his village some sixty miles distant. The Boones were not a family to be trifled with.

2

❦

SOLDIER, SUITOR, HUNTER, EXPLORER

Both England and France were strongly pressing their claims to the Ohio Valley, part of which was later to become Kentucky, and Daniel Boone would get his first taste of Indian warfare all too soon. England asserted its right to the territory under the Virginia charter of 1609 and the explorations of Thomas Batts and Robert Fallam, who took possession of the region for the Crown in 1671. They claimed English sovereignty over the lands drained by the New River and the lands associated with the waters into which that river emptied. By claiming the New River, a tributary of the Ohio, they were in effect claiming the entire Ohio Valley. France, which cited the exploration of the Ohio River by La Salle in 1669 as authority for its continued presence, had perhaps validated its title more effectively than England by establishing a series of sparsely settled frontier outposts from New Orleans to Canada. England had no permanent settlements to buttress its contentions.

The 1670s and 1680s also witnessed a native versus native conflict for control of the Ohio River Valley as Iroquois war parties made repeated raids upon the Shawnee towns. They did so for traditional economic and cultural reasons, but also for ones directly related to European contact. The Iroquois sought to replenish the numbers of their tribe, which had fallen off drastically due to European diseases and warfare, by taking and adopting captives from other tribes. The extensive and continued nature of these raids took on an ironic European coloring as well because an additional intent behind the Iroquois invasion was nearly the same as that of England and France: to seize control of the Ohio Valley's great wealth as a hunting and trapping ground. Pressure from white settlements did cause the dispersed Shawnees to move their new homelands and to begin to relocate in the valley about 1715. By this time many of the new villages were mixed and, by the time of the American Revolution, they eventually became multi-lingual, incorporating different tribes, captives, economic systems, and cultures.

France's close-knit alliances with native peoples increased its ability to control the Ohio region, and the French had actively courted Indian support since the beginning of the eighteenth century with a good deal of success. Unlike the British, they accepted the tribes more readily (even though the Jesuits kept up a steady effort to convert them to Catholicism), intermarried, and did not consistently seek to displace them from their lands. And the French offered better trading terms than the English. The relatively small number of Frenchmen in the Ohio Valley—fur traders, Jesuit missionaries, and government officials—posed no immediate threat to the natives' land because the areas they took for settlement, sometimes by force, were proportionally small. By comparison, between 1745 and 1754 the Council of Virginia granted in excess of 2.5 million acres in the Ohio Valley to speculators.

England and her colonies had no united policy in regard to the Indians, and those colonies that emphasized trade, such as Virginia and Pennsylvania, competed for furs with each other as well as with the French. English influence, originally great among the Iroquois, Cherokees, and Shawnees in the seventeenth century, waned early in the eighteenth. By then, the Iroquois, though still strong, were no longer the overlords of various tribes nor the dominant force they once had been. When Pennsylvania recognized them as the sole rightful claimant to the land drained by the Delaware River, the Shawnees were disillusioned. The French exhibited very different views than the British—who did not openly seek friendship with a race they thought barbaric in action and culture—and successfully wooed many tribes to their cause.

In 1748 the Treaty of Aix-la-Chapelle brought the outright hostilities of King George's War to a halt in the New World, but still left the struggle for control of the Ohio Valley unresolved. Major merchants in England urged the immediate resumption of the war to eliminate France as a commercial rival, and their pleas were aggressively seconded by colonial leaders who hoped for large territorial gains. Although war was not declared, the Greenbrier, Loyal, and Ohio companies began to make significant efforts to settle the Ohio region, and concurrently, from 1748 to 1753, the French moved to consolidate their position with the various tribes with shows of strength designed to intimidate the Indians and prevent trade with the English.

Disputes along the border between the French and their Indian allies and the British over control of the Ohio Valley escalated rapidly. The French had to keep the English settlers east of the Appalachian Mountains; they would brook no migration that would drive away the game upon which their immensely lucrative fur trade depended. Great Britain's position, on the other hand, was more complex. While clearly not wanting a hostile power established in the Ohio Valley, the prospect of governing interior western colonies and defending them from Indian attack was far from attractive. Viewing America as a vast source of raw materials and a large market for English products, Great Britain as a sea power naturally preferred coastal colonies; but as the population of these colonies increased from both reproduction and immigration, the pressure for new land was sure to increase as well, land that the settled seaboard regions could no longer offer.

These military and consequent economic considerations meant that the lines of battle had effectively been drawn. The October 1753 mission undertaken to demand French withdrawal from Fort Le Boeuf at the Ohio River's headwaters in Waterford, Pennsylvania, by George Washington, a relatively unknown young colonial major of militia, climaxed in his bloody defeat by the French and Indians at Fort Necessity in July 1754 and snuffed out the last flickering hope of peace. In effect, the French and Indian War had begun.

Meanwhile, the government of North Carolina was busy repairing forts and raising troops to aid Virginia in repulsing attacks. Three hundred men under Col. James Innis marched to the Virginia backcountry but arrived too late to help Washington at Fort Necessity. Most of the men were recalled to defend the North Carolina frontier, but Capt. Hugh Waddell and his men remained to help as late as September 1754. Daniel Boone may have been a part of this group.

Maj. Gen. Edward Braddock had arrived in Virginia with two regiments of British regulars and taken charge of all British and colonial troops in America by April 1755. He was an arrogant, overbearing bulldog of a soldier, and a master of European warfare. He informed Benjamin Franklin, who was helping to provide supplies and transportation for the army's baggage in Pennsylvania, that "After taking Fort Duquesne [later named Fort Pitt and on the site of Pittsburgh], I am to proceed to Niagra, and, having taken that, to Frontenac. Duquesne can hardly detain me above three or four days, and then I see nothing that can obstruct my march to Niagra." Knowing Braddock's unfamiliarity with frontier fighting, Franklin recorded in his autobiography that he tried tactfully to warn the brash officer that

> The only Danger I apprehend of Obstruction to your March, is from Ambuscades of Indians, who by constant Practice are dextrous in laying and executing them. And the slender Line near four Miles long, which your Army must make, may expose it to be attack'd by Surprise in its flanks, and to be cut like a Thread into several Pieces, which from their Distance cannot come up in time to support each other.
>
> He smil'd at my Ignorance, and replied, "These savages may indeed be a formidable Enemy to your raw American Militia; but, upon the King's regular and disciplin'd Troops, Sir, it is impossible they should make any Impression."

Men destined to affect each other's fate were among Braddock's forces. Washington, twenty-three years old and now a colonel, was attached to Braddock's staff, and a British lieutenant colonel named Gage commanded the advance guard. Twenty years later the Virginian would besiege Gage in Boston. Kentucky's past and future also were represented. Dr. Thomas Walker, who served as one of the commissaries for Braddock's army, had penetrated the Cumberland Gap in 1750. And two lesser personages, Daniel Boone and John Findley (or Finley), had signed on as wagoners for the expedition and were among the one hundred North Carolinians making their way to the front under the command of Capt. Hugh Waddell.

Findley, an Irish adventurer and Indian trader, had recently returned from the hunter's paradise—Kentucky. In Boone his stories found an avid audience. From him Daniel learned that one could get to Kentucky through the great gap in the Cumberland Mountains, and from there follow the "Warriors' Path," a major native war road, to the Ohio River in present-day Mason County, Ohio. These fireside tales of a fertile land where buffalo and deer were so plentiful that they were there just for the taking excited Daniel's imagination and ambition beyond measure.

Boone's meeting with Findley was, in retrospect, perhaps the one bright spot of Braddock's campaign. The general's blunders were legion. He had no conception of forest warfare and no intention of using the colonial militia, the only troops experienced in Indian fighting. He humiliated them by stationing them far to the rear in his column, saying they possessed "little courage or good will." He added contemptuously: "I expect from them almost no military service, though I have employed the best officers to drill them." The march from Virginia began on April 2. Boone and his baggage wagon trailed close behind the British artillery as they crawled toward Fort Duquesne for weeks. The historian George Bancroft commented that Braddock's army stopped "to level every molehill, and erect bridges over every creek" before proceeding. On July 9 the force finally passed the Monongahela River and got within seven miles of the fort, "with colors flying, drums beating, and fifes playing the *Grenadiers' March.*" The British were "the perfection of military discipline, brilliant in their dazzling uniform, their burnished arms gleaming in the bright summer's sun, but sick at heart and enfeebled by toil and unwholesome diet."

Braddock's every move—his deployment of troops, reconnaissance, and bivouac—was a model military maneuver. The French were terrified and willing to surrender. Only a subordinate officer named De Beaujeu was valiant enough to rally a band of French soldiers, Canadians, and Indians to attack Lieutenant Colonel Gage's advance guard of 350 men. The British were moving along a forest path but twelve feet wide and were ambushed as they entered Turtle Creek Ravine. Their enemies seemed to be behind every tree, bush, and rock; all were under cover. Gage's men, though they outnumbered the attackers, could not mobilize to rout them because they could only fight in a slender line from the narrow ravine; only a portion of Gage's forces could fight at one time.

Little changed when the main column arrived. Braddock and his officers exerted every effort to form their failing ranks of regulars into lines in the open in the finest textbook tradition of European battle. The Indians marveled at the magnificent targets their red coats made, and continued the slaughter. Braddock was mortally wounded, De Beaujeu killed. Washington, rising from his sickbed, rallied the provincials to cover the retreat frontier-style. They followed the motto "Every man to his own tree," slowing but not stopping the rampaging Indian pursuit.

Having been ordered not to retreat, Boone and the other wagoners watched the regulars flee past them to the rear. Realizing that to remain with a heavily laden wagon would be suicide, Boone vaulted onto his team, cut the traces, and galloped to safety. Benjamin Franklin confirmed that the "Waggoners took each a Horse out of his Team, and scamper'd; their Example was immediately follow'd by others, so that all the Waggons, Provisions, Artillery and Stores were left to the Enemy."

Findley and the other teamsters who followed Daniel's lead were truly the fortunate ones. One previously taken captive, James Smith, stated, "About sun down I beheld a small party coming in with about a dozen prisoners, stripped naked, with their hands tied behind their backs, and their faces, and part of their bodies blacked." The historian Draper amplified this firsthand account, noting that the twelve did not comprehend their fate until the first soldier "was tied naked to a stake, with his hands fastened above his head, then tortured with red hot irons, and lighted pine splinters stuck in his body; and the shrieks of the victim, drowned in the horrid yells of his tormentors as they gaily danced around him, gradually became fainter and fainter." One after another, continued James Smith, the prisoners were "burned to death on the banks of the Allegheny River opposite to the fort."

To his dying day, Boone condemned Braddock's decisions and methods and was particularly critical of the lack of scouts and the failure "to employ strong flank-guards." Daniel made his way back to the Yadkin. For him, the results of the campaign were simple. He had his dream of Kentucky and he had kept his scalp.

Back in the Yadkin settlement, Daniel renewed his acquaintance with Rebecca Bryan, the daughter of Joseph and Alice Linville Bryan. He had first met her in the fall of 1753 when his sister Mary married Rebecca's brother William. Rebecca was now seventeen and Daniel twenty-one. She was a handsome young woman, nearly as tall as Daniel and marked by a dark complexion and jet-black hair and eyes. Her nephew later described her "very mild and pleasant speech and kind behaviour." Boone was described as "five feet eight inches in height, with broad chest and shoulders, his form gradually tapering downward to his extremities; his hair moderately black; blue eyes arched with yellowish eye-brows; his lips thin, with a mouth peculiarly wide; a countenance fair and ruddy, with a nose a little bordering on the Roman order." They went picking cherries with a group of young people, but managed to isolate themselves sufficiently to engage in a mild flirtation. Boone was taken with the beautiful girl and wondered what type of wife she would be. Feeling a little uncomfortable talking to Rebecca, Daniel drew his knife and began to slash absentmindedly at the grass around them. It may have been by accident or, as Boone ever after insisted, by design, but the wayward knife cut a large hole in Rebecca's white cambric apron, a rare article of finery on the frontier. He waited for her reaction, he said, for he chose this method "to try her temper." Rebecca neither wept, scolded, nor gave any indication that she was annoyed with the "accident." She was so pleasant about it that she may have seen through the entire scheme. In any case, Daniel had found his future wife.

Very few of the events of their courtship were recorded. One, a patently false story concerning their first meeting that gained widespread belief, seems to have been concocted by Timothy Flint for his 1833 biography of Boone. According to the tale, Daniel was on a "fire-hunt" one night, sighted his prey, and raised his rifle to shoot the "deer" whose eyes reflected the torch's light. Some premonition stayed his trigger finger, and the deer, Rebecca, bounded home yelling that she was being chased by a panther. A variant of the tale has Boone killing the kitten Rebecca held in her arms when he "shined" its eyes. None of the Boone children ever believed the tale.

According to frontier custom, however, Daniel did appear one day at his fiancée's door to demonstrate his skill in dressing out a deer that he had killed to indicate his ability as a provider. He launched lustily into his task, but was mocked by some of the young female onlookers because of the blood and grease that besmeared his hunting shirt. Daniel did not say a word. When the young people later sat down to eat, Daniel picked up the wooden bowl placed before him, studied it, and said, "You are like my hunting shirt—have missed many a good washing." The barb hit home. Rebecca's sisters were shocked at this comment on their housekeeping. Daniel had evened the score.

A justice of the County Court of Pleas and Quarter Sessions in Salisbury, North Carolina, Squire Boone married his son to Rebecca on August 14, 1756. After living for a while in a cabin in the elder Boone's yard, the newlyweds moved a few miles north and settled on Sugar Tree Creek in the Bryan family settlement area of northeastern Davie County, North Carolina. Here they generally resided for ten years except during times of impending Indian invasion. Five of their ten children were born in this period: James (1757), Israel (1759), Susannah (1760) and Jemima (1762), both born in Culpeper, Virginia, and Lavinia or Levina (1766). In the first two years of their married life Daniel farmed, worked occasionally as a wagoner, and made fall and winter hunts. The Yadkin area itself remained relatively undisturbed in 1757, even though the forces of the French effectively drove the English out of the Ohio Valley and captured forts on the Virginia, Pennsylvania, and New York frontiers. Although the English reorganized their efforts the next year and in quick succession conquered the forts at Louisbourg, Frontenac, and Duquesne, warfare soon reached the Carolinas from an unexpected source. Lured to fight for the British by promises of rich presents, the Cherokees eventually became disgruntled when no gifts were forthcoming. Most of the warriors deserted on the way to Fort Duquesne and, as they returned home, raided the frontier settlements of their Virginia allies and then those in North and South Carolina.

With tempers at a feverish pitch on both sides, skirmishes abounded. The period from 1758 to 1760 saw the North Carolina border embroiled in a series of Indian wars brought on by the retaliatory murder of a band of a dozen or more Cherokees by whites. Some Boones and Bryans took refuge in Fort Dobbs, a relatively secure structure that measured fifty-three by forty-three feet. Despite the fort's three stories of loopholes (vertical slits in the walls) that allowed for the simulaneous firing of over one hundred muskets, others of the family sought safety elsewhere. Old Squire Boone retreated to Maryland, and Daniel brought Rebecca and his two young sons, James and Israel, to Culpeper County, Virginia, by wagon.

Daniel may have enlisted as a wagon master in Gen. John Forbes's 1758 expedition against Fort Duquesne. If the story Boone told to a friend many years later is true, it would confirm his participation in the campaign. Daniel said that he killed his first Indian by throwing the attacking brave, who was brandishing a knife, off a bridge spanning the Juniata River and onto the rocks some forty feet below. The only troops near the Juniata at this time were those of Forbes.

When not engaged in a campaign, Daniel supported his family in Virginia by hauling tobacco to the market at Fredericksburg. The only surviving anecdote connected with his stay in Culpeper County chronicles a portion of one such trip. Isaiah Boone, Daniel's nephew, stated that one of Boone's employers sent a slave to give the wagoner "a neck piece of bull beef" for his provision. Boone, suspecting that the clammy meat could only be from one of Noah's cattle that had survived the many years since the Flood, told the slave to lay it down. The slave put it on a stump and gazed dumbfoundedly as Boone grabbed a piece of firewood and beat the bull beef all around the ground at a furious pace. His strokes kept the man dodging artfully from place to place to protect his shins. When done, Boone replied offhandedly to the slave's question as to the reason for his curious action by saying, "I thought it looked plaguy tough and I was only trying to see if I could possibly make it tender; but it's all to no purpose." The slave reported the incident to his master, who took the rather broad hint and saw that Boone ever after dined on decent fare. The scene is a telling one, both as one of the few recorded instances of Daniel's humor and as a none-too-subtle demand for fair treatment by his employer.

Hostilities broke out in the fall of 1759 because of atrocities committed by British troops and settlers upon Cherokee men and women. Although Attakullakulla (Leaning Wood or Little Carpenter) argued to keep his people at peace with the English, another chief, Oconostota (the Great Warrior), led the younger warriors against their supposed allies.

Daniel had returned to the Yadkin from Culpeper County by October 12, 1759. He purchased the 640 acres of land on Bear Creek "from his father for 50 pounds" on that date and served as a juror of the Rowan County Court on October 20. That Daniel continued to do his civic duty in serving several times as a juror is also noted in the book recording the minutes of the court. He likely enlisted in the militia about this time to help reinforce Fort Dobbs at the head of the South Yadkin River.

Although his family remained in Virginia during these dangerous times, Daniel always appeared to be too restless to enjoy the farmer's or tradesman's life. During the temporary cessation of Indian hostilities, he plunged into his beloved wilderness and made his first journey across the Blue Ridge, penetrating as far as Boone's Creek in the present Washington County, East Tennessee. About a hundred miles from the Cherokee towns on the Little Tennessee River he carved the now famous fourteen-by-nineteen-inch inscription: "D. Boon cilled a Bar on tree in the year 1760." The hunting was fine.

On his return to Culpeper and passing through the Yadkin Valley, Boone learned that a mopping up operation against the Cherokees was imminent. In Virginia he sold the fruits of his hunt and provided for his family, and then returned to North Carolina by late summer to enlist under Hugh Waddell, now a colonel. By November 1760 the Cherokee nation was broken, having been badly beaten on all fronts and driven into hiding in the mountains. Their villages and crops had been burned, and surrender was inevitable. Boone's contributions to this campaign are unknown. He perhaps took part in the expedition led by Col. William Byrd III of Virginia to rescue Fort Loudon from a siege by the Cherokees. Boone was present, however, on November 19, 1760, for the signing of the peace treaty at Fort Robinson, a newly constructed outpost on the Long Island of the Holston River that was built according to the instructions of Lieut. Gov. Francis Fauquier. The treaty with the Cherokees called for the return of prisoners and the restoration of trade. To show the good intentions of the English and at the request of the Cherokees, an official, Ensign Henry Timberlake, traveled to the native towns. He also endeavored to assure the return of all the white captives. By the next spring, estimates were that all but forty had been freed.

After Waddell's regiment returned to North Carolina and disbanded, Daniel celebrated with another hunt. Heading a group of Yadkin men, he again roamed through East Tennessee and then into southwestern Virginia. One of his companions was Nathaniel Gist, the son of Christopher Gist, Washington's famous scout. Led by a man named Burrell, a slave who worked as a herdsman in the backcountry, they made their way along a buffalo trace to the headwaters of the Yadkin. Continuing to follow the trace, they evidently entered Virginia at Whitetop Mountain, now a part of the Mount Rogers National Recreation Area, and from its treeless crest had a commanding view to the west. Then they made their way to what would later become the site for Abingdon, Virginia, and Daniel also explored along the Holston River into Tennessee. Thoughts of Kentucky may have been in Boone's mind throughout this excursion. Nathaniel undoubtedly spoke of his father's explorations in the land beyond the mountains, and he and Daniel probably made Kentucky a main topic of campfire conversation.

Concluding the hunt in the spring of 1761, Boone returned to his home on Sugar Tree Creek, put in and harvested a crop, and went to Culpeper to retrieve his family. They arrived at the Forks of the Yadkin sometime in 1762. The main business at hand was setting the farm in order; the next year in the life of the Boones was generally uneventful.

It was also a time of growing families. Jemima was born that fall, and rumors abounded that Daniel was not the father. It may have been, as some of the stories related, that Rebecca thought the long-absent Daniel was dead and was comforted by his younger brother, Ned. One source quoted Rebecca as saying that Ned's close resemblance to Daniel was the cause: "He looked so much like *Daniel*—she could'nt [*sic*] help it." All in all, the data was conflicting and too sparse to allow for accurate judgments. The only true agreement in the stories, assuming for the sake of argument that the indiscretion did occur, was that Daniel took the "surprise" in stride, gently comforted Rebecca, and happily accepted the newest Boone as his own.

While the Boones and most frontier inhabitants resolutely began the normal routine of farming, the constant flights to the forts during the French and Indian War had also bred a criminal element. To be able to reap a crop was so unlikely in those troubled times that some found it not worth the effort to sow. Even worse, they found an easy source of income through "appropriating" and selling the abandoned horses, cattle, tools, and furniture of the absent settlers. After the war as the thieves continued to ply their trade, irate border citizens in the Carolinas banded together, called themselves Regulators, and sought to bring immediate justice to the criminals. When horse thieves and other desperadoes were caught, they were tried by a kangaroo court and, if found guilty, punished on the spot. The Regulators justified their actions on the grounds that some judges and sheriffs were in league with the bandits or easily bribed. Some officials practiced their own brand of thievery by charging exorbitant fees or taxes for issuing marriage licenses, registering land claims, and acting on other matters that required legal approval. The people were polarized, often along political lines. The upheaval would last for five years before a truce could be arranged and courts could be established.

It was all too much for Daniel Boone. He tolerated no robbers, but took little interest in political intrigue. He had a simple solution to governmental oppression that was an excellent match for his wanderlust and desire for land—to move beyond the reach of the government and its agents. But matters were not that bad, at least not yet.

An organized group of a dozen thieves became the scourge of the Yadkin country about this time. Two of the outlaws even kidnapped the daughter of a neighboring farmer. Boone, stung by the audacity of the deed, headed one of the pursuing parties. They boldly pressed along the trail and came across the girl, who had escaped while her captors battled over the possession of their prize. Led back to the spot by the girl, they found one kidnapper disabled and bleeding profusely; the other had fled. The wounded brigand was jailed, but his eventual fate is not known.

A cache of stolen goods was found under the hay stack of a Yadkin man named Cornelius Howard nearly a year later. Confronted with the evidence, he confessed his guilt and agreed to lead a band to the thieves' fortress, which was hidden in the distant mountains under an overhanging cliff and protected by a stockade. The robbers were so careful in all their raids that they never created a path or trail that might mark the location of their plunder. When he later examined the hideaway, Daniel said that he admired the robbers' ingenuity almost as much as he hated their deeds.

With Howard's help, Boone and his men surrounded the camp, rushed it, and captured several of the band, including a couple named Owens. Large quantities of stolen goods were recovered from the stockaded cave and various other hiding places in the surrounding area. Mrs. Owens, evidently feigning illness, asked to see Howard. When he appeared, she tried to kill him with a concealed pistol. Frustrated when the gun was snatched from her hand, "she gave him a pretty fair specimen of low invective, branding him as a second Judas." The name stuck. All the captured criminals except "Judas" Howard were taken to the Salisbury jail to await trial. Howard, freed because of his cooperation in breaking up the gang, was ambushed and killed several years later as he was crossing a stream on his horse. The assassin was never apprehended.

Increasing settlement on the Yadkin forced Boone to range farther and farther for game. On these long rambles he acquainted himself thoroughly with the Great Smoky Mountains of western North Carolina. On shorter hunts, perhaps as early as 1764, he began to initiate his eldest son James in the ways of the woods. Sometimes the winter weather was so severe that Daniel could keep his little son warm only by buttoning him inside his buckskin hunting jacket as they lay before their campfire. As James grew up, he continued to accompany his father on fall hunts of several months' duration and gave every indication of developing into a true frontiersman. No one, certainly, could fault the credentials of his tutor.

Perhaps in part because of the rising number of settlers and the consequent decrease in effective commercial hunting, Daniel and Rebecca sold the Bear Creek tract of land to Aaron Vancleave on February 21, 1764. Rebecca signed the bill of sale with an X mark. The fact that Daniel was sued for a debt of fifty pounds in the Rowan County Court in March, perhaps for unpaid taxes, may also have spurred on the sale. The same county court minutes revealed numerous lawsuits over Boone's debts of usually less than twenty pounds that may have stemmed from supplies advanced for his exploring and hunting trips. Debt would plague him throughout his life.

On January 2, 1765, Daniel's father, Squire, died at his home at the age of sixty-nine. His wife, Sarah, would live on for another twelve years. Both were buried in the Joppa cemetery in the present city of Mocksville in Davie County, North Carolina.

Later in 1765 Daniel Boone had an unexpected run-in with a well-known old hunter named Samuel Tate who lived in the Sugar Tree Creek settlement. Returning from one of his hunts, he learned that Tate, a man who hardly ever left the woods, had neglected to lay by enough food for his family. Since he planned to thresh out some rye on his father-in-law's land for his own family's use, Boone asked for and received permission to cut additional grain for Mrs. Tate. Samuel Tate returned, was outraged at Boone's action, which placed Tate in a poor light as a provider, and evidently began muttering around the settlement that Boone was paying too much attention to another man's wife. Daniel was furious. He beat Tate severely and threatened to do so again if Tate mouthed any more of these petty jealousies over an act of kindness for which anyone but a fool would be extremely grateful. The incident was closed, but it added a bit more encouragement for Boone to move on.

Another tale involving Tate ended in a similar fight, but in this instance the argument involved shared hunting territory. Daniel supposedly kept deferring to the older Tate, giving him the best ground, but Tate continually enlarged his territory into Daniel's and bragged about his greater hunting skills. His words led to blows, and Daniel gained the whole range for himself, at least until the swelling of Tate's face went down enough that he could open his eyes.

A timely and unique opportunity presented itself at Boone's door in the person of Maj. John Field in the late summer of that year. Field, William Hill, a man named Slaughter, and two of Boone's other militia comrades from Culpeper County were off to explore Florida, recently ceded to Britain by Spain, with an eye toward the hundred acres of free land granted by Gov. James Grant on behalf of the British government to each new Protestant immigrant and an additional fifty acres for each slave the family owned. Grant was well known in the Carolinas because as a colonel four years earlier he had led an expedition against the Cherokees. Field had already explored a different area of Florida and was eager to return. Daniel quickly accepted Field's invitation to join the group. The Yadkin was becoming far too civilized to suit his tastes and Florida might just prove to be the solution. His younger brother Squire, recently married at the age of twenty-one, and their new brother-in-law, John Stuart, also decided to try their luck to the south. Daniel bid Rebecca goodbye and promised to try to be home in time for Christmas dinner.

Mounted on horseback and reasonably equipped for travel on mostly open roads, the men likely took a route south of Salisbury, North Carolina, past Charlottburg, taking part of the Cherokee path to the north and northwest to skirt the Catawba lands. Heading south, the party rode to Fort Moore, Augusta, and then Savannah, and circled inland along the Savannah River through Midway Church, across the Altamaha at Ft. Barrington, and into East Florida. Crossing the St. John's River at Cowford, approximately forty miles later they reached St. Augustine after a total journey of more than five hundred taxing miles.

The band of eight explored the eastern, central, and western portions of the colony and was amazed at the contrasts they found. At times strangely beautiful natural fountains and luxuriant flowers and foliage gladdened their view, but much of the country was wretched swampland, a nearly impassable quagmire. Along the many waterways the soil was rich, but two hundred yards inland it was too sandy to support a crop. On one leg of their journey to Pensacola they found so little game that they nearly starved to death. Stuart lost his way searching for food and stumbled back upon his companions days later in a pitiable state. When they encountered a camp of Seminole Indians, Squire Boone fortuitously gave "a small shaving glass" to a young girl of the tribe, allaying the suspicions of the Indians and gaining a store of venison and honey for the woebegone travelers.

Despite the paucity of game and inestimable numbers of alligators, bullfrogs, and stinging insects of the inland areas, the coastal regions, especially the bay at Pensacola, pleased Daniel. On the spur of the moment he bought a house and town lot and seemed intent upon making Florida his new home. Like St. Augustine, Pensacola was still in the midst of transition from Spanish to English rule, but it was more of a frontier town, as the movements of Choctaws, Creeks, and Chickasaws through it testified, and perhaps more attractive to Boone.

The eight weary explorers turned toward Carolina and may have struck out to the north and northeast on the most direct route home. Generally following the Escambia River through what would become Alabama, they made their way back to Augusta and Fort Moore and their previous route, arriving in the Yadkin Valley some four months after their August departure. Along the way, Slaughter, a gambler with luck on his side, won almost enough money in the towns along the way to offset their total expenditures. If the few deerskins taken along the way were added in, the account books balanced out.

Boone slowed his pace as he neared Sugar Tree Creek so that he strode into his cabin on the stroke of noon on December 25, giving his "little girl" Rebecca and his children their best Christmas gift. Throughout a joyful dinner he described the hardships and privations of his Florida adventures. Imagine Rebecca's surprise when Daniel announced his purchase and his desire to relocate the family there. For the first time, and also the last insofar as history records, Rebecca flatly refused to support her husband's wishes. She saw nothing favorable about the place for her, the children, or Daniel. They would be too far from friends and relatives. Boone mulled over his spouse's comments and agreed. The house, lot, and migration to Florida were abandoned.

Elizabeth Wilcoxen, a niece of Daniel Boone, married Benjamin Cutbirth about this time. Boone, often a lover of solitude, found in Cutbirth one of his most compatible hunting companions. On one unsuccessful trip into East Tennessee, a party of Cherokees robbed the two friends of a large quantity of furs and skins and all their equipment. They also hunted together for bears in Ashe County in the far northwestern corner of North Carolina. There Boone would often use any spare time to gather ginseng for market. For some reason Daniel did not accompany Cutbirth and three other Long Hunters—John Stuart, John Baker, and James Ward—on an astounding journey that began in the summer of 1767. They made their way through the wilds of Tennessee to the Mississippi River and spent one or two years in winter hunts and spring descents by river to sell their goods at New Orleans. The spring floods of the Mississippi River sometimes bedeviled their attempts; they nearly capsized on one occasion and on another would have done so if their main cargo was other than lumber. The ship floated even after it was totally engulfed by the storm-driven waters. The Mississippi gave Cutbirth a final example of its power as he stood on the bank and saw three acres of the opposite shore fall into the river "as quick," he said, "as the crack of a gun." Although the four men had amassed considerable wealth, the Choctaws stripped them of all their property. They also suffered badly at the hands of the Creek nation on their return to Carolina and vowed never to make the trip again.

Boone meanwhile decided to explore Kentucky in the autumn of 1767. After a dozen years he still remembered Findley's grand stories. He set out with his brother Squire and William Hill, who was Daniel's frequent hunting partner and who, according to son Nathan Boone, "was a man after my father's own heart. He was fond of the wilderness, hunting, and wild adventure—a jolly good companion for such a lonely life." Nathan also remembered that Hill and Boone "made an agreement that whoever should die first would return and give the other information about the spirit world. Hill died first, but Father used to say he never received the promised intelligence from the spirit land. I would suppose he [Hill] died not long after this trip to the Big Sandy River, as I heard no more of him. I would assume if he had been living, he would probably have been on the Kentucky hunt in 1769–1771, as he and father were such great cronies."

Daniel, Squire, and Hill crossed the Blue Ridge and Allegheny Mountains and the Holston and Clinch River Valleys and reached the Russell Fork in Virginia of Kentucky's Big Sandy River. He believed the Sandy would lead them to the Ohio and provide a natural entrance into Kentucky. They followed its banks for about one hundred miles on a journey that put them west of the Cumberland Mountains. Here they were "ketched in a snow storm" and elected to keep winter camp near a salt spring ten miles west of the present town of Prestonsburg, Kentucky. Since great numbers of buffalo and deer frequented the spring, there was no want of fresh meat. Boone killed his first buffalo here. But as the winter weather mellowed, the journey west was hampered by increasingly rugged terrain. The forbidding hills, overrun with laurel, forced them to abandon their quest and trudge back to the Yadkin.

Boone and the others did not realize that they had been in Kentucky. Only a few days' journey would have brought them to the fertile plains of bluegrass and cane that Findley had used to captivate his imagination.

3

∽∽ ∾∾

"IN QUEST OF THE COUNTRY
OF KENTUCKE"

Boone had now explored to the north, south, east, and west. Daniel weighed the advantages and drawbacks of emigration in each general direction and determined that his new home would be to the west, to the land of greatest risk and greatest reward—Kentucky. Boone and many other Americans who drew the same conclusion were, in effect, willing to disregard the British Proclamation of 1763, which forbade settlement west of the Alleghenies.

According to Lord Barrington, England intended, after conquering and winning the Ohio Valley, to maintain the region from the mountains to the Mississippi as a desert for the Indians to hunt in and to inhabit. Any wholesale incursion into the natives' hunting grounds by the colonists would ignite a destructive war that would in turn disrupt the lucrative fur and Indian trade that occupied so much of the London Board of Trade's attention. This Indian "preserve" theory stemmed in part from contemporary English thought on the appropriate economic role of the colonies. Completely subservient to the commercial needs and desires of the mother country, colonies existed only for the purpose of trade. The colonists and the natives were the suppliers of raw materials and the market for products manufactured in England.

Commercial worries also often were tinged with political concerns. Practically speaking, the West and Canada were limitless areas whose remoteness from the Atlantic seaboard would place aggressive settlers beyond English mercantile control. The fear was that they might organize trading with the Indians that would limit the availability of cheap raw materials, or might even set up primitive factories that would reduce the colonies' demand for British manufactured goods. Underlying all these apprehensions was the disturbing concept that emigration to the distant territories would make the new settlements all but ungovernable. Unthinkable as it was at the time, such a migration also would inevitably encourage the independence of the colonies.

The Proclamation of 1763 was untenable at the time of its decree. The Carolinas, Virginia, Connecticut, and Pennsylvania had charters that originally granted them land west of the Allegheny Mountains. Even though Parliament overrode the charters, the British could spare no troops to enforce the ban on migration because of the mounting crisis over colonial taxation. Additionally, the Crown previously had no uniform Indian policy and had left negotiations and agreements up to each of the colonies. The resulting overlap in alliances and boundaries threw the actual ownership of various tracts of land into doubt and made the natives suspicious of the whites' true intentions in the Ohio Valley. To many colonists it seemed that possession would determine legal title in this ambiguous situation. An additional incentive to settlement in the forbidden region was the growing discontent of people with their present lot. New outposts sprang up rapidly as settlers sought a better life in the West.

No exception to this trend, Daniel Boone moved westward three times from 1766 to 1768. Game was getting scarce in North Carolina around Sugar Tree Creek and the increasing population was more and more oppressed by the extortions of court clerks, tax gatherers, sheriffs, and lawyers. In one common example of fraud at the time, land agents issued patents and later discovered that one of the many titles of the landholder (the Earl of Granville) had been "mistakenly" omitted. The patents had to be reissued and a second fee paid or the title would be declared worthless. To avoid such problems, Boone first moved sixty miles northwest toward the headwaters of the Yadkin, to a cabin in the foothills of the Brushy Mountains. The next year the family traveled five miles farther upriver, where Daniel erected another cabin about a half mile up Beaver Creek. He finally settled on the southern bank of the Upper Yadkin just above the mouth of Beaver Creek.

His new situation pleased Boone a great deal. He had more game, less aggravation, and increased freedom to seek the exhilaration of long hunts. On one such trip in early autumn, Daniel observed an unusually large bear in ragged condition making its way generally to the west. Still using the camp in late December, Boone and his party saw the bear returning on the exact same route. There could be no mistaking the rare and distinctive white stripe on its nose. One of the men shot and killed the bear. It was so well-fattened that Daniel knew that it had traveled a great distance because there was no respectable mast of nuts to feast upon that year closer than the westernmost reaches of the Cherokee territory "of the Tombigbee River and Bear Creek." Always one to learn from nature, Boone ever after took note of the westward autumn routes of bears and was always certain of taking fine game on their return.

The hunter, of course, could also become the hunted. On another winter night, near the present city of Jonesborough in East Tennessee, Daniel was aroused from a deep sleep when his snow-covered blanket was gently raised by a Cherokee brave. The warrior recognized Boone and delightedly exclaimed, "Ah, Wide-Mouth, have I got you now?" Undaunted, Daniel got up and gave each of the band a hearty handshake and stated how happy he was to see his brothers. After exchanging civilities, news, and comments on the hunting (Daniel undoubtedly knew a little of the Indian tongue, and the Cherokees probably spoke some English), Boone was allowed to depart. He lost no time in putting a considerable distance between himself and his "brothers."

The Boones received an unexpected visitor during the winter of 1768–1769. Over thirteen years had elapsed since Braddock's defeat, but somehow John Findley, now an itinerant peddler, had found his old comrade's rustic cabin on the Upper Yadkin. He had again descended the Ohio in 1767 and carried on a far more successful fur-trading business with the Indians than he had in 1752–1753. But one man in a canoe could bring out only so much in goods. He wished to return to that land of quick profit by an overland route but readily admitted he was no expert woodsman. Rivers or Indians had always been his guides. When he heard Daniel and Squire relate their failure to reach Kentucky by way of the Big Sandy, Findley explained, in more detail than he had years before, how the Warriors' Path, a north-south trail used by the Cherokees to attack the Shawnees and other northern Indian tribes, led through a gap in the Cumberland Mountains and into Kentucky. But Findley was unsure of how to find an overland route to the Warriors' Path. He knew it was farther west than the Boones had penetrated in 1767, but that was all. He needed a guide. Daniel did not have to be asked twice.

Certainly Findley's visit was a turning point in Boone's life. Daniel's "scratch" farming, never vigorously pursued, barely provided for his family. He was being sued for unpaid debts at the court in Salisbury and consequently was mired deeper in debt by the fees he owed to Richard Henderson's law firm. Judge Henderson was himself interested in western land speculation on a grand scale. As early as 1764 Boone may have been gathering information about the trans-Appalachian wilderness from hunters and trappers; one source stated that Boone said that he was employed by Henderson and company at the time to explore this region. However, Daniel declared that he did not work for Henderson until 1774.

No matter what the level or the time frame of Boone's involvement with Henderson, the problem remained that the land Henderson sought to gain through a royal grant was acknowledged as belonging to the Cherokees by the treaty signed in October 1768 at Hard Labor, South Carolina. This treaty, coupled with the ever-increasing white migration, made it imperative that Henderson negotiate directly with the Indians as quickly as possible. When Boone appeared in court in March 1769, he was accompanied by his brother-in-law John Stuart, the husband of his sister Hannah, and by John Findley. Henderson was to defend Boone. Although no one can be sure, it is likely that the coincidence of Boone's desires and Henderson's needs made Kentucky a far more discussed topic than the lawsuit. Henderson, probably also at this meeting, may have agreed to finance an expedition.

Boone, Stuart, and Findley, with three other men—Joseph Holden, James Mooney, and William Cooley or Cool, who were employed as cooks, camp keepers, and hunters—constituted the band of adventurers. All the men put in their corn crops and Squire remained behind to help all the families with the harvest. According to Daniel's autobiography, the six men left Boone's cabin on the Upper Yadkin on May 1, 1769, "in quest of the country of Kentucke." They likely followed the Route of the Great Traders and Warriors' Path west-northwest generally along the Yadkin River, scaled the Blue Ridge, crossed the three forks of New River, and "passed over Stone Mountain at a place called *'The Stairs'.*" They proceeded over Iron Mountain, across Holston Valley to Wolf Hills, traveled west on the Warriors' Path through Moccasin Gap, and across the Clinch River, Powell's Mountain, and Walden's Ridge. Upon entering the Powell River Valley, they found Joseph Martin's party erecting the then westernmost settlement of Martin's Station and ran across a hunter's trail that led them through Cumberland Gap to the Warriors' Path. In so doing, they walked in the footsteps of Dr. Thomas Walker, who in 1750 had explored some of the region and named the Gap to honor the Duke of Cumberland. Boone's party followed the path north for a few miles, cut a new trail to the west, and finally camped at Round Stone Lick Fork on the west branch of the Rockcastle River.

Believing that the meadowlands of Kentucky were close at hand to the camp, Daniel set off to climb the highest knob on the distant ridge separating the Rockcastle and Kentucky Rivers. From the summit of what became known as Pilot Knob or Pilot View, he saw his dream. He could see what is now Garrard and Madison Counties, and beyond. Findley, meanwhile, had gone off in search of his previous trading site on what became known as Lulbegrud Creek. Rather than a Native American name, the word was a sounded-out frontier version of the city of Lorbrulgrud, the capital of the gigantic Brobdingnagian people in Jonathan Swift's *Gulliver's Travels,* a book that was among Boone's favorites.

Findley had an easy task. The Warriors' Path, which ran along the west bank of a creek and crossed the Kentucky River, led straight to the Shawnee town of Eskippakithiki on Lulbegrud. He returned about ten days later with his report. The adventurers soon crossed the ridge near Pilot Knob, which Boone had previously ascended, and by June 7 made their first base camp near the creek Findley had followed. Its name still bears testimony to their presence—Station Camp Creek.

Of necessity (and pleasure for Daniel), hunting was their immediate task. Deerskins were now in prime condition and were needed in quantity to repay the money needed to finance the journey, and deer abounded in the Kentucky and Red River regions to the north of their camp. Since the average skin weighed roughly two and one-half pounds and brought forty cents a pound at market, each was worth one dollar, or, in hunter's parlance, "one buck." The hunters worked in pairs. Boone and Stuart formed one team and Findley and one of the camp keepers the other. The remaining camp keepers had the job of preparing the skins for market and "jerking" enough meat for winter and spring supply. All went well. Over the course of six months, no matter how many hunts and excursions Boone made, he continued to marvel at the beauty around him. The "autobiography" recorded that even in winter he could say, "Nature was here a series of wonders, and a fund of delight."

Boone and Stuart went hunting on December 22 as they had done so many times before. They had yet to see the first sign of Indians. But near the Kentucky River at the end of that day, they were surprised by a mounted party of Shawnee braves on their way home to Ohio from hunting on the Green River. Capt. Will Emery, their leader, demanded to see their camps.

Poised tomahawks indicated the consequence of refusal. Calm in the face of danger, Daniel "cheerfully" agreed and set slowly about leading the Shawnees to each of their outcamps, where the plunder would be insignificant. At the first stop, Boone managed silently and unnoticed to warn off the camp keeper. He felt sure that the man would head immediately to the main camp on Station Camp Creek, warn the others, and remove the accumulated skins of six months' hunting.

Boone was amazed and dismayed, when they ultimately came to the main camp, for nothing had been taken away. He later remarked that truly "the time of our sorrow was now arrived." The Indians confiscated the skins, guns, ammunition, horses, and every other article of value. Captain Will, technically at peace with the English and well pleased with his good fortune, equipped each captive with a small trading gun, some powder and shot, a doeskin for patch leather, and two pairs of moccasins. He then issued a parting order: "Now, brothers, go home and stay there. Don't come here any more, for this is the Indians' hunting ground, and all the animals, skins and furs are ours; and if you are so foolish as to venture here again, you may be sure the wasps and yellow jackets will sting you severely."

Findley and the camp keepers, who were evidently too frightened to take the time to hide their goods, soon reappeared. These four wanted to give up and go home. Boone, however, persuaded them to stay near the camp while he and Stuart attempted to raid the Indian band and retake at least one or two horses. After two days they overtook the braves during the night and stole four or five horses while the warriors slept. A full day's and night's hard ride later, they stopped to rest the animals. Stuart bent down to tie his moccasin and, with his head near the ground, thought he heard a heavy rumbling or roaring noise. The next instant the Shawnees thundered down upon them. They had discovered the theft almost immediately and had pursued the whites with their swiftest horses. Laughing at the hunters' failure, they tied a horse bell around Boone's neck and forced him to caper about and jingle it while they repeatedly chided, *"Steal horse, eh?"*

Told they would not be released until they reached the Ohio, the prisoners passed the next seven days under close surveillance and were bound each night. While the warriors were making camp near the present town of Maysville, Kentucky, Boone and Stuart each grabbed a gun at a prearranged signal and bolted into a thick cane patch, where they remained until the braves finally gave up the search. They retraced the seven days' trip in less than a day, only to find their camp abandoned by the others, who thought the two were dead. The flickering embers of the campfire encouraged them to follow the eastward trail quickly, but the weary duo struggled on for thirty-five or forty miles before overtaking their companions on the banks of the Rockcastle River. Daniel was overjoyed to find his brother Squire, who, coming out to Kentucky with Alexander Neely, had crossed paths with Findley and the retreating party. The "autobiography" captured some of his emotion: "Notwithstanding the unfortunate circumstances of our company, and our dangerous situation, as surrounded by hostile savages, . . . sorrows and sufferings vanish at the meeting. . . ." Squire's appearance with more horses, traps, and ammunition gave Boone the option to remain in the wilderness to hunt and trap rather than go back to Carolina in debt. Squire, Stuart, and Neely also decided to stay, while Findley, Holden, Mooney, and Cooley chose to depart for civilization. The latter three had had their fill of adventure and never set out to the west again. The more stalwart Findley made two more trading trips west, but was never heard from again after his journey into the wilderness in 1772.

Remembering all too well the costly lesson of setting up camp too close to the Warriors' Path, Daniel made his base camp on the north bank of the Kentucky River near its juncture the Red River and devoted himself to the normal winter hunt of trapping beaver and otter. In top condition, beaver pelts were worth about two and one-half dollars each and otter pelts three to five dollars. Thus winter trapping was the most lucrative of hunts. A horse normally could carry one hundred deerskins, or about 200 to 250 pounds, a load valued at one hundred dollars. A horse load of beaver pelts was worth five times as much. It was no wonder that the hunting party built a canoe to make their trapping more efficient.

Boone and John Stuart continued as a team but, well acquainted with the country, agreed to divide their traps and meet at an assigned place about every two weeks. Near the beginning of February 1770, Stuart loaded his traps into the canoe and crossed the Kentucky. Boone attributed his failure to return to the rain-swollen river. But Stuart never came back. When Daniel could ford the river, he began a search. All he found was a cold campfire and the initials "J.S." freshly carved in a nearby tree.

The mystery remained unsolved until the spring of 1775 when one of Boone's axmen, who was helping to cut the Wilderness Road, found a man's bones in a hollow sycamore near the Rockcastle River crossing, miles from Stuart's former campsite. A powder horn was also found in the tree;

engraved on the brass band encircling it were Stuart's initials. The discoloration produced by a leaden ball was visible at a break in the left arm, but no other injury could be discovered. Boone surmised that Stuart had been wounded by Indians and escaped, but in trying to get to a place to cross the river was forced to crawl into the tree for protection from the elements and died from loss of blood.

Although obviously upset and distressed, Daniel and Squire Boone were able to deal with their brother-in-law's disappearance. Men died in the wilderness. It was that simple. Neely's ability to cope was not the equal of the Boones' and he set off alone for home. The Boones erected a sturdier cabin, or "cottage," as Daniel called it, for the winter and kept busy trapping. Anxiety over the danger of Indian attack understandably was everpresent, but Filson noted that according to Daniel, the fear was more than soothed by their beautiful surroundings: "Thus situated, many hundred miles from our families in the howling wilderness, I believe few would have equally enjoyed the happiness we experienced."

In February 1770, Daniel may have returned home for a time. He is named in the Rowan County records as one of the men chosen to "Lay of[f] a Road from the Road which leads from the Shallow ford to Millers about Two Miles Below said Millers the Nearest and Best way Through the Great Gap of said Brushy Mountains the Nearest & Best Way to George Boons at the Mouth of Be[a]ver Creek, to Strike Mr. Mongomerys Road near the Main Yadkin River." Whether Daniel was simply appointed to do the work in absentia or was in North Carolina in February cannot be determined.

In any event, the winter and spring trapping was a great success for Daniel and Squire, but soon their ammunition was nearly exhausted. They packed the pelts, and Daniel stated in the "autobiography" that "on the first day of May, 1770, my brother returned home to the settlement by himself, for a new recruit of horses and ammunition, leaving me by myself, without bread, salt or sugar, without company of any fellow creatures, or even a horse or dog." Why did he not accompany Squire to help market the pelts and settle some of their debts? He missed his family, he did not have enough powder and shot to hunt commercially, and he could not trap this late in the season. Evidently he stayed to explore, to learn all he could about Kentucky. It clearly was a time of adventure for Daniel. As he said in the "autobiography": "I continued this tour, and in a few days explored a considerable part of the country, each day equally pleased as the first. I returned again to my old camp, which was not disturbed in my absence. I did not confine my lodging to it, but often reposed in thick cane-breaks, to avoid the savages, who, I believe, often visited my camp, but fortunately for me, in my absence. In this situation I was constantly exposed to danger, and death."

By night Boone made Indian-style camps and slept in the cane, by day he traveled throughout the Kentucky and Licking River Valleys and examined the Ohio as low as the Falls (present-day Louisville). There he found the remains of an old trading house, evidently abandoned for some twelve to fifteen years, but still recognizable as mute testimony to the presence of previous white men. Although fresh signs and the sounds of Indians were all around him here and throughout his tour, he was not discovered. At any hint of danger Daniel would head for a canebrake. The dense, entwined masses of cane stretched on for miles in places and grew ten, twenty, and sometimes even thirty feet high. It was next to impossible to track a man who took refuge there. Following buffalo traces when he could to speed his journey, Boone also visited the Upper and Lower Blue Licks to watch immense herds of buffalo come to lick the salty ground or drink the brackish water. He inspected the famous Big Bone Lick and was intrigued by the huge quantity of the fossil remains of mammoths.

After exploring the Ohio and then reaching the Kentucky River near Leestown, just north of Frankfort, Boone observed a brave fishing from a fallen tree that partially extended over the water. All he ever said of the incident was that "while I was looking at the fellow, he tumbled into the river, and I saw him no more." Daniel's tone and expression assured his family that he had been looking at the Indian over the sights of "Old Tick-Licker," his favorite rifle. Revenge? Self-defense? Boone never revealed his motives for the act.

Boone soon penetrated farther up the Kentucky River, camped in a large cave in Mercer County, and carved "D.B.—1770" on a nearby tree. One story records that while roaming along the high ridge of Dick's (now Dix) River, Daniel found himself cut off by Indians. He had two choices—surrender or jump. He jumped, landed where he had aimed, in the thick top of a small sugar maple on a second bank far below, quickly clambered down the tree, and stole off unseen beneath the overhanging boughs. The warriors peered over the cliff and knew that this must be a charmed white man. The bank was sixty feet down.

Daniel's time of adventure and exploration allowed him to enjoy his surroundings to the utmost. In the "autobiography" he stated, "I was happy in the midst of dangers and inconveniences. In such diversity it was impossible I should be disposed to melancholy. No populous city, with all the varieties of commerce and stately structures, could afford so much pleasure to my mind, as the beauties of nature I found here." The nineteenth-century southern novelist William Gilmore Simms perhaps best captured the romance of Boone's solitary stay: "His life was one of excitements, and a certain sense of insecurity heightened his enjoyment. He lived in sight of loveliness, but on the verge of danger. Beauty came to him, with Terror looking over her shoulder. . . . He pursues no old paths, but, reconnoitering the country, gathers a new horizon with every sunrise."

As they had agreed, Boone continued his exploring until he met his brother at their old camp on July 27, 1770. Squire told Daniel that their families were well and had been provided for, that he had paid some debts and procured new supplies. They moved the camp a few miles down the Kentucky to another cave near the mouth of Hickman Creek in Jessamine County. Once when they returned to one of their outcamps, they thought that it had been ransacked by Indians. Moccasins, leggings, blankets, and even the camp kettle were gone. They soon saw wolf tracks. Following the trail, they found the full kettle licked clean and the blankets ripped in shreds, the better to line a den full of cubs. They killed the old thief, but could not train the cubs; Daniel said that despite his best efforts they were wolves still. He always seemed to have bad luck with wolves. Another raided the camp and made off with his hat. Boone, who hated coonskin caps and always insisted on a hat, was not about to let this one get away and be without a replacement until he reached the settlements. A quick shot decided the matter. Daniel's "civilized" hat was back in its proper place.

The season yielded good hunting. In autumn Squire once more took the skins back to the Yadkin and purchased new supplies. His return was delayed beyond the allotted time, probably because of heavy rains, and Daniel set off to the east either to meet his brother or to continue on home rather than spend another season alone in the wilderness without proper provisions.

Along the way, he came upon an ancient Indian who had been left behind by his tribe to die. Pitying the old man's situation, Daniel retraced his steps a half mile to a deer he had just killed and brought the rest of the meat back to the helpless man, who manifested sincere gratitude for the gift. Such concern seemed in direct contrast to his killing the brave who was fishing, but typified the ambivalent attitude that existed in Indian-white relations at the time. A sense of kinship through the common activity of hunting could allow these men to see themselves as "brothers" in a certain sense. Why did Boone help the old Indian and in other much more equivocal circumstances show similar compassion? Why did Captain Will recapture Boone and Stuart rather than kill them outright for disobeying his commands? Perhaps as fellow woodsmen and hunters they recognized and respected their mutual love for untamed nature. And perhaps the recent experience of the French and Indian War made both sides more eager for a peaceful solution and the sharing of the fruits of hunting and trapping that the wilderness provided.

However, the pressures toward violence were increasing. Hundreds, perhaps thousands, had violated the British Proclamation of 1763 and settled on the Indian side of the Appalachians. Moreover, Boone and many of the other Long Hunters who had penetrated deeply into Indian country were not just commercial hunters but also speculators in land or, at the very least, men whom the speculators would follow. They were the harbingers of civilization before which the wilderness had to retreat. Both sides knew or suspected that conflict was inevitable and both were capable of initiating what would logically appear to be unwarranted violence.

Continuing his journey, after his good deed in helping the old brave, Daniel pressed on until he saw a large dry tree on fire. Creeping cautiously forward he found Squire trying to warm himself on the chilly December day. After their reunion the Boones probably trapped for a while on the Kentucky before exploring the regions along the Green and Cumberland Rivers. They were not alone. Early in the fall of 1770 a party of about forty Long Hunters had embarked for Kentucky under the leadership of Joseph Drake and Henry Skaggs. These hunters did not cut trails, but used those already in existence. A normal route would follow the Warriors' Path from the Cumberland Gap to Flat Licks to get through the Cumberland and Pine Mountain ranges. Then Long Hunters could head north into Kentucky by various routes or travel down the Cumberland River, depending on their destination. Their de facto mapping of the wilderness unintentionally helped tame the frontier.

The Drake and Skaggs party was equipped with three packhorses for each man, rifles, ammunition, traps, dogs, blankets, and salt. They hunted along the Rockcastle and Dick's Rivers and southwesterly to and down the Green River, where they erected a camp and took many deer, elk, and buffalo. By February 1771 only fourteen of the original hunters remained. Charles Ewing, who was said to be jealous of Henry Skaggs's superior success in hunting, may have previously exerted enough influence to lead off the rest of the group or they may have grown tired of the wilderness. The camp of the remaining band was later raided by a band of braves supposedly led by Capt. Will Emery, the same half-blood Cherokee who had frustrated Daniel's long hunt. When the white hunters who had decided to explore the region for a few weeks returned, they found their five comrades who served as camp keepers gone. Two were captured or unaccounted for and three had escaped to the settlements; the camp was ransacked and the skins exposed to the elements and spoiled. The men carved the following inscription on a large beech tree over their initials as a mute testament to their misfortune: *"Fifteen hundred skins gone to ruination."*

Previously hunting along the Green River that same winter, some of these Long Hunters—Henry, Charles, and Richard Skaggs, Casper Mansker, James Knox, James Dysart, William Miller, and two others—were likely among those who, according to one story, were once startled by a noise none of them could identify. Mansker told the others to keep still, grabbed his rifle, and glided bravely into the woods to investigate. It could not be an animal since the noise came from a single unchanging direction. Could it be a new Indian trap? Mansker peered from behind a tree and saw a man stretched flat on the ground singing at the top of his lungs. Daniel Boone was entertaining himself while he waited for his brother to come back to camp.

Although the Boones joined forces with the Long Hunters for a short time, they avoided their fate of a raided camp and left the Cumberland Valley for home in March 1771 with a fine load of furs. Sometime in May they reached Powell's Valley near Cumberland Gap. Here Squire came upon a skeleton-like creature whom he recognized as his friend Alexander Neely. Neely had become separated from his hunting party and, bewildered and lost, had fired away all his powder hoping to attract his companions' attention. He survived on the meat of a stray dog that he managed to kill. Squire took Neely into camp and nursed him back to health with Daniel's help. Neely lived another twenty-five years until he and his son James were killed by Indians near their home in the present Sumner County, Tennessee, in the spring of 1796.

The brothers continued their hunting but, despite all that had happened to their friends, were not cautious enough in choosing the location of their camps. A portion of the Warriors' Path led through Powell's Valley and was far too close for comfort to one of the Boones' nightly camps. The almost constant raiding of northern and southern war parties, of Iroquois against the Cherokees and Catawbas and of Shawnees and Delawares against the Cherokees among others, made the path as dangerous as it was convenient for natives and whites alike. One evening, not too far from the Cumberland Gap, the Boones were surprised while cooking their dinner by "six or eight northern Indians," who accepted their invitation to share the meal. Soon the Indians proposed swapping guns—their worthless ones for the Boones' good rifles. Daniel and Squire refused and the warriors stripped them of their skins, horses, rifles, and all their equipment. Told to go, they hid behind a log to observe the course the marauders would take, then hurried to a border settlement and raised a sympathetic band to pursue them and try to recover the goods. A few miles beyond the camp, one of the whites shot a deer that had passed too temptingly near their route. The others, realizing that the report of the rifle had warned the Indians, thought it fruitless to continue the mission, and the Boones agreed. Their withdrawal was fortunate. They later learned that the small Indian band had been reinforced and was lying in ambush for the outnumbered whites just a mile or two ahead.

Except for one man who stayed with the Boones, all the party returned to the settlement. The remaining three stopped to spend the night in a deserted cabin and, glancing through the chinks in the logs a short while later, spotted two armed Indians bedecked in fine ornaments. Retribution was often swift on the frontier. They fired simultaneously and killed both braves. Daniel and the unnamed companion each took a rifle as his booty; Squire took the silver trinkets.

Some jewelry and a rifle —the last half year had been less than profitable for the Boones. Daniel had, according to Isaac Shelby, been "robbed of all the proceeds of this hunt of two years." The statement was not exact, for Squire had managed to bring back two packloads of skins and pelts. When Daniel arrived in the Upper Yadkin in May 1771 to greet his family, however, he was deeper in debt than when he had departed to find the Cumberland Gap. He could not help being greatly discouraged. Yet he had seen Kentucky. He had explored the land, knew it better perhaps than any other white man, and realized its potential. That was a great deal to think about.

One surviving story also attests that Daniel's hardships neither dampened his homecoming nor his sense of humor. Returning in the midst of a settlement dance, he wore an impenetrable disguise of thoroughly over-grown hair and beard that he had gained from his time in the wilderness. He pushed through the crowd to face Rebecca and silently extended his hand to request a dance. She stoutly refused the stranger. Boone laughed and said, "you have danced many a time with me." Recognizing his voice, Rebecca threw her arms around the grizzled backwoodsman, much to the bystanders' astonishment. After the truth came out, Daniel spent the night entertaining his family and friends with "the story of his hardships and adventures."

4

⫷⫸

HENDERSON'S "INFAMOUS COMPANY OF LAND PYRATES" Transylvania

For the next two years Daniel farmed and hunted, each in its season, and undoubtedly kept a keen eye out during his travels for new lands to explore and settle. Although little information survived about Boone's activities during this period of time, he did often go hunting with an old weaver named Joe Robertson, who had a celebrated pack of bear dogs. The two hunted in the Brushy Mountain and Watauga areas and once ventured as far as "the French Lick" (now Nashville) on the Cumberland before returning with a load of skins. Daniel also may have used these years to sound the Cherokees' willingness to sell Kentucky. But one prospective backer could not help: Henderson's judicial appointment ran for another two years and effectively prevented his active involvement.

Others did not delay. The growing shortage of cheap land in North Carolina, the prospect of better land to the west, and the conflicts involving the Regulators helped to push settlers into the valleys of the Upper Tennessee River. They quickly overran the boundaries of the latest cession of the Cherokees in the 1770 Treaty of Lochaber and pressed even farther to the west.

By 1772 Daniel had changed his residence to Sapling Grove in what is now Tennessee, but he eventually moved back to the Yadkin. Store accounts indicate that his food purchases in Tennessee were for a family; they also dispel the contention of Boone's early biographer, John Mason Peck, that the pioneer never indulged in strong drink. An entry for January 26, 1773, read "2 quarts of Rum."

Early in 1773 Boone reexplored Kentucky with Benjamin Cutbirth and a few other men including Samuel Tate and young Hugh McGary. They camped in the same cave he had previously used on Little Hickman Creek in the present Jessamine County; Daniel observed his custom of recording the visit by cutting his initials and the date into the cave wall, and McGary followed suit. Boone was again enormously pleased with the country and resolved to settle there without Henderson's help. On the way home he met Capt. William Russell, the pioneer of the Clinch Valley in southwest Virginia, who became enthralled by Boone's descriptions of Kentucky and agreed to join him in attempting a settlement.

The coming of spring in 1773 heralded renewed and substantial interest in Kentucky. Capt. Thomas Bullitt led his relatively large company of about forty men on the first surveying mission into the area. James and Robert McAfee split off from Bullitt's party for a while and, hiring Hancock Taylor as their surveyor, laid out tracts near the present Frankfort and Harrodsburg, Kentucky, before returning home that summer. While these ventures did not signal a land rush comparable either to the California gold rush or the claiming sales orchestrated by the government in the nineteenth century, they built upon the exploits of the Long Hunters to bring settlement of the wilderness one step closer.

The McAfee brothers met Boone on or about August 12 on their return from staking out land in Kentucky. They informed him that they were not alone in the endeavor. James Harrod's party and at least one other had been likewise engaged. Sensing that all the best land might be taken before he even got under way, Boone redoubled his efforts to complete the necessary preparations. He recruited a number of his wife's relatives at the Bryan Settlement in the Lower Yadkin and rushed back north to sell his farm and whatever goods could not be transported easily. Five neighboring families joined him, as did William Bush and Michael Stoner (George Michael Holsteiner). They departed for Kentucky on September 25, 1773. For the sake of speed, the Bryan party of about forty men would meet them in Powell's Valley, allowing them to travel the most dangerous part of the journey together.

Extraordinary difficulties marked their migration. The route was a serpentine hunter's trace that was too narrow for a wagon, so a single-file packtrain of horses carried their provisions. Some of the party rode; most walked. Near Powell's Valley, Boone sent his son James, along with John and Richard Mendinall, to Captain Russell's at Castle's-woods to get more flour and to tell him of their advance. Russell provided the flour and sent a few cattle and several horses loaded with farming implements and provisions. His seventeen-year-old son, Henry, a young man named Drake, Isaac Crabtree, and the family slaves, Charles and Adam, were sent to help in transporting the goods. Captain Russell, accompanied by Capt. David Gass, would hurry to overtake the party as soon as his business was completed.

James Boone, Henry Russell, and their party camped on the northern bank of Walden's (or Wallen's) Creek, along what is now U.S. Highway 68, about five miles east of Jonesville, Virginia, on the night of October 9. They were unaware that Daniel's company was but three miles ahead and equally unaware that their steps were silently shadowed by a force of Indians, who had tracked them most of the preceding day. At dawn they were attacked while still asleep. Drake and one of the Mendinalls apparently were killed outright; the other Mendinall crept off, mortally wounded. Crabtree, although wounded, escaped back to the settlements. Charles, the older slave, was captured and later tomahawked to death, while Adam hid in some driftwood piled on the creek's bank and became an unwilling audience for a grisly spectacle. He later said that he heard James tell Henry that he thought his mother, brothers, and sisters must already be dead.

James Boone and Henry Russell had both been shot through the hips and were unable to move. James recognized one of the warriors, a Shawnee named Big Jim, who had been a frequent visitor at the Boones' farm, and begged him to spare his life. He soon begged him to end it. The boys' bodies were slashed and stabbed countless times, with great care taken not to injure a vital organ, and their toenails and fingernails were torn out. A merciful death by tomahawk finally ended their ordeal. The events did not become clear until Adam stumbled home in shock eleven days later.

As was generally the case, murder continued to beget murder and vengeance was confused with justice. The following spring one of the survivors, Isaac Crabtree, flew into a rage and killed the unarmed relative of a Cherokee chief at a gathering held near the present Jonesborough, Tennessee, designed to maintain peace with the tribe. Crabtree soon placed himself beyond the reach of Virginia's laws by moving to Kentucky.

Boone first learned of the boys' fate and that of their companions from a petty thief who had deserted Daniel's party after being apprehended with goods stolen from other members. The young man left before sunrise, paused long enough to pilfer a few deerskins Daniel had left by the trace for James to bring along, and headed for home. Reaching Walden's (now Indian) Creek apparently just after the Indians had left, he dropped the skins and dashed back to the camp with his tragic news. Daniel organized the people to repel a possible attack by fortifying themselves behind fallen trees and sent Squire with a few men to bury the dead and ascertain the strength of the enemy. Squire arrived on the scene to find Captains Russell and Gass staring in disbelief at the mangled remains of the boys. The dead had not been scalped; braves would not bring white scalps into their towns in time of peace. James and Henry were buried together, wrapped in a linen sheet provided by Mrs. Boone.

Distraught, the settlers held a general council in the main camp. Daniel noted in the "autobiography" that "this unhappy affair scattered our cattle, brought us into extreme difficulty, and so discouraged the whole company, that we retreated. . . ." Boone was the only one who voiced a strong desire to push on, and the expedition disbanded. Daniel accepted Captain Gass's offer to stay temporarily in a cabin on his farm near Castle's-woods, probably hoping to convince Gass and Russell to make another try to settle in Kentucky.

Boone's dream was slipping from his grasp. The McAfees, Harrod, and Bullitt were only the first to explore Kentucky in 1773: George Washington traveled down the Ohio to Fishing Creek, where George Rogers Clark was already located; Simon Kenton and fourteen others were examining northeastern Kentucky; and James Douglas and James Smith were also surveying and claiming the choicest lands they could find.

All these men sought land under a law passed in 1705 that entitled every Virginian to settle up to five hundred acres of uninhabited frontier land for himself and granted two hundred additional acres for each slave or tithable servant, up to a maximum total of four thousand acres. They also could gain preemption rights—the right to the land on which they had settled—for three years by improving it. Captain Bullitt sought land for officers and enlisted men who had received land warrants from the governor for their service in the French and Indian War. Kentucky was bustling with surveyors, speculators, men hired to improve land as quickly as possible to establish preemption rights for others, and with future settlers. It would be nearly eighteen months before Boone cut the Wilderness Road through to Boonesborough.

Colonials were not the only people interested in staking claims in Kentucky. Across the Atlantic, influential London speculators joined forces with prominent Americans such as Benjamin Franklin to form the Vandalia Company and petitioned for a royal charter for a huge tract of land bordered by the Ohio River on the north and the Kentucky River on the west.

Clearly, the boundary set by the Proclamation of 1763 was by this time academic. Virtually no active attempt was made to prevent western settlement. Also, it had become increasingly clear that the Ohio Valley could not be settled without a war with the Shawnees who were, at least in one sense, caught in the middle of a land grab by Pennsylvania and Virginia. George Croghan and his associates, as well as other Pennsylvania merchants, knew that their trade would be disrupted by any conflict. They also were attempting to colonize large areas of Pennsylvania and western Virginia (including eastern Kentucky), some of the same land that Virginia claimed for its veterans of the French and Indian War. The supporting forces of the Virginia surveying expeditions in Kentucky began to attack Shawnee hunting parties, and Lord Dunmore, the royal governor of Virginia, sent militia as further protection for its citizen-surveyors on the frontier. The Pennsylvanians accused their competitors of attempting to destroy the Indian trade; the Virginians countercharged that Pennsylvania merchants had purchased goods stolen from them by the Indians (with Captain Russell's horses turning up as part of the evidence) and had incited the Shawnees to try to drive them from the Ohio Valley.

The outright conflict with the Indians, termed Lord Dunmore's War, essentially commenced with the murder of young Boone and Russell. According to Col. Arthur Campbell, "the Murder of Russells, Boones, and Drakes Sons" was truly "in every ones mouth." Their fate was literally the talk of the frontier. In an unusual action, two Cherokees eventually were executed for the crime by their own chiefs, who bowed to extreme pressure from the Virginia colonial government. The undeclared war that had existed along the borders since 1764 escalated as both sides committed the most inhumane acts to avenge previous atrocities. By early 1774 in Kentucky "no questions were asked on either side—but from the muzzles of their rifles."

Williamsburg's *Virginia Gazette* recorded the tension. The March 17 issue noted that "Captain Russell, from Fincastle, brings the disagreeable Intelligence, that a general Discontent appears among the Indian Nations; that the Cherokees and Shawanese have combined together; and that, in short, the Frontier Inhabitants are under the most dreadful Apprehensions, from the ill Temper prevailing amongst those *Barbarians*." A week later a writer used the newspaper to urge Governor Dunmore and the assembly to prepare for a full-scale assault. He wrote that recent events left "no room to doubt that the storm which has been so long gathering, will, ere long, break forth in all its fury. . . . Should an instance of any hostile act of theirs be demanded, I need only mention the unhappy murder of young Russell, committed not long ago, and, as has since been ascertained, was perpetrated by a Cherokee chief."

The event that precipitated all-out hostilities was the murder of the family of Tahgahjute, a famous chief who gave himself the English name of Logan. On May 1, 1774, Daniel Greathouse persuaded some friendly Indians to come to the white settlement near Yellow Creek, got them hopelessly drunk, and then shot them all. Among the group were Logan's brother and pregnant sister or sister-in-law. At least one of the natives was scalped. Braves who attempted to cross the creek to help their comrades were driven back with numerous fatalities, and the unborn child was cut from its dead mother's womb and impaled on a stake. Indians had no monopoly on cruelty and, like their adversaries, had long memories. Although their attack was likely a random one, they exacted their revenge seventeen years later, boarding Greathouse's flatboat, killing his crew, and torturing Greathouse and his wife to death.

News traveled slowly on the frontier. When Daniel Boone set out in May to hunt and to visit his son's grave, he had not heard of the massacre of Logan's kin. He found that the logs covering James's grave had been disturbed by wolves but the boys' bodies were untouched. While he finished re-covering the grave with more logs, he was caught in a sudden violent storm; nature seemed to support the melancholy associations the place held for him. He was more depressed then, he said, than at any other time in his life. The noise of approaching warriors who had discovered his small fire startled Boone out of his reverie. He stole off, driving his belled horse well before him through the creek to confuse his trackers. Gaining some distance on his pursuers, he silenced the bell, mounted his horse, and escaped. Ever after, Daniel credited the storm with saving his life by delaying the braves.

Sometime before Boone's return, Capt. William Russell had received orders from Col. William Preston, on the authority of Governor Dunmore, to choose "two faithful woodsmen" to warn the Kentucky surveyors—such as Hancock Taylor, James Douglas, Isaac Hite, and John Floyd—of their imminent danger. Russell replied to Preston, "I have engaged to start immediately on the occasion, two of the best hands I could think of—Daniel Boone and Michael Stoner." Russell, immensely confident in Daniel, wrote again to Preston about the surveyors on July 13: "If they are alive, it is indisputable but Boone must find them."

Boone and Stoner set out on June 26. A surviving story about the trip recorded that on their way to Kentucky they stopped at a place near the Blue Licks where the buffalo had licked away so much of the salty ground that deep trenches separated only by a narrow ridge were formed. Stoner peeked through a small hole in the partition and saw a buffalo calmly feeding on the salt. Stoner, a Pennsylvania German, said to Boone, "Shtop, Gabtain, and we will have shum fun." Stoner removed his hat and thrust his head through the aperture into the face of the buffalo. But the buffalo was not frightened off. Instead, it rammed the wall and burst through the clay bank up to its shoulders. Stoner wheeled and screamed as he ran, "Schoot her, Gabtain! Schoot her, Gabtain!" Daniel saw that Stoner was in no danger and fell to the ground in uncontrollable laughter. Nathan Boone recalled the thick accent of his father's constant friend for Lyman Draper and described Stoner as "an awkward Dutchman, a low chunky man."

The duo made their way along the North Fork of the Kentucky River to Big Lick, where Boonesborough was later located. The legend persists that they reached Harrodstown (Harrodsburg) before July 8, when the Shawnees killed James Cowan and James Hamilton in an attack upon a band of men surveying a few miles north of the settlement. It was more likely that Boone and Stoner arrived after that date. Having started from Castle's-woods on June 26, they probably could not have traveled three hundred miles through rugged terrain in thirteen days. (The men of Harrodstown took twenty-one days to make the return journey to the Clinch River settlements.)

Similarly, while it was true that the major part of Harrod's party, about thirty-four or thirty-five men, had been previously engaged in laying out the town and that each settler was granted "a half-acre in-lot, and a ten acre out-lot," Boone did not pause a short time to register as a settler and to erect a double cabin with Evan Hinton, as many have speculated. The new settlement was disbanded within one or two days of the attack. Further, Boone and Stoner did not find two of the surveying parties, one led by John Floyd and another by James Douglas and Isaac Hite. When Floyd and his men arrived at a prearranged rendezvous point on July 24, they found no sign of the comrades they were to meet. Instead, they discovered a note: "Alarmed by finding some people killed, we are gone down." Floyd's party made for the settlements immediately. Boone and Stoner perhaps found and warned the group headed by Hancock Taylor, but the other parties likely were already on their way home. Two decades later in an April 24, 1794, deposition in Point Pleasant for a land claim, Boone remarked about the trip that he and Stoner found that "the surveyors were driven in by the Indians," a comment supporting the view that he did not contact and warn them of impending hostilities; the majority of the surveyors already knew.

Boone and Stoner returned to the Clinch Valley on August 26. In sixty-one days they had traveled over eight hundred miles and successfully notified some of the surveyors of their danger. Only a few were unable to retreat. Upon his return, Boone was commissioned a lieutenant in the colonial forces. At the request of Maj. Arthur Campbell, he raised a party of recruits and marched off to the front, a defensive line extending from the mouth of the Kanawha River northward to Fort Dunmore (old Fort Pitt). Campbell noted in an August 28 letter to Colonel Preston that "what induced me particularly to apply to Mr. Boone, was seeing his Journal last night, and a letter to Capt. Russell, wherein he professes a great desire to go on the expedition, and I am well informed he is a very popular officer where he is known. . . . I have been informed that Mr. Boone tracked a small party of Indians from Cumberland Gap to near the settlements. Upon this intelligence, I wrote pressingly to Capt. Thompson to have a constant lookout, and to urge the spies strictly to do their duty." Knowing that his position needed bolstering, Capt. John Floyd also wrote to Preston on the same day: "pray let Boone join me and try. Capt. Bledsoe says Boone has more influence than any other man now disengaged."

According to his son Nathan, Daniel raised a small company of men and set out to join in the Point Pleasant campaign. Daniel, however, was overtaken and recalled only two days later to help defend the Clinch region against a number of bloody Indian raids and proved an active commander. Capt. Daniel Smith of Fort Christian on the Clinch River noted the following in his record book: "Sept. 22d. Lieut. Boone, fourteen men, four days, three pounds of beef per day." Standing orders were to issue meat only to scouts or those in pursuit of Indians. In a letter to Colonel Preston, Smith also noted that while he was in the lower settlements, he had seen "a petition signed by many of the inhabitants, representing their situation to be dangerous because they have been so irregularly supplied with the number of men allotted to the district; and also requesting you to appoint Mr. Boone to be a captain, and to take charge of these lower forts, so that he may be at liberty to act without orders from the Holston captains, who, by their frequent absence, leave the inhabitants sometimes in disorder." Preston soon commissioned Daniel a captain and gave him the command of Blackmore's and Cowan's Forts, in addition to that of Moore's Fort, his previous responsibility.

His opposition was now the formidable Logan himself. The avenging chief's war party waylaid three of Boone's men who had made the mistake of going out three hundred yards from Moore's Fort to check pigeon traps. Boone and his other men arrived just after the shots were fired, but were too late. One man, John Duncan, had already been scalped. Daniel pursued the raiders with no success and did so again the next month with the same result.

For the present time, Boone's part in the war, and that of the other commanders of frontier forts, was to maintain a successful defensive posture; they were to react rather than act. The overall strategy of the campaign against the Indians was designed and initiated by Lord Dunmore. On July 24 Dunmore notified Gen. Andrew Lewis that he himself would go to Fort Dunmore to reinforce the defenses of the upper Ohio, gather a strike force of one thousand men from the Monongahela and upper Potomac regions, and march down the Ohio River. Lewis was to march west along the Kanawha River with militia raised from Augusta, Botetourt, and Fincastle Counties in western Virginia and then combine with Dunmore's army at the Ohio to invade the Indian territory.

Cornstalk, a Shawnee chief known to the whites as King Cornstalk, was an excellent general and tactician who knew that his only chance for victory against the enemy columns, either of whose force was numerically superior to his own, was to attack before they could unite. At dawn on October 10 he led a war party, variously estimated from three hundred to eight hundred or more Shawnee, Mingo, Delaware, and Ottawa braves, against Lewis's advance guard near Point Pleasant. Even when Lewis ordered the remainder of his troops into the battle, the immediate result was a standoff. When Isaac Shelby led a flanking movement against the Indians, however, Cornstalk mistakenly determined that his worst fears had come true—either Dunmore's army or reinforcements from Augusta and Botetourt Counties had arrived. He ordered a retreat. Estimates of Lewis's losses ranged from forty-six to eighty killed and from eighty to one hundred and fifty wounded, losses probably comparable to those of Cornstalk. Because the natives as a rule carried away the bodies of their dead, no exact figures concerning casualties could be determined.

The Indians' defeat at Point Pleasant was of great importance because it indicated to both the Indians and the Virginians that Lord Dunmore's offensive would be successful. Cornstalk told his people that they had two alternatives: kill their women and children and fight to the death or seek peace through a treaty. They decided to negotiate. In that same month Dunmore's agreement with the Indians, the Treaty of Camp Charlotte, established the Ohio River as the boundary line between the two groups. Concurrently, Dunmore decided to strengthen the frontier by garrisoning seventy-five men at the fort that bore his name and by erecting Fort Blair at the mouth of the Kanawha River. Traders and speculators, having gained a strong foothold in the Ohio Valley and the protection of forts, were overjoyed.

By November 20, Boone and his men had been discharged from the militia, and Richard Henderson, no longer on the bench, felt the time was ripe for his grand land scheme. In the autumn of 1774, Henderson and Capt. Nathaniel Hart made a preliminary visit to the Cherokee nation and confirmed Boone's reports that Kentucky could indeed be purchased. Henderson's Transylvania Company wished to buy twenty million acres of land, nearly all of the present state of Kentucky and a portion of Tennessee, and to found the fourteenth colony, to be called Transylvania, with the company's officers as proprietors. Proprietary rights mirrored the feudal system and allowed the charging of an annual quitrent on each acre of land sold, a guaranteed perpetual income. This fee freed the tenant from obligatory service to the proprietor. Henderson and his partners, however, would eventually find that they had underestimated the new spirit of independence in these soon-to-be former colonists, especially in assuming that they would accept such a landlord-tenant relationship.

Of more immediate consequence was that Henderson and his partners were flouting the Proclamation of 1763, the Treaty of Fort Stanwix (1768), and the claims of North Carolina and Virginia to the territory. Patriots and Loyalists alike were alarmed by Henderson's dreams of empire. George Washington, himself a significant speculator in wilderness land, wrote, "There is something in that affair which I neither understand, nor like, and wish I may not have cause to dislike it worse as the mystery unfolds." Governor Dunmore feared that Transylvania would lure able industrious people away from Virginia, while Gov. Josiah Martin of North Carolina conversely termed it "an Asylum to the most abandoned fugitives from the several colonies." Martin also put his finger on the most worrisome aspect of the Transylvania enterprise—imitators: "If some effectual stop is not put to those daring usurpations," he said, "such Adventurers will possess themselves soon of all the Indian country." Martin's uncensored feelings came out in a letter to the Earl of Dartmouth in which he spoke angrily of "Henderson the famous invader" and his "infamous Company of land Pyrates."

These royal governors were irate at Henderson's coup and, had it been any other time, would have demonstrated their displeasure through the use of troops. But talk of revolution was becoming more frequent. They could not afford to commit any more of their forces to the frontier. Although the auditor of the colony wrote, "Pray, is Dick Henderson out of his head?" the "famous invader" had coolly recognized his opportunity and seized it. Even Governor Martin acknowledged that there was no law against "leasing" the land from the natives for an indefinite period.

Matters progressed swiftly in Henderson and Hart's meeting with the Cherokees. February or March was agreed on as the time to meet to sign a treaty at Sycamore Shoals (one of the first permanent settlements west of the thirteen original colonies' modern borders) on the Watauga River in what is now Tennessee. The old, wizened chief Attakullakulla (Leaning Wood or Little Carpenter), famous for his wisdom, traveled with the Transylvania partners to Cross-Creek (the present Fayetteville, North Carolina) to look at the goods offered for the land. The merchandise was shipped to the Watauga on December 6. Henderson anticipated success and publicized his desire for settlers by publishing on Christmas Day, 1774, his "Proposals for the Encouragement of settling the Lands purchased by Richd Henderson & Co. on the Branches of the Mississippi River from the Cherokee tribe of Indians." His proposals were ambitious, stating that the company would grant land free and clear (except for the quitrents) as follows: five hundred acres for each of fifty soldiers to defend the settlers; five thousand acres to any person who built a "Furnace or other Iron works" within three years; one thousand acres for a "salt manufactory within twelve months"; and five hundred acres for erecting a grist or saw mill within a year. There were even two prizes of five hundred acres, one for "raising the greatest crop of corn in proportion to the hands he may have under him" and one for "the person who shall carry out the greatest number of sheep." Each settler who was willing to raise a crop of corn and remain through the first day of September would get a grant of five hundred acres for himself and two hundred and fifty acres for each tithable person, but it would cost twenty shillings sterling per hundred acres plus a quitrent of two shillings sterling per hundred per year. Henderson amplified his plans a bit more on February 22, 1775, but did not alter the terms of his Christmas "gift."

At Henderson's instruction, Boone had used the winter to tour the Cherokee towns and urge the inhabitants to attend the treaty. He did his work well. A thousand to twelve hundred braves came to Sycamore Shoals in March. Filson recorded in the "autobiography" that Daniel said he "was solicited by a number of North-Carolina gentlemen, that were about purchasing the lands on the S. side of Kentucke River, from the Cherokee Indians, to attend their treaty at Wataga, in March, 1775, to negotiate with them, and, mention the boundaries of the purchase." Boone also was sure enough of the completion of the sale to have begun assembling woodsmen at the Long Island of the Holston River to cut the Wilderness Road.

While no inventory has survived, the goods offered in exchange for the land were said to have "filled a house." Set in plain sight of the Cherokees, they proved to be the most persuasive bargaining tool that Henderson possessed. He originally anticipated no dissent and was taken aback when Dragging Canoe, an influential young chief, spoke out vehemently against the treaty. His keen eye had seen that the treasure offered, the equivalent of ten thousand pounds sterling, or about fifty thousand dollars, was not a fair price for the land. His speech caused a breakdown in negotiations. In actuality, the often-quoted price that the historian Draper placed upon the goods may have been inflated. The original terms of the Treaty of Watauga declared the sum to be two thousand British pounds, and one observer later wrote that there were "only ten waggons loaded with cheap goods, such as coarse woolens, trinkets, and spirituous liquors."

The next day, March 16, Dragging Canoe and the other opposing chiefs gave in to the demands of the young braves for the finery and some quantity of ammunition that stood so temptingly before them. The treaty-deed was signed on March 17, 1775, by Attakullakulla, Oconostota, and Savanookah (the Raven). It granted "Henderson and company the tract of country from the mouth of the Kentucky or Louisa River to the head spring of its most northerly fork, thence south-easterly to the top of Powell's Mountain, and thence, first westerly, and then north-westerly, to the head spring of the most southerly branch of the Cumberland River, and down that stream, including all its waters, to the Ohio, and up the Ohio to the mouth of the Kentucky." Aptly named, "The Great Grant" was specifically laid out not to infringe upon the land sought by the Vandalia Company.

Henderson then stated that he wished to purchase a right-of-way from the Holston River to the Cumberland Gap, the gateway to "The Great Grant," in exchange for "the value of two thousand weight of leather" and some six or seven hundred pounds to pay the Indians' debt to John Carter. After some brief haggling, the parties agreed to these terms for "The Path Deed."

There was much grumbling among some of the young warriors when the merchandise was doled out. One, whose share was a shirt, complained loudly that on the land sold he could have killed more than enough deer in one day to pay for the garment. Henderson wisely signaled the beginning of the feast he had promised the Cherokees. Many cattle were killed and roasted, and the rum, previously withheld, flowed freely.

At one point early in the negotiations, when the purchase seemed certain, Boone was taken aside by Dragging Canoe, or perhaps by the war chief, Oconostota, and told, "Brother, we have given you a fine land, but I believe you will have much trouble in settling it." The prophetic chief also supposedly remarked that "a black cloud hung over it." No one recognized how true the two statements would prove to be. Boone, undaunted, left for the Long Island of the Holston to mobilize his axmen before the treaty was ratified. A road needed to be cut to Kentucky.

5

~~~~

CUTTING THE WILDERNESS ROAD

Daniel stated the matter simply in the "autobiography": "I . . . undertook to mark out a road in the best passage from the settlement through the wilderness to Kentucke . . . having collected a number of enterprising men, well armed." Thirty backwoodsmen warmly greeted Boone's arrival at Long Island on Holston River. Among those present were Squire Boone, Michael Stoner, Benjamin Cutbirth, Col. Richard Callaway, David Gass, William Bush, Capt. William Twitty and his slave, and Felix Walker, who chronicled the expedition.

On March 10, 1775, the woods began to resound with the ring of axes. Blazing the trail through Powell's Valley and Cumberland Gap, the men widened Boone's previous trail from a footpath to one that would accommodate packhorses for approximately fifty miles before heading west for a short distance near Hazel Patch and then northwest along a buffalo trace to the Rockcastle River. "On leaving that river," wrote Felix Walker, "we had to encounter and cut our way through a country of about 20 miles, entirely covered with dead brush, which we found a difficult and laborious task." They then carved out a path along another buffalo trace for "about 30 miles through thick cane and reed" before eventually reaching the Kentucky River. Walker recorded that as the cane ceased, "a new sky and strange earth seemed to be presented to our view. So rich a soil we had never seen before; covered with clover in full bloom, the woods were abounding with wild game—turkies so numerous that it might be said they appeared but one flock, universally scattered in the woods."

Up to this point, the roadmakers had experienced no Indian trouble; Henderson's larger party, complete with supplies for a settlement, followed about one hundred miles behind. When Boone and his men camped on

Taylor's Fork of Silver Creek on March 24, they were but fifteen miles from their final destination, Big Lick near Otter Creek. A half hour before dawn, war whoops and rifle fire startled them from their sleep. Walker and Twitty were badly wounded, with Twitty shot through both knees; Twitty's slave was shot and fell dead into the campfire. Dazed and only partially awake, the other whites grabbed their rifles and plunged half naked into the forest. Walker crawled to safety. As the Indians rushed the camp to scalp Twitty, his bulldog seized one brave by the throat and threw him to the ground. A second Indian tomahawked the dog, and both attackers fled without their trophy.

The attack ended as quickly as it had begun. Boone reassembled his men and assessed their situation: only a few horses were missing, but Twitty and Walker could not be moved. While Boone nursed their wounds, he had his men erect some small cabins for shelter, which they termed "Twitty's Fort." Twitty died, but by April 1 Walker was well enough to be transported on a litter tied between two horses. In his "Narrative," Felix Walker paid tribute to the man who saved his life: "But let me, with feeling recollection and lasting gratitude, ever remember the unremitting kindness, sympathy, and attention paid to me by Colonel Boon in my distress. He was my father, my physician, and friend; he attended me as his child, cured my wounds by the use of medicines from the wood, nursed me with paternal affection until I recovered, without the expectation of reward."

Walker later recounted another event that occurred during the stay at Twitty's Fort. While gathering kindling, Colonel Callaway's female slave saw a man peep cautiously from behind a tree. She screamed "Indians!" and ran for the camp. Boone snatched his rifle and ordered everyone to take cover. Then the "Indian" announced his name. He was one of their own party who was not certain that the whites had regained control of the camp.

Boone's letter of April 1 to Richard Henderson described the events of the next few days:

> On March the 28th, as we were hunting for provisions, we found Samuel Tate's son, who gave us an account that the Indians fired on their camp on the 27th day. My brother and I went down and found two men killed and sculped, Thomas McDowell and Jeremiah McFeeters. I have sent a man down to all the lower companies in order to gather them all to the mouth of Otter Creek. My advice to you, Sir, is, to come or send as soon as

possible. Your company is desired greatly, for the people are very uneasy, but are willing to stay and venture their lives with you; and now is the time to flusterate their [the Indians'] intentions, and keep the country whilst we are in it. If we give way to them now, it will ever be the case.

Though not yet in mortal danger, Henderson's party experienced difficulties of its own following what became known as the Wilderness Road. William Calk, who was close on the heels of Henderson's band, recorded the problems that he and his group were encountering on the trek to Kentucky:

> April satd first this morning there is ice at our camp half inch thick we Start Early & travel this Day along a verey Bad hilley way cross one creek whear the horses almost got Mired Some fell in & all wet their loads we cross Clinch River & travell till late in the Night & camp on cove creek having two men with us that wair pilates
> Sund 2d this morning is avery hard frost we Start Early travel over powels mountain and camp on the head of Powels valley whear there is verey good food
> Mond 3d we Start Early travel down the valey cross powels River go some throw the woods with out aney track cross some Bad hils Git into hendersons Road camp on a creek in powels valley; Tuesday 4ᵗʰ Raney we Start about 10 oclock and git down to capt martins in the valey where we over take Coln. Henderson & his companey Bound for Caintuck & there we camp this Night there they were Broiling & Eating Beef without Bread; Wednesday ye 5ᵗʰ Breaks away fair & we go on down the valey & camp on indian Creek we had this creek to cross maney times & very Bad Banks Abrams Saddel turned & the load all fell in we go out this Eavening & Kill two Deer
> thurd 6ᵗʰ this morning is ahard frost & we wait at camp for Coln. Henderson & companey to come up they come up about 12 oclock & we Join with them and camp there Still this night waiting for Some part of the companey that had their horses Ran away with their packs; fryday ye 7ᵗʰ this morning is avery hard Snowey morning & we Still continue at camp Being

in number about 40 men & some Neagros this Eavening Comes
aletter from Capt Boon at caintuck of the indians doing mischief and Some turns back

Those of Boone's party who had not turned back arrived at their
destination by April 6. These road cutters eventually received ten pounds
ten shillings for their work, enough money to buy about 420 acres of Kentucky land. Walker's narrative stated that the group had followed Otter
Creek northward and that he "was carried in a litter between two horses, to
Kentucky river, where we made a station, and called it Boonesborough,
situated in a plain on the south side of the river, wherein was a lick with
two sulphur springs strongly impregnated." The site was no doubt selected
for its proximity to the river, creek, and salt lick and because it was a plain,
which required minimal clearing. Walker also described the scene greeting
them at the end of their journey: "On entering the plain we were permitted
to view a very interesting and romantic sight. A number of buffaloes, of all
sizes, supposed to be between two and three hundred, made off from the lick
in every direction; some running, some walking, others loping slowly and
carelessly, with young calves playing, skipping, and bounding through the
plain. Such a sight some of us never saw before, nor perhaps ever may again."
    Greatly encouraged by their surroundings, the party began to build
Fort Boone immediately. The few cabins erected, sixty yards south of the
Kentucky River and fronting it, sat a little below the lick. Despite their
recent trouble with the Indians, the whole party became quite careless in
their defense and kept watch only the first night after their arrival. Such
instances of foolhardiness were not isolated on the frontier: men who were
weary from exposure and the labor of constructing a fort did not want to
stand guard. Also, Boone had little or no actual control over his men,
independent adventurers who recognized his leadership abilities, if not always his orders. This lack of discipline no doubt contributed to the sad
event that ensued: "On the fourth day, the Indians killed one of our men."
    Richard Henderson, who received Boone's letter on April 7, was snow-
bound twenty miles east of Cumberland Gap and even further delayed by
the need to build shelters for the wagons before proceeding with packhorses.
Henderson angrily watched more lightly outfitted settlers pass him by to
claim his land. But in the next few days he counted over one hundred
terrified faces rushing eastward, back to civilization. He wrote in his diary
that, on April 8 alone, he "Met about forty person returning from the

Cantucky on account of the late murders by the Indians. *Could prevail on only one to return.*" Several Virginians in Henderson's party also chose to join the fleeing settlers.

Indian raids and the fear they caused were taking a heavy toll. A subsequent letter from Henderson to his partners in North Carolina revealed that the success of Transylvania hinged on Boone's abilities: "It was beyond a doubt that our right, in effect, depended on Boone's maintaining his ground—at least until we could get to him. . . . It is impossible to make the picture worse than the original. Every group of travellers we saw, or strange bells which were heard in front, was a fresh alarm; afraid to look or inquire, lest Captain Boone or his company was amongst them, or some disastrous account of their defeat."

That Henderson reassure Boone that his party was on its way was imperative. William Cocke offered to carry the message in exchange for ten thousand acres of choice land and a traveling companion. Henderson agreed but could get no one else to volunteer on equal terms, so Cocke reluctantly agreed to go alone. The next morning was gloomy and so was Cocke, who was having second thoughts about his impending 130-mile journey. Noting Cocke's growing hesitation, Henderson "struck whilst the iron was hot, fixed Mr. Cocke off with a good Queen Ann's musket, plenty of ammunition, a tomahawk, a large cut-toe knife, a Dutch blanket, and no small quantity of jerked beef." Fortunately, Cocke reached Fort Boone without incident.

Following Boone's path, Henderson's party crossed the Rockcastle River by April 15. William Calk recorded their progress:

> Satterday 15th clear with a Small frost we Start Early we meet Some men that turns & goes With us we travel this Day through the Plais Cald the Bressh & cross Rockcas[tl]e River & camp ther this Night & have fine food for our horses—
>
> Sunday 16th cloudy & warm we Start Early & go on about 2 mile down the River and then turn up a creek [Trace Branch] that we crost about 50 times Some very Bad foards with a great Deal of very good land on it the Eavening we git over to the Waters of Caintuck & go alittel Down the creek & there we camp keep Sentry the forepart of the night it Rains very har[d] all night—
>
> Monday 17th this is a very Rany morning But Breaks about

11 oclock & we go on and Camp this Night in Several companeys on some of the creeks of caintuck [Roundstone Creek]

Tuesday 18th fair & cool and we go on about 11 oclock we meet 4 men from Boons Camp that Caim to cunduck us on we camp this night Just on the Beginning of the Good land near the Blue lick they kill 2 Bofelos this Eaevening—

Wednesd 19th Smart frost this morning they kill 3 Bofelos about 11 oclock we come to where the indians fired on Boons Companey & Kild 2 men & a dog & wounded one man in the thigh we campt this night on oter creek—

Thursday 20th this morning is Clear & cool We Start Early & git Down to Caintuck to Boons foart about 12 oclock wheare we stop they Come out to meet us & welcom us in with a volley of guns

On Tuesday, April 18, Henderson's force had been met by Boone's friend Michael Stoner and three others, who had brought additional packhorses to assist them and "excellent beef in plenty." As Calk noted, they arrived at Fort Boone at noon two days later. Both groups were at once overjoyed and relieved.

Henderson's diary revealed that the next few weeks were spent improving the fort site. His entry for Friday the twenty-first highlighted important problems in settling the land and ensuring safety:

On Viewing the Fort, and finding the plan not sufficient to admit of building for the reception of our company and a scarcity of ground suitable for clearing at such an advanced season, was at some loss how to proceed. Mr Boone's company having laid off most of the adjacent good lands into lots of two acres each and taking as it fell to each individual by lot was in actual possession and occupying them. After some perplexity resolved to erect a fort on the opposite side of a large lick near the river bank which would place us at the distance of 300 yards from the other fort[,] the only commodious place near or where we could be of any service to Boone's men or *vice versa*.

Thus the fort's location was shifted to higher ground, land was cleared, a fort garden was planted, and a magazine built. Fort Boone, designed to have blockhouses on all four corners, fronted the Kentucky River for 240 to 260 feet and was 80 feet deep.

A great deal of time had been and continued to be spent surveying and arguing over the method of choosing plots. After much contention and two drawings of lots for land, Henderson said on the twenty-fifth that "every body seemed well satisfied." William Calk's journal provided a sense of the early process of settling Boonesborough:

> tuesday 25th in the Eavening we git us a plais at the mouth of the creek & Begin clearing this day we Begin to live with out Bread
> Wednesday 26th We Begin Building us a house & a plaise of Defence to keep the indians off
> thursday 27th Raney all Day But We Still keep about our house—
> Satterday 29th We git our house kivered with Bark & move our things into it at Night and Begin houskeeping Eanock Smith Robert Whitledge & my Self
> monday May ye first I go out to look for my mair and Saw 4 Bofelos the[y] Being the first Ever I Saw & I shot one of them but did not git him when I caim home Eanck & Robin had found the mair & was gone out ahunting & did Not Come in for Days and kild only one Deer—
> tuesday 2d I Went out in the morning & kild aturkey and come in & got Some on for my Breakfast and then went & Sot in to Clearing for Corn—

Pressing external problems added to the difficulties of establishing a settlement. Boone and Henderson's parties were far from alone in venturing into Kentucky in 1775. The McAfees, county surveyors John Floyd, James Douglas, and Isaac Hite, and two other companies of men, one led by Col. Thomas Slaughter and the other by James Harrod, were all busy making or improving their claims. James Harrod and his party were actively erecting the settlement of Harrodsburg to the west, and the group of land seekers led by John Floyd had located temporarily on Dick's River to the southwest. Floyd came to Fort Boone on May 3 to discover the terms on which he and his men might settle on Henderson's land. Quite suspicious of Floyd's intent, since he was in the employ of Colonel Preston (who had tried to defeat the Transylvania enterprise), but taken with his "modesty" and his "honest open countenance and no small share of good sense," Henderson noted in his diary: "We thought it most advisable to secure them to our interest, if possible, and not show the least distrust of the intentions of Captain Floyd, on whom we intend to keep a very strict watch." Henderson had his Cherokee deed, but Harrod and Floyd already occupied the land. Fortunately, by May 9, after a few days' talk, Floyd and then Harrod left Fort Boone, or Boonesborough as it was also called, evidently content.

All did not go smoothly. Henderson seemed particularly upset about his lack of control over the settlers and their ability: "Many men were ignorant of the woods, and not skilled in hunting, by which means some would get lost, others, and indeed at all times, shoot, cripple, and leave the game, without being able to get much. . . . Others of wicked and wanton dispositions would kill three, four, five or half a dozen buffaloes, and not take a half-horse load from them all. These evils we endeavored to prevent, but found it not practicable; many complaining that they were too poor to hire hunters, others loved it much better than work." Henderson also wondered about the benefit of having a Sunday service for "a set of scoundrels who scarcely believe in God or fear a devil, if we were to judge from most of their looks, words, and actions."

Henderson pressed forward with his plans nonetheless and scheduled a general meeting for May 23 to establish a government in Boonesborough. Each settlement needed to elect delegates to the convention. On Saturday afternoon, May 20, Boonesborough chose Daniel and Squire Boone, William Cocke, Richard Callaway, William Moore, and Samuel Henderson as its representatives. Four delegates each were likewise elected in Harrodsburg, St. Asaph (Logan's Station or Fort, which was laid out with the assistance of Floyd), and the Boiling Spring Settlement (founded by Harrod). The "divine elm" at Boonesborough was their point of assembly because its branches could shade a hundred people; Henderson intended it to be their "church, state-house, council chamber, etc." Henderson opened the May 23 meeting with a long, involved harangue spiced with eighteenth-century oratorical devices that gave ample testimony to his legal career. He stressed the need for wise laws, especially to prevent the wanton destruction of game, and the need for courts and a militia, all designed, of course, "without giving offence to Great Britain, or any of the American Colonies."

The four-day session was quite productive. "Transylvania" became the officially designated name of the colony. The minister, Mr. Lythe, introduced *"a bill to prevent profane swearing and Sabbath breaking"*; the bill, which must have been quite forceful, was sent to "a committee to make amendments." Henderson and John Farrar, who had been the Cherokees' attorney at the Sycamore Shoals treaty, performed the ancient rite of "Livery of Seizin": the symbolic handing of a small patch of turf from Farrar to Henderson completed the formal transfer of lands. The Boones prepared some significant bills that were voted into law. Daniel brought in one bill "for improving the breed of horses" and another designed "for preserving the game." Squire followed suit by introducing a bill "to preserve the range." Henderson reported that the delegates "finished the Convention in good order"; Daniel was more positive in his estimate: "I feel pleased with the work we have done here" and "feel sure we can hold against a huge number of savages."

While Daniel's first bill foreshadowed what was to become a passion for wealthy Kentuckians, the second had little effect. Conservation was proportional only to a lack of powder and lead. Commercial and subsistence hunting and the killing of game for sport radically thinned the great herds of buffalo and reduced the number of deer and bear, all of which had flourished under Indian control. Buffalo would essentially vanish from Kentucky by the end of the next decade.

Daniel Boone departed to bring his family to Boones-borough on June 13. Since the birth of his daughter Lavinia in 1766, three more children had been added to the family—Rebecca (1768 or 1770), Daniel Morgan (1769), and Jesse Bryan (1773). Daniel set a rapid pace, for he was soon to be a father again. His importance to Henderson's plans of empire was nowhere more potently underscored than in a joint letter written by Henderson and one of his partners, Colonel Luttrell, to their North Carolina associates: "We are informed that Mrs. Boone was not delivered the other day, and therefore do not know when to look for him; and, until he comes, the devil himself can't drive the others this way." All of Henderson's grand schemes would have to wait.

In the same letter of July 18, 1775, Henderson and Luttrell presented a catalog of the present woes of the new country—Indian skirmishes, abandoned settlements, no salt—and downplayed it as true entrepreneurs. Self-assured that a letter to the Cherokee chiefs simply reminding them of the Treaty of Watauga would put an end to their major problem, they concluded their letter by dangling the lure of fertile land, a powerful part of the American dream:

> The country might invite a prince from his palace, merely for the pleasure of contemplating its beauty and excellence; but only add the rapturous idea of property, and what allurements can the world offer as an equivalent for the loss of so glorious a prospect? Our crop of corn is beyond all description, and will scarcely admit of a deduction for untimely planting, cultivation, and being somewhat pinched with a dry season. In short, a description of our country is a vain attempt, there being nothing elsewhere to compare it with, and therefore can only be known to those who visit it.

The success of Transylvania was predicated upon the new settlers who would follow Boone. They always followed Boone. But Daniel would not budge until the baby arrived.

Rebecca gave birth to little William Boone in early July, but he survived just a short time. Somber moments were seldom long indulged by pioneer families. By the latter part of August the Boones, accompanied by Daniel's twenty young male recruits, had joined other prospective settlers in Powell's Valley. At the head of Dick's River the party separated, with the McGary party choosing to go to Harrodsburg. The rest, led by Boone, came into Boonesborough on September 6 or 7. Boone always boasted that his wife, Rebecca, and his daughters were "the first white women that ever stood on the banks of Kentucke river." (Unbeknownst to him, the captive Mary Ingles may have unwillingly won this title in 1755.) By the eighth of the month he was preparing to stock a larder with meat, as revealed by a charge to Boone in Henderson's books for two pounds of powder and twelve pounds of lead.

Squire Boone shepherded in a number of Rebecca's relatives later in September and Colonel Callaway also guided in his family together with another group of hopeful settlers. The latter party met with a band of Cherokees friendly enough to give the whites part of a buffalo they had killed. About this time, a solitary pioneer and Indian fighter made his way to Boonesborough after spending a season near the present site of Washington, Kentucky. Simon Kenton had earlier fled the Virginia frontier for Kentucky mistakenly believing that he had killed a man in a fight and would be charged with murder. Now only twenty years old, he was said to be more than the equal of all as a frontiersman, save perhaps Daniel Boone. He was a most welcome addition to the settlement.

The autumn of 1775 saw the migration to Boonesborough continue. The frontier for some time remained isolated from the repercussions of events that occurred in the East, but on April 19, the day before Henderson reached Fort Boone, the Revolution began with the battles of Lexington and Concord. On May 28, at the end of the Transylvania Convention, the Reverend Lythe is said to have read the prayer for the royal family for the first and last time at Sunday services in Kentucky. News of the trouble in Massachusetts did not arrive until the next day. Some later voiced suspicion about the inquiries made by certain visitors, believing them to have been Tory spies, intimates of Governor Dunmore, who were there to make friends with the Indians and examine the defenses of the various outposts.

While Daniel was on his way back to Kentucky with his family in August, Henderson, then in North Carolina, met with his partners to discuss matters concerning Transylvania. They voted Boone a present of two thousand acres of land "for the signal services he had rendered to the Company." In other business, the proprietors paid careful attention to the drafting of a memorial to the Continental Congress in Philadelphia. Henderson and his partners, unsure of the outcome of the rebellion, produced a masterpiece of equivocation and fence-straddling. They wished "to be considered by the Colonies as brethren, engaged in the same great cause of liberty and of mankind." They expressed the hope "that the united Colonies will take the infant Colony of Transylvania into their protection." On the other hand, if America remained a dominion of George III, they noted that they could "by no means forget their allegiance to their sovereign" and hoped "that Transylvania will soon be worthy of his royal regard and protection."

Richard Henderson and his associates certainly cannot be condemned for their vacillation. Many of the delegates to the Continental Congress were equally unsure of the future. In fact, upon the advice of leading members of Congress, the memorial was not presented. Congress had just petitioned the king and hoped for peaceful accommodation. To admit a fourteenth colony would have been an act of outright defiance.

Undeterred by the stalemate, Henderson followed through on his promise to publish the exact terms on which Transylvania land could be had. He did so on September 30 in Williamsburg, Virginia, and then concluded his announcement by again promoting Transylvania as an Eden ripe for American enterprise:

> any person who will settle on and inhabit the same [Transylvania], before the first day of June, 1776, shall have the privilege of taking up and surveying for himself five hundred acres, and, for each tithable person he may carry with him and settle there, two hundred and fifty acres, on the payment of fifty schillings per hundred, subject to an yearly quit-rent of two schillings, like money, to commence in the year 1780. . . .
>
> This country lies on the south side of the rivers Ohio and Louisa, in a temperate and healthy climate. It is in general well-watered with springs and rivulets, and has several rivers, up which vessels of considerable burden may come with ease. In different places of it are a number of salt springs, where the making of salt has been tried with great success, and where, with certainty, any quantity needed may be easily and conveniently made. Large tracts of the land lie on limestone, and in several places there is abundance of iron ore. The fertility of the soil and goodness of the range almost surpass belief; and it is at present well stored with buffalo, elk, deer, bear, beaver, and etc., and the rivers abound with fish of various kinds. Vast crowds of people are daily flocking to it, and many gentlemen of the first rank and character have bargained for lands in it, so that there is a great appearance of a rapid settlement, and that it will soon become a considerable Colony, and one of the most agreeable countries in America.

But Daniel Boone, far removed from the politics of Philadelphia and the propaganda published in Williamsburg, had no time to wonder about the outcome of Congress's deliberations with the king or about his future part in Henderson's grand scheme. His problems were immediate.

6

REVOLUTION AND RESCUE
ON THE FRONTIER

The December 1, 1775, opening of a Transylvania land office in Kentucky sparked a rush of claimants. Among the many men issued certificates of settlement for making improvements that year was Daniel Boone. Unfortunately, claim boundaries often overlapped unintentionally, creating "shingled" claims and immense losses for Boone and others in the future. For the time being, however, most of December 1775 proved uneventful in Kentucky, and the uninterrupted peace provided a sense of security. The Indians neither seemed to notice nor mind the growing invasion of their territory; only in December did the tribes north of the Ohio learn that large numbers of whites were constructing permanent settlements on their hunting grounds.

On December 23 Col. Arthur Campbell, accompanied by two boys named McQuinney and Sanders, left Fort Boone and crossed the Kentucky to search out fertile bottomland. They separated, with Campbell heading two hundred yards upstream and the unarmed youths climbing a hill to reconnoiter. No more than ten minutes later the crack of a gun and a scream echoed through the forest. Rescuers rushed from the fort and met Campbell, who, running to the landing with only one shoe on, said that he "had been fired on by a couple of Indians" just three hundred yards away. Boone raised a scouting party, but could ferret out neither the Indians nor the boys. Adding to the party's concern were the dozen hunters who were absent and unaware of the ambush; fortunately, they all gradually straggled in. No trace of the boys was found until McQuinney's scalped body was discovered in a cornfield three miles from the fort. Sanders was never found. Daniel noted in the "autobiography" that the Indians "seemed determined to persecute us for erecting this fortification."

Jesse Benton led a party of rangers dispatched the next day to determine if any force of warriors was in the vicinity. The rangers received two shillings a day and were offered five pounds for each Indian scalp they took. They returned on the thirty-first, sure that the raiders had retreated north across the Ohio and that the raid was not part of any organized attack. At the October Treaty of Camp Charlotte, King Cornstalk of the Shawnees had spoken of a renegade band of warriors over whom he had no control, stating, "if any of them should be killed by the whites, no notice should be taken of it." When the settlers finally learned of the treaty, they believed that these braves were the ones responsible for the incident. Those who could tried to push the whole matter into the backs of their minds. Many could not.

The settlement of Kentucky had progressed quite well: almost nine hundred claims entered for 560,000 acres; 230 acres of corn raised; horses, cattle, hogs, and poultry introduced; and even five hundred apple trees planted by Nathaniel Hart. Civil and military officers were commissioned and the militia had repulsed a few small Indian attacks. But ammunition was running low. How long would the Indian treaties forestall open conflict? The pressure was too great. Soon, of the five hundred people that had ventured into Kentucky, only two hundred remained, twelve of whom were courageous women like Rebecca Boone.

Those who stayed were less than united. Early in 1776, Daniel and Squire Boone accompanied surveyors who were laying out a tract of seventy thousand acres at the Falls of the Ohio for the proprietors. The action angered many of the settlers, who rightly regarded this land as probably the most valuable in Kentucky. The increase in land prices from twenty to fifty shillings per hundred acres also created much bitterness. As a result, a petition of grievances signed by "Capt. James Harrod, Abraham Hite Jr., and eighty-six others" was presented to the Virginia Convention in April. To quell the ire of the discontented, who now took issue as well with the validity of the Transylvania Company's claim, Henderson announced that he would not demand any money for the lands already sold until September.

On or about May 1, 1776, Colonels Henderson and Williams left to try to confirm their claim before the Virginia Convention and, if needed, before Congress. On June 15, the same day that Henderson was presenting his case in Williamsburg, the still embittered men of Harrodsburg elected

Captains John Gabriel Jones and George Rogers Clark to serve as delegates to the convention, giving them a mandate to urge that the territory be organized into a new county of Virginia. Nine days later the convention proclaimed that the Cherokee purchase lacked legislative approval and therefore could not be considered a valid claim. A deathblow was dealt to the company's hopes on July 4, 1776, when the convention "appointed commissioners in eleven frontier counties" to gather information negating Henderson's purchase. When the news of the Declaration of Independence reached Williamsburg, it virtually sealed the fate of the proprietary colony of Transylvania. Henderson's sole salvation rested with Great Britain's fortunes of war. Any rapid resolution of the disputed land claim was most unlikely and, for a considerable period, the matter thus tottered precariously on the brink of disaster.

The American War of Independence in the West was mainly an Indian war. Detroit and the several other scattered outposts lacked enough British regulars to mount a significant offensive against the American settlements. They could, however, furnish supplies and leadership to the Indians of the Ohio Valley, who in many instances were all too ready to go on the warpath against those who had usurped or devastated some of their best hunting grounds.

Although other colonies such as Pennsylvania obviously participated in the Revolutionary War in the West, Virginia bore the brunt of the conflict. Its citizens formed the majority of the settlers and consequently the majority of the militia. The war was fought over lands they claimed in defiance both of British law and other colonies' claims; to Virginians the war was a unique and special cause. When Henry Hamilton, the British lieutenant governor, first arrived in Detroit in November 1775, he accurately sized up the uneasy peace that existed between the settlers and the Indians in a letter to Governor Carleton in Quebec. He wrote that the Indians "are not likely to continue upon terms with the Virginians. . . . The savages have a high opinion of them as Warriors, but are jealous of their encroachments, and very suspicious of their faith in treaties." He also stated that the Virginians "have plundered, burnt, and murdered [the Indians] without mercy. Tis to be supposed from the character of the savages that opportunity only is wanting to retaliate and that there can be little cordiality between them."

English strategists recognized the value of forcing the colonies to fight a war on two fronts early in the struggle, hatching one such plot before

America declared its independence. John Connolly, Lord Dunmore's former Indian agent, received the permission of the British commander-in-chief General Gage to organize the Indians and frontier Loyalists and attack Fort Pitt. Simultaneously, Lord Dunmore, who had fled Virginia and sought asylum on a British man-of-war in Chesapeake Bay, was to lead an attack from the sea. Connolly would march to the east and Dunmore to the west, hoping to crush between them any resistance in Virginia. Fortunately, Patriots recognized and captured Connolly, a well-known figure on the frontier, before he could execute his plan.

However, the failure of grand schemes like Connolly's did little to stop the British from effectively playing upon the Indian-settler antagonism of decades past. The Shawnees were easy to incite and particularly antagonistic to the expansion of Virginia because of their defeat in Lord Dunmore's War. Commencing long before the Revolution, the brutal confrontation over the trans-Appalachian West would continue long after the final echo of the shots "heard 'round the world" had ceased.

Urged on and in part supplied by the British, tribes stepped up their raids on the northern settlements in the summer of 1776. A number of men were killed and several more were missing. Writing from the Holston country on July 7, Colonel Russell, sure of an impending Indian war, advised the immediate abandonment of Kentucky.

Since the December attack on the boys, Boonesborough had not suffered serious Indian trouble. The people had become less and less cautious because they saw no evidence of any imminent threat. While to the east the Continental Congress was in Sunday session on July 14, attempting to provide men and supplies for Washington's army, the residents of Boonesborough indulged themselves in the leisure activities of a sunny Sabbath day. Jemima Boone, Daniel's attractive daughter, convinced Betsey and Fanny Callaway to go with her on an excursion in the settlement's canoe. She wanted to soak her foot, which had received a painful *"cane-stab,"* in the cool river water. A young Virginian, Nathan Reid, promised to join them, but was too busy to do so at the last moment. The three young women felt quite capable of managing the dugout canoe alone. Betsey, sixteen, was engaged to Samuel Henderson, and Fanny and Jemima, both fourteen, had more than their share of serious suitors.

After pushing off from shore the Callaway girls paddled the canoe easily along the Kentucky River while Jemima trailed her injured foot in the soothing water. Nearing a prominent rocky cliff on the northern shore, the girls realized that the current had drawn them about five hundred yards below the fort. Unalarmed, one of the Callaways suggested going ashore to pick wildflowers and young cane. Jemima half-heartedly objected to landing on the Indian shore, saying that she was afraid of the Indians, whom she called "the *Yellow Boys.*" They decided to turn upstream and go home. The current, however, much stronger near the cliff, drew them close to the northern shore no matter how hard they paddled. The cane and bushes rustled and then suddenly parted in an explosion of painted warriors. One dashed into the water, seized the buffalo tug on the prow of the canoe used for mooring, and tried to drag the vessel ashore. Fanny Callaway thwacked the eager brave over the head with her paddle until it broke; her sister followed her example. When the other Indians reached their beleaguered brother, they made clear that they would capsize the boat if the beating continued. The screaming girls were pulled from the craft and hauled onto the shore. After one warrior yanked back Betsey Callaway's hair and gestured with his knife that another sound would forfeit her scalp, their shrieks terminated abruptly.

Forced to climb the riverbank, Jemima refused to move any farther. She pointed to the cane stab and declared quietly that she would rather die than march barefooted. Unswayed by threateningly raised tomahawks, she and Fanny were quickly given moccasins. After cutting off the dresses of all three at the knees for rapid travel and fashioning the remnants into leggins, the Indians hurried them forward, anxious to put a good distance between themselves and the fort. They kept to the harder ground of the ridges to leave less of a trail.

Jemima knew one of the captors, an English-speaking Cherokee named Scolacutta or Hanging Maw, whom she had probably seen at her father's Watauga cabin. The others, another Cherokee and three Shawnees, were unknown to her. Because they had already traveled out of earshot of the fort, she knew that the Indians would now allow her to break silence. Hoping they might be released, Jemima told Hanging Maw who she was; and when asked, she answered that the others were indeed her sisters, perhaps hoping they would all be set free. Hanging Maw only laughed. By accident he had gotten the upper hand over the famous "Wide-Mouth." "We have done pretty well for old Boone this time," he said.

Camping soon, about six miles from the river and about three miles southwest of the present Winchester, Kentucky, the braves took no chances. The historian Draper noted that "the captives were pinioned at the elbows, so that their hands could not touch each other; each of the captives placed beyond the others' reach, with one end of the tug with which they were tied, made fast to a tree, while the other was lain upon by one or more of the Indians, who sprawled themselves upon the ground in a circle around their prisoners." Anxiety made it impossible for the girls to sleep. Jemima tried to reach the penknife in her pocket, but she was bound too tightly.

The trek to the north resumed early the next morning. The girls knew their families would pursue them and devised all manner of excuses for marking a plain trail. They broke twigs and crushed parts of bushes and, when caught, told the Indians that they were "tired" and "had to pull themselves along." Betsey secretly shredded her linen handkerchief and dropped pieces of it strategically near their path. Until she had the heels knocked off her shoes by the Indians, she dug them deeply into every soft spot she could find. Jemima, blaming her wounded foot, frequently fell to the ground with a loud scream, praying that her voice might signal their location. At each of these instances the Indians brought upraised tomahawks and knives into the girls' faces, quieting the trio for a few minutes, but they soon resumed their actions.

Despairing of making any good time with such weak and clumsy white squaws, the Indians happened to find a stray pony, surely a way to increase their speed. Jemima, the most obvious offender, was placed on the animal; Fanny, and sometimes her sister as well, were mounted behind her. They covertly kicked, pinched, and pricked the pony in every way possible to get him to rear or buck and followed the previous pattern of falling to the ground with a piercing yell. At first the Indians merely put them back on the beast, but the tumbles continued. One patient brave mounted the pony to demonstrate to his three very slow pupils how easily it could be managed. Realizing that the use of the pony gained them no time, the Indians set it free in the woods. These must have been the most indulgent kidnappers on record: the girls' behavior was obnoxious enough to warrant death time and again by Indian code. Betsey Callaway was the only one punished—the frustrated pony bit her arm.

After making camp two or three miles south of Hinkston's Fork of the Licking River, the girls were given a meal of smoked buffalo tongue that was hard, unsalted, and barely palatable, before they were bound. By nine o'clock the next morning, Tuesday, July 16, the band was only thirteen miles from the Upper Blue Licks. A few miles farther on, feeling safely beyond the reach of the whites, the braves shot a buffalo, cut out part of the hump, and cooked the first meal since the capture. Their assurance deepened the girls' gloom. Relatives and friends should have overtaken them by now. It was three days since the abduction.

The young women did not realize the extent of activity taking place on their behalf. On Sunday, when the screams were heard at the fort, Daniel Boone jumped from his bed, grabbed his rifle, and stormed down to the riverbank, not even pausing to take his moccasins. Little Caleb Callaway ran to the lick and alerted Captain Floyd and Nathan Reid, who, hastening back, joined in the preparations already under way for pursuit. Samuel Henderson, Betsey's fiancé, stopped in the midst of shaving and ran downriver with Boone. These two, Floyd, Reid, William B. Smith, John Gass, and others first had to reclaim the canoe set adrift by the Indians, since it provided the only quick way of crossing the river and keeping their powder dry. Young John Gass fearlessly plunged into the water while the others flanked the shore with rifles cocked, ready to fire if any Indians should appear. Gass succeeded in bringing the craft back and crossed to the Indian side with Boone, Henderson, and three others.

While Colonel Callaway led a mounted party a mile below Boonesborough to a ford across the river, Boone divided his party to search for some sign of the Indians and their prisoners. Floyd's group found the trail first. Boone, turning back upriver, also came upon the trail and was soon met by Callaway's men. The agitated Callaway insisted on running down the marauders with his band, but Boone overruled him, knowing that the Indians usually posted one brave as a rear guard. At any alarm from him, the captives would be tomahawked. The rescuers decided that Callaway's horsemen should proceed at full speed straight to the Lower Blue Licks to head off the Indians' retreat at the customary crossing point on the Licking River. Boone and his men would cautiously pursue the general direction of the trail on foot.

Daniel eventually overtook Floyd's party, which had followed the tracks about five miles before nightfall. Continuing slowly forward to investigate a barking dog, Boone and the others found nine men, who had not been molested by the Indians, building a cabin. After making camp here, they evaluated their sorry condition: little ammunition, no provisions, and no proper clothing. One's best Sunday pantaloons were hardly suited to the task at hand. The intrepid John Gass made a round-trip journey back to the fort in the darkness of night, returning with gunpowder, shot, hunting attire, jerked venison, and Daniel Boone's moccasins.

Boone's party, bolstered by cabin builders John McMillen, William Bush, and John Martin, resumed the pursuit at Monday's first light and soon reached the spot where the Indians had made camp. Beyond the camp the trail disappeared. Taking full advantage of thick canebrakes, the kidnappers had temporarily separated and vanished without a trace. Daniel vetoed the idea of fanning out and attempting to follow whichever trails might be found as a waste of crucial time. Sure that the Indians were aiming for the Shawnee towns on the Scioto River, he insisted on striking off on a northerly route parallel to what he felt was their true course. The pursuers crossed the trail a number of times and, finding Betsy Callaway's heel prints and other encouraging signs left by the girls, double-timed their pace until darkness forced them to halt. Always the teacher, even at this time of extreme stress, Boone gave Nathan Reid a bit of possibly lifesaving advice, telling him that when scouting "through the country, never look for Indians, but keep a sharp lookout for their guns lying across logs or fallen timber."

Setting off at dawn on Tuesday, they came to Hinkston's Fork on the Licking River by ten o'clock. Boone believed that the Indians would have forded the water slightly downstream. A journey of one-tenth of a mile proved him right. The water was muddy and the moccasin tracks still fresh. Daniel decided to follow directly on the trail again, since the Indians would probably be less cautious after traveling more than thirty-five miles with no sign of pursuit. For the most part, the braves used the Warriors' Path, which led toward the Upper Blue Licks. They would sometimes take a buffalo trace to break the trail, but inevitably returned to the path.

Keeping to the Warriors' Path, Boone and his men soon broke into a trot. After eight or nine miles they came upon a recently slaughtered buffalo; blood was still oozing from the hump where the Indians had taken the choicest cut of meat. Daniel said "that he was certain that the Indians would stop to cook [a meal] at the first water." A mile or two farther on the pursuers found a small snake, which the Indians had crushed, still writhing. The trail stopped at a stream. The warriors had evidently waded along the creek bed, but no tracks left the water in the vicinity. Boone knew that the braves, likely preparing a noon meal somewhere next to the stream, were close.

Daniel, who had previously ordered his men to maintain silence, now reinforced the command with gestures. It was crucial that no sound be made. He motioned the party to divide; Henderson, Reid, and others went downstream, while Boone, Floyd, and the remaining men went upstream. Nathan Boone recorded the situation as told to him by his sister Jemima: "The girls were sitting in the grass on the ground in a small open glade and a few steps from the fire and were apparently guarded by one of the Indians in a reclining posture." Daniel's scout, probably William B. Smith, soon halted and waved the others forward. They crept forward on their bellies, keeping out of sight until the camp was only thirty yards away. Hanging Maw had just taken a kettle to bring cooking water from the stream, one brave was gathering wood, and another was preparing the meat; the sentry had left his post to light his pipe from the newly kindled fire. Jemima, having seen the rescuers, told the other girls to get some water with her so that they could get out of the line of fire. Before the men could reach the scout, Smith fired and missed. (He said the Indians had spotted him and he was trying to drive them away from the captives.) Boone and Floyd fired hurried, but eventually mortal, shots as soon as they were within range of the retreating braves, who were unprepared to repulse an attack despite the alert of Smith's shot. The only other shot, thought to be a distant one probably fired by John McMillen, had no effect.

Boone's men gave a loud yell and rushed the camp. Before he dove into the cane, one warrior flung a tomahawk at Betsey Callaway, barely missing her head. The girls jumped to their feet at the first rifle crack. Jemima joyously screamed "That's Daddy!" and the three captives began to run toward safety. Boone commanded them to fall flat on the ground and to stay there to prevent them from being fired upon deliberately by the Indians or accidentally shot by their rescuers. But the girls quickly bounded up again as the white men took the camp. In the confusion, one man mistook Betsey for an Indian because of her cutoff dress, makeshift leggins, and the red bandanna wrapped around her head. He was about to club her with the butt of his gun when Boone grabbed his arm and exclaimed, "For God's sake don't kill her when we have travelled so far to save her from death!" When the fellow realized what he had almost done, he wept like a child.

He did not cry alone. Jemima told her granddaughter that Daniel said, "thank Almighty Providence, boys, we have the Girls Safe—let us all Sit down by them and have a hearty Cry." The granddaughter also remembered that, according to Jemima, "there was not a dry Eye in the Company—a Cry for joy."

If the Indians had returned during this emotional reunion, Boone's party would have been at a terrible disadvantage. But the surviving warriors were happy to escape. They left knives, tomahawks, some moccasins, and two small worthless shotguns that were smashed over a tree. "We sent them off," Floyd wryly remarked, "almost naked." Recovering his composure, Daniel pointed to a bush, stating that there "I fired at an Indian." Drops of blood and a rifle were found at the spot indicated. Both Matthew Arbuckle and Chief Cornstalk later confirmed that his victim and Floyd's were Shawnees.

Now a bit calmer, the girls told of their English-speaking captors bragging about the Cherokee war parties supposedly assembling on the Kentucky and near the Upper Blue Licks, and about the raids in the Watauga region. With this knowledge, Boone determined to set out for home as soon as possible. (Strangely, no further word was heard of such war parties.) Exhausted from their ordeal, the girls and rescuers went just a few miles before making camp.

Luckily, along the way back to Boonesborough the party encountered the same pony used by the girls to vex their captors; the animal was now quite docile when pressed into service. Callaway's mounted band overtook them as they neared the fort. Discovering tracks of a solitary Indian fleeing from the Blue Licks, they surmised that the braves had been routed and the girls rescued, and had proceeded home. July 17, when all returned, was a day of joy at Boonesborough.

Interestingly, in recalling the whole episode for her young niece about a half-century later, Jemima seemed to echo her father's understanding view. She bore no grudge against her kidnappers and even spoke favorably of their behavior throughout her life, saying that "the Indians were really kind to us, as much so as they well could have been, or their circumstances permitted."

Samuel Henderson heard many jokes on the return trip, and no doubt inside the fort as well, about the three days' growth of beard on half of his face and several additional days' on the other. But Betsey's ardor remained undampened. On August 6 or 7, 1776, they were the first couple to be married in Kentucky, and Daniel Boone officiated "as magistrate under Transylvania authority." Colonel Callaway consented to the match only after exacting an oath from Henderson that a more recognized authority would solemnize the marriage as soon as possible.

Jemima, Betsey, and Fanny's adventure caused a sensation on the frontier and seaboard alike, further heightening Daniel Boone's reputation as a wilderness scout and Indian fighter. Years later, James Fenimore Cooper used the episode as the basis for the captivity and rescue of Alice and Cora Munro in *The Last of the Mohicans,* and the main character of his Leatherstocking Tales always seemed to bear a strong general resemblance to Boone.

Not long after the Henderson-Callaway wedding, a traveler brought to Boonesborough a copy of the *Virginia Gazette* that contained the first news of the Declaration of Independence. Eastern politics and turmoil did not yet play a major role in the thinking of Kentuckians, however. In the summer and fall of 1776 Boone commented in his "autobiography" not upon the continuing struggle for independence from Britain, but that the Indians had "attacked several forts, which were shortly before this time erected, doing a great deal of mischief. This was extremely distressing to the new settlers."

John Floyd recorded another source of trouble in a May 27, 1776, letter to Col. William Preston. Although the right of the settlers to four hundred acres of vacant land on the frontier would be upheld by the Virginia Convention in June, Floyd found maintaining order to be nearly impossible. He wrote Preston that it was

> The D——l [Devil] to pay here about land—pray try to get something done by the Convention with regard to selling those lands, or there'l be bloodshed soon. . . . Hundreds of wretches come down the *Ohio & build pens* or *cabins*, return & sell them; the people come down & settle on the land they purchase; these same places are claimed by some one else, & then quarrels ensue. In short they now begin to pay no kind of regard to the officers land more than any other. Many have come down here & not stayed more than 3 weeks, & have returned home with 20 cabins a piece, & so on. They make very free with my character, swearing I am engrossing the country [with military surveys] & have no warrants for the land, & if I have, they will drive me & the officers, too, to hell.

Over fifty years passed before the courts settled the majority of these and ensuing land disputes in Kentucky.

No major Indian attacks occurred in the latter part of 1776, but successive raids took a toll upon the feeble Kentucky settlements. Seven stations broke up; only Boonesborough, Harrodsburg, and McClelland's Station remained. Construction of palisades began at each of the three outposts, but after the alarm subsided only McClelland's Station finished theirs. The concentration of the two hundred settlers in three locations had at least one beneficial effect: three forts could be defended more easily than the previous ten.

A dwindling supply of ammunition threatened the concentrated defenses. In early July, before the capture of the girls, George Rogers Clark and John Gabriel Jones, the delegates to the Virginia Convention from the western parts of Fincastle County, left for Williamsburg to ask for support. When they arrived, they found a new constitution for a new state and a new government at work under a new governor—Patrick Henry. The convention, however, had adjourned. Clark visited Governor Henry at his residence in Hanover County and then returned to Williamsburg to try to convince the Executive Council of Kentucky's importance to the defense of Virginia. The council was hesitant at first to supply stores, already having a war on its hands, but granted the determined Clark five hundred pounds of powder on August 23.

Maj. Arthur Campbell of Holston had meanwhile sent a small supply of powder and lead to Kentucky. On September 7 Captain Boone reported that he had sold all of it to the people, except for a small amount reserved for scouts, at "six shillings per pound" for powder and "ten pence" per pound for lead. In fairness to Henderson and his associates, it should be noted that they provided the powder and shot for the entire countryside during most of 1775 and 1776. According to Draper, "These accounts remain unclosed upon the books in every instance, shewing a condition of no little indebtedness for the colonists of Transylvania to the great proprietors."

The Virginia legislature soon repudiated the Transylvania Company's claim to Kentucky. Captains Clark and Jones laid a petition before the legislature, and although they were not given seats, at their request in October or early November 1776 a bill was introduced to form the county of Kentucky out of the area incorporated as Fincastle County, Virginia, in 1772. Although Henderson's vigorous opposition delayed passage of the bill for one month, on December 23 county officers were appointed. John Bowman became the first official Kentucky colonel (though Boone may have held the title under Henderson's authority), Clark was made a major of militia, and Boone a captain.

For Henderson, his now frustrated dream of empire was reduced to a salvage operation from which he hoped to receive some compensation for his efforts and considerable expenses. Eventually, after the Virginia legislature closed the final business relating to the Transylvania Colony in late 1778, he and his partners received a grant of two hundred thousand acres at the mouth of the Green River, far less than they had requested as restitution. They no doubt now wished that they had been politically astute enough to include their determined opponents—Patrick Henry and his influential friends—in their grand project early in 1775 when Henry had stated that he believed the Transylvania claim was valid and, though he later denied it, had perhaps showed interest in participating in their venture. Sadly, Daniel received none of the compensatory tract of two hundred thousand acres, not even the two thousand acres for what Henderson had previously called Boone's "signal services." His efforts over the years apparently forgotten, Daniel ultimately was left landless in Kentucky.

Sometime probably in mid-December 1776, Clark and Jones left the legislative session to go to Pittsburgh to attempt to descend the Ohio River with the much needed supply of powder and other goods. Noting a continued Indian presence, Clark secreted the cargo in various places near Limestone (now Maysville, Kentucky), set their boat adrift, and continued on to Harrodsburg for reinforcements. Jones and some other men remained at Hinkston's deserted settlement on the Licking River. Joined by John Todd and others, Jones concluded that ten men were a sufficient force to convey the stores to the settlements and set out to retrieve them. A band of forty or fifty Mingoes under the command of the notorious Pluggy surprised and defeated the whites on Christmas day five miles east of the Lower Blue Licks. Although most escaped, two settlers were killed and Joseph Rogers and Josiah Dixson were taken prisoner.

Pluggy then attacked McClelland's Station on December 29. Luckily, Clark had just arrived with the men from Harrodsburg on his way to get the powder. Reinforced, the station's forces repulsed the warriors and killed Pluggy, among others, but numbered Capt. John McClelland, who received a mortal wound during the battle, among their casualties.

Worried that the captives, Rogers and Dixson, might reveal the locations of the stored powder, Simon Kenton and a companion trailed the remnants of Pluggy's raiding party back to the vicinity of Limestone and remained there long enough, despite the danger, to be sure that the caches of powder stayed safely hidden. Later Kenton returned to the settlements and then went out with about thirty men to bring in the powder. He refused to allow the group to use the shorter but more exposed Warriors' Path on the homeward trip. If the powder was lost, so was Kentucky. They returned safely by a longer route.

Likewise in January 1777, the settlers abandoned McClelland's Station, fearing that another attack was imminent. Only Boonesborough, Harrodsburg, and perhaps Price's Settlement on the Cumberland were yet occupied, with barely more than one hundred and fifty men fit for duty in the country. The bloody time, remembered afterward as "the year of the three sevens," had begun.

Blackfish, war chief of the Shawnees, irate over the defeat of Pluggy, took it upon himself to rid Kentucky of all whites. In a February 27 letter asking Patrick Henry and the Council of Virginia for aid, Capt. Hugh McGary stated: "We are surrounded with enemies on every side; every day increases their numbers. . . . Our fort is already filled with widows and orphans; . . . [and] a continuation of our woes threaten us—a rueful war presents itself before us."

A strong Indian war party, the first ever seen near Boonesborough, assembled in early March; however, Harrodsburg suffered the most during this month. On March 2 or March 6 seventy of Blackfish's warriors ambushed four young men near there, capturing Thomas Shores and killing and scalping William Ray. William Coomes managed to hide in a treetop and observed the disfiguring of Ray's body. James Ray, the dead boy's brother, outran all of the Shawnee warriors and escaped. Toward evening, thirty settlers on horseback went in search of their missing friends. Captain McGary blanched at the sight of the mangled remains of William Ray, his stepson. When one man mistakenly identified the body as that of Coomes, he was startled as the "dead" man came out from cover exclaiming, "No, they haven't killed me, by Job! I'm safe!" But at least three other men from Harrodsburg fell victim to the Indians that month.

A detachment of Blackfish's force killed a black fieldhand and wounded another person at Boonesborough on March 7. Near the same time, some Harrodsburg men who were making sugar were attacked; and among those horribly killed was another of Hugh McGary's stepsons. When Shawnee warriors fired the cabins outside the fort the next day, a brave wearing the stepson's hunting shirt was killed. Unable to control his fury, McGary savagely dismembered the brave's body and fed it to his dogs.

The outlying settlers now came in to "fort up," and all remained fairly quiet until April 24. Having left the fort early that morning to bring in the horses grazing nearby, Daniel Goodman and a companion were fired upon. Untouched, they fled toward the stockade, but Goodman was tomahawked two hundred feet from the gate. Simon Kenton, who was just setting out on a hunt, killed the Indian about to scalp Goodman. Boone, Stoner, Bush, and about ten others rushed out to help Kenton pursue the retreating braves and ran straight down a path between two fields. Reloading after killing a warrior who had Boone in his sights, Kenton saw that a large number of the one hundred hidden Indians had circled behind them. Boone yelled, "Boys, we are gone—let us sell our lives as dearly as we can!" and ordered a charge through the enemy to the fort. Each man fired and then clubbed down anyone in his way with his gun. An Indian's shot broke Boone's left ankle. Kenton killed a Shawnee who tried to tomahawk Boone, clubbed down another brave who was after Daniel's scalp, and then picked Daniel up and ran for the fort. As the pair neared the palisades, Jemima Boone darted out of the fort and helped them in. Two men still remained exposed. Bush faked a covering shot with his discharged rifle to allow the wounded Stoner to hobble into the fort and then made a mad dash for the safety of the walls.

Blackfish and his men retreated, as was usual with even a large Indian raiding party, once the element of surprise was lost. The chief knew that there was little chance of taking a fortified settlement defended by Kentucky long rifles and that even a successful attack would cost too many warriors' lives. There would be other and better opportunities to capture Boonesborough.

After the whites were safe inside the fort, their wounds were dressed. Captain Todd and Isaac Hite were among those shot, and Michael Stoner had taken disabling fire twice—once through the wrist and once to his hip. Fortunately, the ball extracted from Boone's ankle had flattened as it hit the bone. Daniel sent for and thanked the young man who had saved his life three times that day in a disarmingly understated fashion: "Well, Simon, you behaved like a man to-day: indeed you are a fine fellow." The painful wound disabled Boone for a number of weeks, serving ever after as an unpleasant barometer for bad weather or fatigue.

Daniel knew that food would soon be in short supply and divided the people into two companies—one to act as guards and scouts, the other to plant and cultivate corn. On May 23, or perhaps July 4 (the date is uncertain), the reflection of the sun from an Indian's rifle near the cornfield revealed the secret approach of a war party later estimated at two hundred braves. All the whites fled to the fort, but three were wounded before they could reach it. The Indians besieged the compound for two days until giving up in disgust and contenting themselves with destroying whatever cattle they could find. Boone's fellow sharpshooters had decreased the number of Blackfish's war party by seven.

Raids continued, but sustained, full-scale Indian attacks were few. Half-truths that spread along the frontier, such as "Boone was badly wounded" and "the people of Kentucky were penned up in forts," may have helped persuade Virginia to send reinforcements. Colonel Bowman arrived on August 1 with two companies from Virginia totaling one hundred men. He probably informed the population that a "New Commission of the Peace" had been appointed by the Council of Virginia on June 4 and that Daniel was one of the new members.

Capt. William Bailey Smith returned on September 13 from a trip to the Yadkin with forty-eight of Boone's kindred and friends. They entered Boonesborough single file, keeping six feet between horses to give the illusion of a larger force. The ruse worked—Indian scouts reported the arrival of two hundred white warriors. Learning "the superiority of the Long Knife, as they called the Virginians," Blackfish and his band relegated themselves to guerilla warfare, or, as Boone continued in the "autobiography," "Our affairs began to wear a new aspect, and the enemy, not daring to venture on open war, practised secret mischief at times." Parties of armed whites now aggressively pursued Indian marauders.

In his "autobiography" Daniel Boone could nevertheless truly state for the people of Kentucky that "we passed through a scene of sufferings that exceeds description"; the suffering apparently would continue. The Indians had destroyed cattle and crops; food was scarce and it was too late to plant. Starvation threatened to succeed where the tomahawk had failed. In December Col. John Bowman wrote from Harrodsburg to General Hand at Pittsburgh requesting corn: "I think it proper to order some corn to this place for our support. We intend to keep possession of the country, and plant crops the ensuing spring, as we have no other place from which to expect relief. If we are denied this request, we must do without bread till we can get it from what we intend to plant."

Boonesborough, however, had a partial source of grain. The previous year's cornfield, unlike the new fields, had not been burned by Blackfish. In some instances spillage and natural seeding produced seven or eight barrels to the acre. Some years later, Gen. Charles Scott probably drew upon this situation when making his now famous remark about the fertility of Kentucky's soil. "If planted," said he, "and cultivated as you Virginians do yours, twenty barrels would be an ordinary yield; if planted and not cultivated, ten barrels; *and if not planted at all, seven barrels!*"

Fertility of the soil notwithstanding, life remained difficult for the settlers, who were more hopeful despite having no reason to believe the Indian attacks would cease. Even when Daniel Trabue arrived in Boonesborough on Easter Sunday, 1778, the situation had changed very little. He noted that "The people in the fort was remarkable kind and hospitable to us with what they had but I thought it was hard times no bred no salt no vegetables no fruit of any kind no ardent spirits indeed nothing but meat." But none of the fresh meat could be preserved without salt, an ingredient essential to the Kentucky settlements' survival.

7

SHEL-TOW-EE
SON OF BLACKFISH

To try to remedy the lack of salt, Boone and thirty men set out on January 8, 1778, for the lower salt spring of the Blue Licks on the Licking River. They were to be the first of two contingents from Boonesborough to make salt for the different garrisons that constituted the Kentucky settlements, whose weakened state ruled out the normal trip to the North Holston wells as too long. Boonesborough's own salt lick, created by a sulphur stream, would not produce salt for human consumption. The water at the Blue Licks was very weak; 840 gallons had to be boiled to make one bushel of salt. That bushel, however, commanded a formidable price—a cow and a half. To boil down the huge quantities of briny water, Col. John Bowman had requested and received large kettles from the Virginia government. The large force of men accompanying Boone was required not so much to work the boiling operation as to cut the wood for the fires and to prevent Indian attack. Licks were a favorite spot for all hunters because of the game they attracted, but winter was an unlikely season for trouble.

This winter would prove far from typical, unfortunately for Boone and his party. The previous June the American brigadier general Edward Hand had arrived at Fort Pitt to consolidate defenses on the upper Ohio but was unable to follow through on his plan to attack the Indian villages of the Wyandots and of the confederacy of mixed tribes that formed Pluggy's Town. Successful raids by the Indians—their September 1 assault on Fort Henry, in which twenty-three of the garrison were killed, and the ambush later that month of Capt. William Foreman's scouting party, in which he and twenty of his men died—forced Hand to use what troops he had to defend vulnerable perimeter areas.

British officials coordinated the intensification of Indian attacks. Governor Hamilton of Detroit, particularly adept at playing upon the tribes' hatred for the white settlers, dispatched fifteen well-supplied war parties to the frontier in July 1777; within six months he reaped a bounty of 129 scalps and seventy-seven prisoners. Although British plans for the year had been stymied by Burgoyne's defeat at Saratoga on October 17, the news of his surrender did not slow Indian attacks in the West.

Their fury was fired in part by a particularly brutal action by the Americans. That same October, Cornstalk, accompanied by two other Shawnee chiefs, Old Yie and Redhawk, had come to Fort Randolph at Point Pleasant to tell the Americans that their tribe was yielding to British pressure and the chiefs could no longer urge neutrality. The commandant, Capt. Matthew Arbuckle, had no wish to hurt Cornstalk, who had proved faithful to his treaties in the past and had helped the Kentuckians, but faced with this declaration, held the three hostage. He later also detained Cornstalk's son, Elinipsico, who came to the fort searching for his father.

In early November Indians killed and scalped a soldier from the garrison close to the fort. After the attack, the captain of his company, a man named Hall, burst by the protesting Arbuckle with a group of his men and savagely murdered the four captive Shawnees. As Brig. Gen. Edward Hand wrote in his December 24, 1777, letter to the secretary of war, "From this event we have little reason to expect a reconciliation with the Shawanese, except fear operates on them; for if we had any friends among them, these unfortunate wretches were so." After these murders, the Shawnees needed no further justification to become full allies of the British.

These events made the Kentucky settlements one of the first lines of defense in the West, and their situation was growing increasingly desperate. A petition to the Virginia General Assembly, endorsed on November 25, 1777, and signed by Boone, emphasized their plight: "your Petitioners are and have for some time past been almost destitute of the necessary Article Salt. That by reason of the Incursions of the different Nations of Indians this year past we have been prevented from making what Quantities would be necessary for ourselves and Families as we formerly did, for small parties would be in great Danger of being cut off and larger ones could not be spared from the defence of the Families." The ability to hold Boonesborough and the other Kentucky forts would be in some respects proportional to the success of Daniel Boone and his party at making salt.

No remarkable event occurred for several weeks after their arrival at the licks. Daniel appointed himself one of the three hunter-scouts for the party, and on February 7, 1778, he left camp with a packhorse to resupply his band with fresh meat. (This duty gave him a chance to check his string of beaver traps as well.) He rode ten miles below the Lower Blue Licks before he could bring down a buffalo. Snow fell heavily by the time he had butchered the carcass and fastened about four hundred pounds of meat to his horse with strips of buffalo hide cut from the animal.

Well satisfied with the kill, he started back for camp. After traveling through a narrow path past a fallen tree, his horse spooked. Looking over his shoulder, Daniel saw four Indians coming at him, their movements muffled by the quickly falling snow. He furiously tried to throw off the meat and escape on horseback but found that the buffalo tugs had frozen. Reaching for his knife to cut the straps, he could not draw it from the scabbard. It too was frozen fast; he had forgotten to clean the blood off the blade and the grease off the handle and his hands. All this took but a moment. With no option other than surrender, the forty-four-year-old Boone took to his heels. But the Shawnees were young and swift. After a half mile, they closed the distance and their warning shots kicked up the snow on either side of Boone. One brave had cut loose the meat and was using Boone's own horse to pursue him. The next shot cut the strap of Daniel's powder horn. There would be no further warning. Exhausted, he dodged behind a tree and placed his rifle in front of it as a sign of submission. The braves came up laughing and whooping; "Wide-Mouth" had been captured.

When ushered back to their nearby camp, Daniel was stunned at what he saw: "a party of one hundred and two Indians, and two French-men, on their march against Boonesborough." The situation was worse than Daniel's count of combatants, which he provided for his "autobiogra-phy." The fully armed Shawnees, painted for war and under the command of Blackfish himself, numbered more than one hundred and two strong. And, in addition to the two Frenchmen in British employ, the war party included two "white Indians," James and George Girty, the brothers of Simon Girty, the terror of the frontier, to help direct the attack. As the traditional amenities of the handshake and "How d'do" greetings were ob-served with the chiefs, Boone recognized his old captor from 1769. Daniel accosted him by name, saying, "How d'do, Captain Will?" No Indian was more astonished than Captain Will at this greeting. After Boone reminded him of their encounter, he shook hands again with increased cordiality. Following his lead, each chief repeated the ritual.

Stepping forward, Blackfish came up with Pompey, a black adopted into the tribe who served as his interpreter, and informed Boone that he was on the march against Boonesborough. The unusual winter expedition was meant to avenge the murder of Cornstalk and his companions. The war chief then asked Daniel if the salt boilers at *"Pe-me-mo Lick,"* the general Shawnee name for the Lower Blue Licks, were his men. Ignoring the question until he was told that Indian scouts already knew their number and location, Boone granted that they were his. When Blackfish stated in a matter-of-fact tone that he would kill them, Daniel thought quickly. He had to forestall the attack on Boonesborough, whose fort still lacked one wall and whose settlers lacked any expectations of attack; moreover, most of the defenders were making salt. The case of his own men was equally hopeless: outnumbered four to one and ignorant of the presence of any hostile force, the salt boilers would be taken by surprise on Sunday, their day of rest. Any who escaped the initial onslaught would easily be tracked down in the woods because of the newly fallen snow.

His mind racing, Daniel decided to try a bit of duplicity, saying that he would persuade his men to surrender if Blackfish promised that they would be well treated and exempted from the tradition of running the gauntlet. He also said that all of his people would be happy to live with the Shawnees, but that the women and children would not survive a winter march. He offered to ride with the warriors to the fort in the spring to arrange a peaceful surrender. Blackfish agreed, but told Boone that he would forfeit his own life if he did not convince the salt boilers to give up.

Trudging through half a foot of snow, the Indian force arrived at the Blue Licks at noon the next day. They surrounded the salt makers and remained undiscovered only two hundred yards away. The men, seeing Boone and others approaching, thought the relief column from the fort was at hand. Then they saw the Indians. As they leaped to their feet and snatched up their rifles, Boone yelled "Don't fire!—If you do, all will be massacred!" He explained the situation, told them of the terms that he had negotiated, and persuaded them to surrender. Twenty-six additional prisoners were thus taken. Two scouts and two salt packers were absent— Boonesborough would be warned.

The licks now became the site of an Indian council convened to determine the fate of all the prisoners except Boone, who was needed for the spring capitulation of the fort. Such a betrayal of trust seemed impossible to Daniel. The action, however, was the repetition of what American soldiers had done to Cornstalk and his party. Pompey was allowed to translate the two hours of deliberations for Boone in a low voice. Blackfish also let Daniel make the final speech, an indication that he wished to keep his word despite the protests of many braves. Boone's plea, as recorded later by Joseph Jackson, one of the salt boilers, gave his men the first hint that their lives hung in the balance. He addressed the Indians:

> "*Brothers!*—What I have promised you, I can much better fulfil in the spring than now. Then the weather will be warm, and the women and children can travel from Boonesborough to the Indian towns, and all live with you as one people. You have got all my young men; to kill them, as has been suggested, would displease the Great Spirit, and you could not then expect future success in hunting nor war. If you spare them, they will make you fine warriors, and excellent hunters to kill game for your squaws and children. These young men have done you no harm, they were engaged in a peaceful occupation, and unresistingly surrendered upon my assurance that such a course was the only safe one for them; and I consented to their capitulation on the express condition that they should be made prisoners of war and treated well. I now appeal both to your honor and your humanity; spare them, and the Great Spirit will smile upon you."

Sentence by sentence, Pompey translated the speech to the Shawnees, who then voted. Fifty-nine voted to kill the prisoners, sixty-one to let them live.

After the British agents argued to no avail for an attack upon the weakened fort, the Indian party prepared for the return march by dumping three hundred bushels of salt into the snow, dividing the booty, and assigning a load to each white. Daniel refused to carry the sizeable brass kettle that was his portion. A brave shoved it at him. He returned the shove so forcefully that Indian and kettle were both sent spinning to the ground. Blackfish intervened at this point to take Boone under his care. His partiality to Boone, when combined with Daniel's speech, aroused suspicions of the pioneer's loyalty among some of the captives. Boone never had the opportunity to divulge his plans to them.

Boone noticed some braves clearing a three-hundred-foot path in the snow at that night's camp. He took Pompey with him and gently complained to Blackfish about the promise that his men would not run the gauntlet. Blackfish replied, "O Captain Boone . . . this is not intended for your men but for you." Boone had forgotten to include himself in the exemption. Indians armed with tomahawks, clubs, and switches formed two lines about six feet apart along the path. Boone stripped to the waist and began the race, running in a zigzag pattern that gave few braves a chance to inflict a severe blow. One brave near the end of the line, who was determined that Daniel should not pass unscathed, stepped directly into the path. Daniel pretended not to notice him and, at the last moment, butted the fellow full in the chest with his head and ran over him to safety. The Indians roared at their companion's discomfort, called him a squaw, and complimented Boone as a "vel-ly good so-jer."

"The same evening," according to Daniel's son Nathan, "a dispute arose as to whether to trim the ears of the prisoners, that is, to split the rim of the ear fully two inches in length, in which, when healed, to hang bobs and things as was the Indian custom. The two French officers argued this point, one for and one against. They became so heated that they drew swords against each other." The Shawnees had to step in to prevent bloodshed, and the captives' ears evidently remained intact.

The two missing scouts, Flanders Callaway and Thomas Brooks, soon alerted Boonesborough to the disastrous capture of the salt makers, but little could be done. Kenton and others followed the trail to the Ohio River before giving up.

The Shawnee towns were ten days distant, and the march to them was described by Boone in the "autobiography" as "an uncomfortable journey, in very severe weather." The ears of some Shawnees froze. William Hancock, one of Boone's fellow captives, noted that Daniel often shared his small ration of food with the others. Daniel added that they "received as good treatment as prisoners could expect from savages." Always a man of few words, Daniel's summation does not do justice to the hardships faced on the bitterly cold journey. The historian Draper pieced together a fuller account. In addition to the temperature and the snow,

> worse than all, no game of any kind happened in their way. In consequence of the depth of the snow and the plunder the party had to carry, their progress was necessarily slow and tedious,

which was greatly aggravated by the pinching of hunger. It is related that the Indians killed and ate their dogs. Then both whites and Indians subsisted for several days on slippery elm bark, the tendency of which was to relax the bowels, which effect was counteracted either by chewing the inner bark of the white oak, which, possessing a stringent quality, was denominated *oak-ooze*, or using a decoction made from the oozings of this bark, when, Boone used to say, he could travel with the best of them. At length, the Indians shot a deer and boiled its entrails to a jelly, of which they all drank, and it soon acted freely on their bowels. They gave some to Boone, but his stomach refused it. After repeated efforts, they forced him to swallow about half a pint, which he did with wry faces and disagreeable retchings, much to the amusement of the simple savages, who laughed heartily. After this medicine had well operated, the Indians told Boone that he might eat but that if he had done so before, it would have killed him. They then all fell to and soon made amends for their long fast.

They arrived at Chillicothe on the Little Miami River on February 18. The Shawnee town was larger than any of the Kentucky settlements and, built on the elevated ridge of the river, was easy to defend. Not since the defeat of Braddock's forces in 1755 had so many prisoners been taken. Despite Daniel's protests, all the other captives were now forced to run the gauntlet; fortunately, no one was seriously hurt. Soon the tribe adopted Boone and sixteen of his men, with Chief Blackfish adopting Boone, an act that reflected and added to the regard that the Shawnees had for the pioneer.

Daniel was given the name "Shel-tow-ee," or "Big Turtle." One of Boone's early biographers, John Mason Peck, who had had a number of conversations with the frontiersman, described the adoption ceremony:

The hair of the head is plucked out by a tedious and painful operation, leaving a tuft, some three of four inches in diameter, on the crown, for the scalp-lock, which is cut and dressed up with ribbons and feathers. The candidate is then taken into the river in a state of nudity, and there thoroughly washed and rubbed, "to take all his white blood out." This ablution is usually performed by females. He is then taken to the council-house, where the chief makes a speech, in which he expatiates upon the distinguished honors conferred on him, and the line of conduct expected from him. His head and face are painted in the most approved and fashionable style, and the ceremony is concluded with a grand feast and smoking.

Daniel accompanied Blackfish and forty Shawnee braves to Detroit on March 10 to sell to the British the ten prisoners who had not been adopted. Of this exploit, Boone said in the "autobiography" that "During our travels, the Indians entertained me well; and their affection for me was so great, that they utterly refused to leave me there with the others, although the Governor offered them one hundred pounds Sterling for me, on purpose to give me a parole to go home. Several English gentlemen there, being sensible of my adverse fortune, and touched with human sympathy, generously offered a friendly supply for my wants, which I refused, with many thanks for their kindness; adding, that I never expected it would be in my power to recompense such unmerited generosity."

Governor Hamilton, known as "The Hair-Buyer" because the settlers believed that he gave rewards for American scalps or prisoners, obtained permission to interrogate Boone to see if he knew anything about the fate of Burgoyne's army. Daniel told him "it was a well-known fact in Kentucky before I was taken, that Burgoyne and his whole army had surrendered to General Gates." With his fears confirmed, Hamilton urged Boone not to tell the Indians. "You are too late, Governor," Daniel answered, "I have already told them of it." Boone was said to have shown Hamilton his old commission from Lord Dunmore as a British captain and to have hinted that the Kentuckians might be won over to the British cause.

These developments undoubtedly sparked Hamilton's desire to ransom Boone. Blackfish, however, would not part with his newly adopted son even for one hundred pounds, five times the usual bounty for captives. In describing the situation at Detroit to his superior, Sir Guy Carleton, on April 5, 1777, Hamilton noted that the chief had plans for Shel-tow-ee: "These Shawanese delivered up four of their prisoners to me; but took Boone with them expecting by his means to affect something." Daniel was the key to the taking of Boonesborough.

Further, according to Hamilton, Blackfish had good reason to expect success. The governor wrote, "By Boone's account, the people on the frontiers have been so incessantly harrassed by parties of Indians that they have not been able to sow grain; and at Kentucke will not have a morsel of bread by the middle of June. Cloathing is not to be had, nor do they expect relief from the Congress—their dilemma will probably induce them to trust to the savages, who have shown so much humanity to their prisoners & come to this place before winter."

Boone, who previously refused the private offers of aid from English gentlemen, accepted "a horse, saddle, bridle, and blanket" from the governor before returning to Chillicothe, as well as some "silver trinkets" to use as trading currency. His favorable treatment by the British indicated that they believed he would influence Kentucky to support the Crown. Some of the American prisoners also began to share that belief. On April 10 Blackfish and his son left for home, stopping along the way to notify a number of Mingo, Delaware, and Shawnee villages of the time to meet at Chillicothe for the grand expedition against Boonesborough. The return trip, according to the "autobiography," "was a long and fatiguing march, through an exceeding fertile country, remarkable for fine springs and streams of water." No matter what his situation, Daniel always had a keen eye for good land.

They arrived in Chillicothe on April 25 to discover that Pe-Cu-La, or "Little Duck," who was one of the captive salt boilers, had escaped. Pe-Cu-La, whose name was Andrew Johnson, had led the Shawnees to believe that he was both young and a fool by pretending that he was terrified of entering the forest alone and demonstrating such severe gun-shyness that his lack of marksmanship was the laugh of the camp. His captors felt that he was not smart enough to escape and paid him little heed. Even after the fact the Shawnees did not believe that Johnson had escaped; they felt that he had wandered off. His Indian father honestly believed that he was the cause of what surely would become Pe-Cu-La's death. Angry at his son's disobedience in coming to a dance, he had told him to "take a dance, go home, and not to come back," but did not tell him which home he meant. Pe-Cu-La knew the home to which he wanted to return and did so with his father's gun, powder, and ammunition, as well as his tomahawk, knife, and blanket-coat.

Andrew Johnson, in reality a compact, veteran frontiersman rather than a befuddled boy, escaped, rafted the Ohio, and made it safely to Harrodsburg. After about two weeks there, he began to lead raids against the Indian war and hunting parties and towns. Blackfish himself was nearly killed in Pe-Cu-La's first surprise attack and escaped back to Chillicothe with two fewer warriors. When a warrior wounded in an encounter not involving Pe-Cu-La later recognized Johnson and his armed band and brought the news back to Blackfish's tribe, it was proclaimed that Pe-Cu-La "was a *little man*, but *a great rogue*."

Boone later declared that bringing the salt boilers to the Indian villages was a crucial mistake for the Indians: never "did the Indians pursue so disastrous a policy, as when they captured me and my salt-boilers, and learned us, what we did not know before, the way to their towns, and the geography of their country. . . ." The "calamity" of their captivity proved a blessing in disguise.

In the "autobiography" Daniel recorded that he fit in well with his Indian family and tribe:

> I became a son, and had a great share in the affection of my new parents, brothers, sisters, and friends. I was exceedingly familiar and friendly with them, always appearing as chearful and satisfied as possible, and they put great confidence in me. I often went a hunting with them, and frequently gained their applause for my activity at our shooting-matches. I was careful not to exceed many of them in shooting; for no people are more envious than they in this sport. I could observe, in their countenances and gestures, the greatest expressions of joy when they exceeded me; and when the reverse happened, of envy. The Shawanese king took great notice of me, and treated me with profound respect, and entire friendship, often entrusting me to hunt at my liberty. I frequently returned with the spoils of the woods, and as often presented some of what I had taken to him, expressive of duty to my sovereign. My food and lodging was in common, with them, not so good as I could desire, but necessity made everything acceptable.

When Boone was allowed to hunt alone, he received a carefully limited supply of powder and shot. By using light loads and sometimes recovering the spent balls, however, he amassed the supply of ammunition he felt he needed to escape. Once, he stocked a rifle for one of his tribesmen and received more ammunition as a payment. He also requested a flint, ostensibly to test the gun, but that soon found its way into his cache of ammunition, lock, and rifle barrel.

Part of Daniel's acculturation into the tribe as the son of the chief may well have also included marriage. Boone's great-granddaughter wrote, "Grandfather Boone said he had a squaw that claimed him as her buck; said she mended and dried his leggins and patched his moccasins." And Stephen Hempstead, who lived near Daniel in Missouri in 1809, remembered that Boone had said that during his captivity he "had been obliged to be married in Indian fashion."

Daniel evidently adapted so well to his new life that suspicions about his loyalty continued among some of the other adopted salt boilers. Capt. Will Emery's "son," William Hancock, "used afterwards to say that he could not understand how Boone could go whistling about apparently so contented among a parcel of dirty Indians when he (Hancock) was constantly melancholy." Blackfish and his wife treated Boone with kindness, the chief always addressing him as "my son," and as a brave, Daniel did not have to do any farming, as that was women's work in Shawnee culture. As Black-fish said to Boone when he saw him working in the fields with his Indian mother: "You need not hoe corn—your mother can make enough both for my family and yours also when you bring them out."

Hancock's views were understandable on two levels. First, Hancock was a poor woodsman who, as his words make clear, viewed the Shawnees only as savages. Ill-suited to wilderness life, he was predisposed to think the worst about Boone's behavior. Secondly, Hancock was right. Whatever the circumstances and no matter how much he missed Rebecca and his children, Daniel was foremost a hunter, not a farmer, and his place in his new family allowed him to do what he loved. Events, however, soon revealed the other motives behind Daniel's actions.

By June the Indian army began to assemble for the Boonesborough assault. On the way back to Chillicothe from salt making on June 16, Daniel stated in the "autobiography" that he was "alarmed to see four hundred and fifty Indians, of their choicest warriors, painted and armed in a fearful manner, ready to march against Boonsborough." His decision had been made for him: "I determined to escape [at] the first opportunity."

He did not have long to wait. The Shawnee band of salt makers scared up a flock of turkeys near the present Xenia, Ohio. The braves pursued them about three-quarters of a mile until the birds landed in some trees. Busy shooting the turkeys, they were unaware that Boone judged this moment his best chance to escape. Daniel cut the lashings that held the brass kettle to his horse and answered his "mother's" agitated questions about his actions by saying "I am going home; I must go and see my squaw and children, and in a moon and a half, I will bring them out here to live with you." As he said goodbye, the squaws raised a loud yell that made him urge his pony forward at the best possible speed.

According to Jimmy Rodgers, a white taken captive earlier and now enculturated into the tribe, the Shawnees followed Boone's trail for some distance, but returned because they thought he would get lost. Rodgers knew better. Boone rode all that night and did not slacken his pace until his horse gave out at ten o'clock the next morning. He turned the pony loose and put the saddle, bridle, and blanket in a tree with the thought that they might prove useful to someone else. He pushed on, frequently breaking his trail by walking on trees that had fallen perpendicularly to his intended path. Reaching the Ohio near darkness, he swam the river, pushing before him a small raft he had made to carry his clothes and belongings. Another story says that he crossed the river in an abandoned canoe he happened upon.

After a sound sleep, he treated his "scalded" feet with an ointment prepared by pounding peeled oak bark into a jamlike ooze. He also cut down a sourwood sapling, carved a rough stock for his gun barrel, and tied the barrel and lock to the stock, using the thongs that secured his blanket to his back. His superior skills as a gunsmith served him well here and throughout his life. He was quite proud of his new rifle's accuracy and soon brought down a buffalo, which supplied him with very welcome food. According to the "autobiography," Daniel arrived at Boonesborough on Saturday, June 20, "after a journey of one hundred and sixty miles; during which I had but one meal."

8

⤳⤳

PATRIOT OR TRAITOR?
Boonesborough Besieged

On his return to Boonesborough, Daniel found that Jemima, who had wed Flanders Callaway, was the only immediate family member who had not gone back to North Carolina. All had thought he was dead. Returning to his empty cabin, he received an unexpected greeting when the family's old cat, which had not been found since Rebecca and the children went back to the settlements, jumped into his lap.

Daniel had no time to indulge his emotions and his loneliness. During the four and one-half months of his captivity the lack of leadership had taken a heavy toll on Boonesborough. Little progress had been made on the defenses of the fort and the fort itself was filthy and unsanitary. That March a visitor said he "found a poor, distressed, half-naked, half-starved people."

Boone stirred the settlers to action with the news of the impending attack and directed their hasty preparations. One side of the fort was still not enclosed with palisades; two additional blockhouses had to be built; the gates needed strengthening; a new well had to be dug inside the fort; and the brush and stumps outside the stockade, which would provide any attackers excellent cover, needed to be cleared. The most pressing improvements were completed in ten days; during that time some fifteen to twenty men came as reinforcements from Logan's Fort and Harrodsburg.

The suspense was unbroken until July 17, when William Hancock, a new escapee from Chillicothe, brought word that the Indian expedition had been delayed three weeks because of Boone's escape. Hancock, who barely survived his nine-day trek, was nursed back to health for three days by his brother Stephen, Colonel Callaway, and Daniel. Hancock also said that Blackfish had sent runners to Governor Hamilton to apprise him of the new situation. In a July 18,1778, letter to Col. Arthur Campbell, Daniel cited more of the intelligence that Hancock had provided and noted his assessment of the situation: "He [Mr. Hancock] informed us of both French and Indians coming against us to the number of near four hundred, whom I expect here in twelve days from this. If men can be sent to us in five or six weeks, it would be of infinite service, as we shall lay up provisions for a siege. We are all in fine spirits, and have good crops growing, and intend to fight hard in order to secure them."

Although Boonesborough was at the ready, the war party did not come. In the "autobiography" Boone said that "the Indians had spies out viewing our movements, and were greatly alarmed with our increase in number and fortifications. . . . [They] determined utterly to extirpate the whites out of Kentucke. We were not intimidated by their movements, but frequently gave them proofs of our courage." He suspected that the scouts' reports to Blackfish were the real reason for the delay in the attack rather than his own escape, and toward the end of August he determined to head a raid against Paint Creek Town on the Scioto to take Indian prisoners, gain information, and seize enough horses and furs to pay for the effort. It was risky business that would weaken the fort's defense. Colonel Callaway bitterly opposed the plan, for he had grave doubts about Boone's motives and loyalty. But Boone prevailed.

Thirty volunteers set out on August 31. By the time they reached the Blue Licks, eleven had decided to turn back. Boone, Kenton, and the others continued on. As usual, Kenton took the point. When within four miles of their destination, he heard a bell tinkle, hid himself, and soon discovered two Indians, one riding, one walking. The Indian on foot suddenly jumped on the back of his friend's pony, greatly startling him. Both laughed. Both were now lined up in Kenton's sights. He fired, killing one and badly wounding the other with a single shot. When he ran up to take their scalps, he heard the cane rustle behind him, and just as he dove into the brush, two balls whistled past his head. Thirty or forty more warriors came up, but so did Boone and his men. "A smart fight ensued betwixt us for some time," according to Daniel in the "autobiography." "At length the savages gave way, and fled. We had no loss on our side: The enemy had one killed and two wounded. We took from them three horses, and all their baggage. . . ." The raid also began to erase the doubts about Boone's loyalties.

The Indians had been on their way to join the main attack column and the absence of braves from Paint Creek Town told Boone what he wanted to know—the attack force was on the move. He made all possible speed to outpace them to Boonesborough while Kenton and another man remained to try to secure horses or a prisoner. Boone's party slipped by the Indians at the Lower Blue Licks on September 5 and got to the fort the next day. The inhabitants now frantically cleaned and repaired guns, molded and trimmed bullets, brought in vegetables, and filled all available containers with water.

Comprised mainly of Shawnees, but also of Cherokees, Wyandots, Miamis, Delawares, and Mingoes, the war party arrived about ten o'clock on September 7, a beautiful Monday morning. Boone numbered the Indians at 444 and the French Canadians in British employ at an even dozen. Pompey, also known to his tribesmen as Black Dick, advanced under a flag of truce and hailed Boone, asking him to come out to see his father and to receive letters from Governor Hamilton. Boone hesitated until Blackfish called out to Shel-tow-ee to come and meet him. Due to the time they had spent together, the two men could understand each other reasonably well. Daniel went to meet Pompey and both went to a designated stump about sixty yards from the fort to confer with Blackfish. After a handshake and initial greetings, Blackfish asked, "My son, what made you leave me in the manner you did?" "I wanted to see my wife and children so bad, that I could not stay any longer," replied Shel-tow-ee. "If you had let me know," said the chief, "I would have let you go at any time, and rendered you every assistance."

Reminding his son of his bargain and oath to deliver the fort, Blackfish then proffered a letter and proclamation from Hamilton stating that the people would be "taken to Detroit, become British subjects, and be treated well," and that any officeholders would continue "at the same rank." The alternative was a massacre. Blackfish asked how Boone liked the terms. Daniel answered that he had been kept a prisoner for so long that new commanders had been appointed and he must first consult with them. Blackfish agreed and then mentioned that his warriors were hungry. Boone, who knew they would take whatever they pleased, kept up the pretense of friendship saying, "There, you see plenty of cattle and corn; take what you need, but don't let any be wasted." He went back to the fort as the Indians began killing cattle and gathering corn.

In a tense meeting inside the fort, Daniel said that he preferred to fight, but would abide by the decision of the majority. Squire Boone, who now styled himself a Baptist preacher, said hotly that "he would never give up; he would fight till he died." All the men agreed. "Well, well," mused Daniel, "I'll die with the rest." Expecting to receive help from Virginia, they also agreed to try to stall the negotiations to gain time.

Maj. William B. Smith went out with Daniel to treat with Blackfish, Moluntha (who had replaced the slain Cornstalk), and the Canadian commander, Antoine Dagneaux de Quindre. Adding further tension to the negotiation was Moluntha's knowledge that Boone's Paint Creek Town raiding party had killed his son; he had tracked the force back to the fort. The talks began with the Boonesborough negotiators seated upon a panther skin covering a log and with bushes held over their heads to shade them from the sun. Blackfish spoke to them, again urging the capitulation of the garrison. He exhibited a wampum belt with three rows of beads—black symbolizing a warning, white meaning peace, and red representing the blood that would flow if resistance was encountered. Blackfish said that one end of the belt "represented Detroit and the other Boonesborough." Which row or path would the whites choose?

Smith evaded the question by remarking that it would be very difficult to transport the many women and children to Detroit. "I have brought forty horses," countered Blackfish, "on purpose for the old people, women and children to ride." Boone asked for time until the following day to confer with the many white commanders. Blackfish granted the request and agreed on a line thirty yards from the fort over which neither side would pass. He even presented Daniel with a gift of seven tongues of jerked buffalo for the white squaws as a sign of his sincerity. Some believed the meat to be poisoned, but such was not the case. The interview ended with both sides smoking together as friends, with each group unknowingly covered by an opposing band of riflemen.

The people of Boonesborough rose the next day and tried to create the impression that the fort contained many defenders. Only sixty individuals could bear arms, forty of whom would be effective. But Blackfish had brought forty horses to transport the women and children; he probably had believed Boone's inflated figures of the garrison's size. To encourage this belief the women, dressed in surplus hunting garb and hats, marched back and forth in front of the fort's open gate armed with rifles. Daniel soberly noted in the "autobiography" that "It was now a critical period with us.—We were a small number in the garrison.—A powerful army [was] before our walls, whose appearance proclaimed inevitable death, fearfully painted, and marking their footsteps with desolation. Death was preferable to captivity; and if taken by storm, we must inevitably be devoted to destruction. In this situation we concluded to maintain our garrison, if possible. We immediately proceeded to collect what we could of our horses and cattle, and bring them through the posterns into the fort."

That evening Blackfish demanded their decision. He was shocked both by Boone's reply that his people refused to go to Detroit and would defend the fort to the last man and by Shel-tow-ee's sarcastic thanks for the extra time to strengthen the settlement's fortifications and for reinforcements to reach them. Unexpectedly Blackfish offered to negotiate a treaty and the peaceful withdrawal of his army with nine white representatives. Boone eagerly grasped at the additional time and remarked that the proposition "sounded grateful in our ears."

A place near the sulphur licks and about sixty yards from the gates was finally selected for the next day's meeting. During the conference Squire Boone announced that George Rogers Clark was leading an army to Boonesborough—a false tale but one very disturbing to the braves present. Daniel and his friends vigorously protested Blackfish's demand that he be accompanied by eighteen Indian deputies. He said that number was necessary so that each Indian town would be represented; otherwise the treaty would not be binding. The white men returned to the fort knowing that they would be outnumbered two to one on the morrow and fully expecting the worst. Although the Indians' original offer was probably genuine, the last was extremely suspect. Blackfish was seen walking slowly around the palisades and scrutinizing the fort's defenses. The Shawnees even performed a war dance. Neither of these actions bolstered confidence in Blackfish's good faith; both sides were equally capable of duplicity.

Negotiations resumed on the following morning, Wednesday, September 9. Few other Indians made themselves visible. After sharing a sumptuous meal prepared by the ladies of the fort to demonstrate their "vast" store of foods, young warriors replaced the older counselors at the talks. When Boone objected, Blackfish told him that the change was made at the request of the warriors, who wished to witness the historic negotiations. With such a switch, Boone must have been glad he had given explicit orders that twenty-five of his best sharpshooters man the bastions nearest the treaty ground with their rifles cocked. At the first sign of hostility, they were instructed "to fire at the lump." He was gambling. The odds were two to one that an Indian would be the victim.

The peace pipe was passed when all were seated and Blackfish proposed that they "forever bury the tomahawk, and live as brothers should live." Boone said that he agreed and asked what terms would be stipulated. The war chief said he would give the settlers six weeks to leave Kentucky, for they had no right to the land. The whites refused and reminded him of the treaty with the Cherokees. Blackfish pretended not to have heard of the document, but when a Cherokee who was present confirmed its existence, he said that "that entirely alters the case; you must keep it, and live on it in peace." He then set the Ohio River as the boundary between whites and Indians that was not to be crossed with hostile intent. Hunting, trading, and trapping were to be permitted on either side of the river. The only other demand was that the people of Boonesborough take the British oath of allegiance. After some discussion these stipulations were accepted by the settlers.

Blackfish said that he had to make a speech to inform his men that a firm peace had been made. After he concluded, he went up to the white commissioners and cautioned them not to be afraid, for it was customary, he said, at the conclusion of a treaty that was to be long and lasting, that they shake "long hands," a grip in which two Indians embraced each white man in a way that brought their hearts close together. Blackfish and another brave advanced toward Boone, and the other Indians paired off similarly with each white. The handshake turned out to be a grappling hold. Blackfish yelled "Go!" A warrior on the perimeter of the treaty ground fired a signal shot and all the braves now tried to drag the whites down a clay embankment a few yards distant, out of range of the fort's guns.

Blackfish's plan failed. The immediate volley from the fort's sharpshooters killed one Indian and so disconcerted the others that the settlers were able to break free. The fact that Boone had thrown his father to the ground hard enough to stun him added to their confusion, convincing some braves that the chief had fallen victim to a shot from the fort. An Indian wielding a pipe-tomahawk struck Daniel as he was about to dash for the fort. Its handle cut a two-inch gash across the back of his head and the blade "inflicted a lesser wound between the shoulders." Squire was hit and knocked down by a bullet that lodged in his shoulder, but jumped up and ran for the gate. It was shut. He and John South then ran to a previously designated cabin door to gain the relative safety of the fort. The braves hidden all around the treaty ground fired an estimated two hundred rounds at the fleeing whites.

Daniel summarized this dangerous scrape in the "autobiography" by saying that "although surrounded by hundreds of savages, we extricated ourselves from them, and escaped all safe into the garrison, except one that was wounded, through a heavy fire from their army." Squire was the one seriously hurt. In a slack moment Daniel had to make a sizeable incision to cut the ball out of his brother's shoulder. Forced to retire to his bed, Squire took a light broadax with him, vowing to use it as long as he could if the Shawnees penetrated the fort.

William Stafford had fired the first shot from the bastion, having drawn a bead on a chief sitting a bit beyond the treaty council and squeezing the trigger at the Indians' signal shot. The ball was fatal. But a number of Indians had been thinking along similar lines. Ambrose Coffee had unconcernedly stretched himself out on the highest log of the bastion to view the proceedings. At the first fire, fourteen balls pierced his clothing. Incredibly he fell into the compound without a wound, receiving no small amount of abuse for his foolhardiness.

As he made his rounds of the garrison, Daniel Boone had an encouraging word for everyone . Only then did he have his wounds dressed. The Indians' first charge was repulsed. Unfortunately, the settlers had not had time to clear all the shrubs, stumps, and trees from around the fort to lessen the available cover. The smell and smoke of gunpowder soon permeated the air. An old Dutch potter named Mathias ("Tice") Prock could not stand the odor, or perhaps the danger, and was discovered by Mrs. Callaway hiding under a bed. She encouraged him to his duty with her broomstick and ousted him as well from his next haven under the bellows of Squire Boone's smithy. Daniel Boone and Colonel Callaway intervened at this point and upbraided Tice for his cowardice, telling him to finish digging the new well if he would not fight. He did so with gusto—the deeper he dug, the safer he would be. At a lull in the fighting, Callaway noticed that Tice had left the well. Questioned, Prock replied that he would not dig while others did nothing. Callaway, who ordered him back to work, became infuriated when the potter refused, drew his tomahawk, and chased Prock about the compound until he jumped back into the well and dug at a furious rate.

Nathan Boone recalled his father saying, "The first day Indians rushed the fort and attempted to scale the walls but were beaten back. They made frequent attempts to set fire to the fort at night by carrying the fire under a blanket, and several got killed in this way." When the Indians saw that two days of constant fire produced no tangible results, they pursued some new schemes, such as putting the settlers' flax along a fence connected to the fort and setting fire to it, hoping that the flames would spread to the nearby blockhouse. The men inside foiled their design by tunneling under the palisades and pulling down the section of fiery fence near the wall. The Indians then tried to lure the people out of the fort by pretending to withdraw, but the racket they made "departing" assured the settlers that all that was in store for them outside the gates was a deadly ambush. The people of Boonesborough outwaited the Indians, who, realizing that their ruse had failed, began once again to bombard the fort with a seemingly limitless supply of powder and shot.

The muddied water of the river revealed a new tactic on September 11. De Quindre had convinced the braves to dig a mine from the riverbank to the palisades sixty yards distant. The settlers quickly erected a rough observation tower on the roof of the cabin that had originally served as Richard Henderson's kitchen. They could now see the dirt being thrown into the river and adopted the only practical defense—a countermine. Begun in Henderson's kitchen, the ten-foot-deep and two- or three-foot-wide mineshaft ran parallel to the river.

London, one of Henderson's slaves, had crept down into the passage dug the previous day to pull down the burning fence and had remained there all night to get a shot at an Indian sniper. He finally fired at the muzzle flash of his foe and in turn became a target by the flash of his gun; a fatal shot penetrated London's neck. A sentry named David Bundren was also mortally wounded when he peered through a partially closed porthole in the wall. The attackers used their weapons quite well, and Boonesborough could not afford to lose any of its able defenders.

The heaviest fighting since the beginning of the siege occurred that night. Rapid flashes from the rifles completely lit up the interior of the fort. Boone ordered a cease-fire just before daybreak to conserve ammunition and the Indians, as usual, followed suit.

After the defenders had built the watchtower, the Shawnees were especially careful not to expose themselves. Pompey, however, constantly popped his head up near the opening of the mine to observe the fort and verbally taunt his enemies, drawing a few ineffectual shots. William Collins, an excellent marksman, took careful aim at the place where Pompey's head had last emerged and fired the instant it reappeared. The men in the fort soon abused their opponents by asking in a mocking tone where Pompey was; the Shawnees yelled back that he had gone for reinforcements, gone hog hunting, or gone to sleep. It was not until the end of the siege that they said, "Pompey nee-poo," that Pompey was dead. The Shawnees had lost one of their best marksmen.

Another version of Pompey's demise stated that he was perched in a tree sniping at the inhabitants of the fort and that it was Boone, using "Old Tick-Licker," his favorite rifle, who dispatched him. The episode may be inextricably confused with one described by Draper in which an Indian, not Pompey, was firing into the fort from a tree. The brave varied his attack by "pulling up his breechclout, and exhibiting his person in a bantering, derisive manner." Boone's "Tick-Licker," which carried a one-ounce ball, was pressed into service, given an extra charge of powder, and used to end the striptease. Presumably it was Daniel who pulled the trigger.

This same morning Boone had a box rigged to dump the fort's excavated earth over the stockade walls to inform the attackers that the appropriate measures to nullify their mine were under way. John Holder and others picked up large stones as they were dug up and heaved them over the stockade walls and down the riverbank at the Indians. Irate curses verified their aim. Old Mrs. South, a simple soul, begged Holder "not to throw stones at the Indians, for they might hurt them, make them mad, and then they would seek revenge." The men took up her remark as a catchphrase and then parodied it in many a sarcastic taunt and jeer flung at the Indians.

Still the mine came closer with the enemy penetrating more than one hundred feet, or two-thirds of the distance to the fort, in several days. The settlers, both on the battlements and in the countermine, could hear them digging and would sometimes bawl out to the Indians, "What are you doing down there?" "Digging a hole," came the reply. "Blow you all to hell before morning, may be so! And what are you doing?" "O, as for that," rejoined the settlers, "we are digging to meet you, and will make a hole large enough to bury five hundred of you sons of bitches!" Luckily for the defenders, rain fell almost every night during the siege. A particularly heavy downpour eventually caused major cave-ins in the Indian tunnel, forcing them to resort to their rifles. They again took full advantage of the fort's ill-chosen location to fire down upon the compound from the river bluff and the hill southwest of the lick. Jemima Boone Callaway, seemingly unconcerned about exposing herself to enemy fire, fearlessly busied herself carrying ammunition and food to the men. One spent ball struck her as she stood in her cabin doorway. Facing inside to help supply her father with ammunition, Jemima had exposed what most biographers have gallantly referred to as "the fleshy part of her back." A tug on her linen undergarment was enough to make the bullet, which had barely penetrated the skin, fall out. The Indians managed, however, to sever the flagpole and cheered as the American colors fell to the ground. The men in the fort soon took down the pole, reattached the flag, and raised a loud cheer of their own as they set their standard back in its place.

Given his abilities as an inventor, Squire Boone had made his own preparations for the siege by building "a wooden cannon from a tough black-gum tree." Although reinforced with iron bands, the makeshift artillery piece cracked at its first trial. He then made another that was tested and found effective. Squire waited for a good target. One morning he spied a large group of Indians a bit more than five hundred feet from the fort. The cannon was brought out and loaded with a swivel cannon ball and a score of bullets, aimed and fired. The Indians fled in all directions. Several were thought to have been killed or wounded. But either at this discharge or the next, the barrel cracked, rendering the weapon useless. Furthermore, to thwart any attempt to burn down the buildings of the fort, Squire had disassembled a number of old muskets, fitted their barrels with small pistons, and found to his delight that they could discharge "from a pint to a quart of water" at each use. He gave the squirt guns to the women so they could extinguish any fire arrows or torches that lodged on the cabin roofs. Since the roofs sloped in toward the fort for greater protection, burning torches flung by the warriors that did not roll off could usually be swept off with long poles. If sweeping or squirting failed, a sharp blow with a pole from inside a cabin usually dislodged the flaming shingle for removal, as only a single peg fastened each long shingle.

The Indians tried their best to burn the defenders out for several nights while digging the mine, but fortunately, nightly rains kept the roofs damp. Some of the fire arrows had a small load of gunpowder tied in a rag attached to them, which was ignited by a crude time fuse made of punk. Such arrows would set a number of shingles ablaze. Still, the settlers were safely able to knock them loose. Extinguishing the torches thrown against the stockade was another matter, often requiring a trip outside the fort. John Holder took such a risk to douse a torch thrown up against a cabin door. He seized a bucket of water, flung open the door, and put out the blaze, roundly cursing the Indians the entire time. Mrs. Callaway heard him and he came in for a protracted tongue-lashing from the pious woman, who could tolerate his profaning the name of God little more than abiding Tice Prock's cowardice.

Night and day the sharpshooting from the fort exacted a small but steady toll on the warriors. On Thursday night, September 17, the Indians made a final unsuccessful effort to set fire to the fort. Defiant yells of the whites within answered the attackers' war whoops as they rushed the stockade and flung torches at the cabin roofs. It was again so bright that it was said a pin could be seen anywhere within the fort. William Patten, or Patton, who was out hunting when the Indians appeared, viewed from a distance this incredible scene—the repeated attacks of the Shawnees with their torches as they "made the Dreadfullest screams and hollowing that could be imagind," the screams and yells from within the settlement—and concluded that the fort was taken and its inhabitants massacred. He hastened to Logan's Fort with his sad news. Benjamin Logan prepared his people for the battle that he was sure would come. Only a few straggling Indians, however, were encountered.

At dawn on the eighteenth, almost no Indians could be seen near the fort. Hoping to keep up the pretense of the siege, they retreated gradually. By noon the victorious settlers emerged from their quarters for the first time in nine days. Some of the men "procured a quantity of cabbages and fed the more than half-starved cattle" that had been penned up within the stockade; others picked up the bullets on the ground outside the walls. British lead could be melted and recast into American bullets. In the "autobiography" Boone said that they "picked up one hundred and twenty-five pounds weight of bullets, besides what stuck in the logs of our fort." An additional one hundred pounds of lead was said to have been embedded in the bastion nearest the river. Daniel also summarized the battle statistics: "During this dreadful siege, which threatened death in every form, we had two men killed, and four wounded, besides a number of cattle. We killed of the enemy thirty-seven, and wounded a great number." Since the Indians carried away their dead, the figure was a guess. All other accounts, however, supported the number as a reasonable estimate.

As Kenton and his companion made their way back from Paint Creek Town where Daniel had left them, they saw the signs of a large war party heading for Boonesborough and changed their course for Logan's Fort. After Patten brought his grim tidings there, they set out to confirm his report. Reaching Boonesborough, the two men happily found that the story was false. A few days later the reinforcements arrived from Virginia.

Even after the detachment sent from Logan's Fort to help Boonesborough returned home, however, a band of warriors remained active for a time and seriously wounded Captain Logan as he attempted to drive cattle back into the fort that bore his name.

Since the immediate Indian danger had passed, and perhaps reinforced by William Hancock's account of Daniel's favorable treatment at the hands of the Shawnees, suspicions of Boone's activities were again voiced. Colonel Callaway, who had strenuously objected not only to Boone's Paint Creek expedition but also to his willingness to conduct a treaty with Blackfish, preferred formal charges. Both Callaway and Capt. Benjamin Logan insisted upon a trial. Both also had nephews who were still held captive as a result of the surrender of the salt boilers orchestrated by Boone.

The court-martial of Daniel Boone convened at Logan's Fort, with charges as follows:

> i. That Boone had taken out twenty six men to make salt at the Blue Licks, and the Indians had caught him trapping for beaver ten miles below on Licking, and voluntarily surrendered his men at the Licks to the enemy.
>
> ii. That when a prisoner, he engaged with Gov. Hamilton to surrender the people of Boonesborough, to be removed to Detroit, and lived under British protection and jurisdiction.
>
> iii. That returning from captivity, he encouraged a party of men to accompany him to the Paint Lick Town, weakening the garrison at a time when the arrival of an Indian army was daily expected to attack the fort.
>
> iv. That preceding the attack on Boonesborough, he was willing to take the officers of the fort, on pretence of making peace, to the Indian camp, beyond the protection of the guns of the garrison.

Boone's response to the charges and to Callaway's insistence that "Boon was in favour of the britesh government, that all his conduct proved it," was recollected and recorded by Daniel Trabue, who witnessed the trial.

> Capt. Daniel Boon sayed the reason he give up these men at the blue licks was that the Indeans told him they was going to Boonsbourough to take the fort. Boon said he thought he would

use some stratigem. He thought the fort was in bad order and the Indeans would take it easy. He (Boon) said he told the Indians the fort was very strong and too many men for them, that he was friendly to them (and the officers at Detroyt) and he would go and shew them some men—to wit, 26—and he would go with them to Detroyt and these men also, and when they could come to take Boonsbourough they must have more warriers than they now had. Boon said he told them all these tails to fool them. He also said he Did tell the Britesh officers he would be friendly to them and try to give up Boonsbourough but that he was a trying to fool them.

After a full investigation, Boone's defense of his actions and loyalty was upheld and he was honorably acquitted on every charge. In fact, he was even promoted to the rank of major for his faithful service. Whether from jealousy, frustration, or some other motive, Callaway and Logan were much displeased with the disposition of the case. Boone's conduct, however, had been fully exonerated and the salt boilers themselves, most of whom eventually escaped from captivity, generally agreed that Daniel had consistently chosen the best course for their survival and for that of Boonesborough.

The thought of Rebecca and the children soon hurried Daniel back to North Carolina. He went by way of Watauga to see an old friend, Capt. James Robertson, and eventually inspired him to visit the Cumberland country and later become one of the early pioneers and promoters of settlement in Middle Tennessee. Daniel soon arrived at the Bryan Settlement at the Forks of the Yadkin and found his family living comfortably at William Bryan's. News of Daniel's escape had come to the settlement, but the story of the defense of Boonesborough, his court-martial, and his promotion was now probably heard for the first time.

Richard Henderson and John Williams filed suit at the court in Salisbury on September 5, 1778, against Daniel Boone, J. Lewis Beard, and Robert Johnson for a debt of twenty pounds, and the *Records of the Moravians* noted that Daniel was in Salem on November 9, 1778; but other than these two facts, very little is known of Boone's and his family's activities from the winter of 1778 through the fall of 1779. They seem to have stayed in the settlements of North Carolina. In the "autobiography" Daniel maintained "nothing worthy of a place in this account passed in my affairs for some time." But, almost as an afterthought six paragraphs later, he added, "The history of my going home, and returning with my family, forms a series of difficulties, an account of which would swell a volume, and being foreign to my purpose, I shall purposefully omit them."

Faced with such a passage, a reader can only wonder at the apparent contradiction. It may be, of course, that John Filson received no information from Boone about this period in his life in their interviews and was merely trying to achieve a smooth transition in the "autobiography." But if not, what "difficulties"? Why "purposefully omit them"? Boone must have had to make a report to the authorities in Virginia about the present state of affairs in Kentucky. Accurate firsthand information was hard to come by. Were his actions called into doubt again? Some suggested that the "difficulties" had to do with the British sympathies of the Bryan clan, many of whom were Tories. Such a problem may have been one that Boone did not care to pursue. But all statements of this nature are speculative. The fact remained that after a long delay, for whatever reasons, Daniel Boone began to move his immediate family and a large number of Boones, Bryans, and others back to Kentucky after the fall harvest was completed. He needed to confirm his claims before the Virginia Land Commission, whose members would meet in Kentucky that winter.

9

FROM PAUPER
TO LEGISLATOR

Daniel's absence from Kentucky was marked by many changes. In the spring of 1779 Colonel Bowman mounted an attack on Old Chillicothe with two hundred men. He burned the village and destroyed the crops but withdrew without forcing a surrender. During the raid a shot ripped Blackfish's leg open from knee to thigh. Boone's "father" died a few weeks later from the resulting infection.

A successful campaign north of the Ohio River in the summer of 1778 by George Rogers Clark had brought about the capture of the British outposts of Cahokia, Kaskaskia, and Vincennes. Governor Hamilton of Detroit, however, retook Vincennes from Capt. Leonard Helm, one of Clark's subordinates, on December 17. Hamilton's victory was the first phase of a campaign to be mounted in the spring in which he hoped to unite all the pro-British tribes, have them meet on the lower Ohio, and, with an estimated 1,000-man force equipped with cannon, drive the Americans back to the seaboard. Clark, who had to attempt to reconquer Vincennes with only 170 men, said that if his effort failed, "this country as well as Kentucky I believe is lost."

He began his march on February 5, 1779, attacking on February 23 and taking Hamilton completely by surprise; after two days of fighting and negotiating the governor was forced to surrender. Detroit, the cornerstone of the British position in the West, offered a tempting but illogical next target. Clark's men were exhausted, and a number of them would have to be left behind to guard their prisoners. That expedition was postponed.

Clark's recapture of Vincennes, combined with other victories by him and his officers, had a significant effect upon the war in the West. Dealing from a position of strength that at times was based more on bravado than manpower, they won many Indian tribes away from British influence— the Kaskaskia, Peoria, Chippewa, Ottawa, Potawatomi, Miami, Kickapoo, Wea, Piankeshaw, as well as the more distant Sauk, Fox, Winnebago, and others. They had not broken the British domination of the large tribes, but had raised considerable doubt in the Indians' minds as to the ultimate success of the British cause. Indian support became more half-hearted and reluctant than enthusiastic and willing. Clark's victories also encouraged many new immigrants to come to the West, many of whom entered Kentucky following Boone's Wilderness Road.

In the fall of 1779 Daniel himself led his family and a group of new settlers on the road he had blazed to Boonesborough. Abraham Lincoln, the grandfather of the sixteenth president, is said to have been in the party, a story made credible by the fact that the Boones and Lincolns were long-time friends and related through marriage. One of the settlers, eighteen-year-old Peter Houston, later recollected the preparations for the journey:

> . . . on the morning of September 22, 1779, we started for Kentucky with six horses, twelve milch cows and a bull. The bull was my father's and being a good work animal we should need him in Kentucky. His burden for the journey was two large kettles we had used in making malt (my father directed a part of his time in making malt). These kettles were strapped over a pack saddle on the bull's back—Boone, also, had two kettles used for ordinary purposes, which were strapped over one of the horses backs, and over the backs of others were strapped various articles indispensable to our journey and to our wants after our arrival in Kentucky. And among other things were fire chopping axes, some cane hoes, a sifter and churn. (The last two articles and the two family kettles were Mrs. Boone's.) Thus armed and equipped we began our journey all afoot except the women and small children, who were added to the other burdens of the horses.

The trip was generally uneventful, except for the fall of Jemima Boone and eight-year-old Jane Dodson from Jemima's horse into a rain-swollen stream. Their rescue by Peter Houston and John Dodson, the child's father, the death of one of Boone's horses, and a three-day delay when Jane came down with measles were the only newsworthy events. Houston noted that "All slept in the open air with buffalo rugs for bedding except on unclear wet nights we constructed sheds of poles and bark. . . . The women baked Johnny cakes before our nightly fires and the men cooked the wild turkey and deer by running sharp sticks through the slices of meat and roasting it over the fire. We thought we were living in luxury until we had exhausted the salt with which we started."

The party arrived safely at the fort on October 22, 1779. The first view of Boonesborough may have pleased Houston and the Lincolns but could only have disheartened Daniel. In his absence the town he had founded had become a bustling settlement that was too hectic for his liking. The game had retreated and soon so did he. He moved north, near the present town of Athens, to erect Boone's Station on one of his claim sites.

Hurrying back to Kentucky to confirm his now invalid Transylvania land claims before the Virginia Land Commission, which began its hearings in the various forts on October 13, Boone quickly established a valid title to fourteen hundred acres for himself and an additional twenty-four hundred acres for his brother George and son Israel. Although Daniel hoped that the matter was finally settled, the vagueness of the certificates issued by the commission argued otherwise. His claim was described as "on the Waters of licking [River] including a small spring on the North East side of a small branch[,] a Camp & some Bushes Cut down at the same about 20 Miles East from Boonesborough." Not surprisingly, subsequent surveys generated lawsuits that clogged the court system of Kentucky for decades to come. A September 29, 1779, letter of Richard Henderson to Col. Robert Burton underscored the problems: "It is with me, a great doubt whether we shall finish the boundary line—There is no probability of the Virg^{ans} obtaining their quota of men to guard them. People here are so disgusted with the Land Law that they will not turn out on any account. . . . Upon the whole, am affraid the business will fall through, which will be very hurtful to myself as well as the rest of our Transylvania Company."

In 1779–1780, a hard winter set in around the middle of November. Lured by an exceptionally mild autumn, the fourth consecutive Indian summer, many immigrants were now snowbound or stopped by drifts in the mountains. Hunting became the main source of food as many of the cattle and remaining livestock were killed and the supply of corn ran very short. As far south as Nashville the rivers froze solid. Exposure, starvation, and disease took a heavy toll on beast and man as the heavy snows and bitter temperatures did not relent until March.

Those that did arrive after the thaw were often in ragged shape and ill prepared for their new situation. William Clinkenbeard remembered that "Pressly Anderson was barefooted & bare-legged—(rolled up his pantaloons.) His w. [wife] was walking & carrying her child. They passed us pretty nigh every day. . . . The women, the 1ˢᵗ spring we came out, wo'd follow their cows to see what they ate, that they might know what greens to get. My w. & I had neither spoon, dish, knife, or any thing to do with, when we began life. Only I had a butcher knife." Families led a primitive existence, subsisting on hunting and the bit of corn that they could grow, and always lived under the cloud of possible Indian attack.

The awful weather that winter allowed Daniel to try to improve the marginal existence of his family. As bad as the weather had been, it also kept the speculators away and gave Boone time to sell his land to buy warrants for new tracts. He started for Virginia early in 1780 to purchase the land at "forty pounds for every one hundred acres," the price set by the new law. From his land sales he had raised about twenty thousand dollars, in the depreciated paper currency of the day, and Nathaniel Hart and other friends had given him additional money to purchase warrants in Williamsburg. Daniel's saddlebags held between forty and fifty thousand dollars in cash when he began his journey. He and his companion got as far as an inn in James City, Virginia, where they stopped, perhaps to get a good night's rest, before entering Williamsburg the next day. They locked the door of their room and placed the saddlebags at the foot of their bed. In the morning they awoke to find the door ajar and the bags gone. Some of the currency was found stuffed in jugs in the cellar of the inn, but the vast majority of the sum was never recovered. Nathan Boone recorded, "It was my father's opinion that the landlord was the chief plotter of the scheme, and that an old white woman was the instrument, and that she must have hidden in the room, either under the bed or elsewhere. . . ." Boone could prove nothing. The backwoodsmen may have been drugged to ensure an easy theft.

Daniel seems always to have suffered at the hands of civilization. Everything he had struggled to maintain since first entering Kentucky in 1769 was now gone. In his own words, after the robbery he "was left destitute." Fortune, the wealth he had hoped to derive from the land he was to purchase, was never to be his. He was especially forlorn over the loss of the money belonging to his friends, many of whom held him accountable. Daniel paid them all back, one at a time, over the years. The Hart brothers, who had lost the most, saw the matter differently. In a letter dated August 3, 1780, Thomas Hart summed up their position on the robbery: "I feel for the poor people who perhaps are to loose even their preemptions by it, but I must say I feel more for poor Boone whose Character I am told Suffers by it." Hart went on to chastise Daniel's critics and to praise him: "much degenerated, must the people of this Age be, when Amoungst them are to be found men to Censure and Blast the Character and Reputation of a person So Just and upright and in whose Breast is a Seat of Virtue too pure to admit of a thought So Base and dishonorable[.] I have known Boone in times of Old, when Poverty and distress had him fast by the hand, And in these Wretched Sircumstances I ever found him of a Noble and generous Soul, despising every thing mean." He concluded his comments by stating that "therefore I will freely grant him a discharge for Whatever Sums of mine he might be possest of at the time."

Boone soon returned to Kentucky, where he had a number of encounters with Indians. While hunting with a large party south of the Kentucky River, he discovered a band of braves advancing toward the camp one night. He quickly directed his men to build a fire and stuff their blankets with beaver pelts to make it appear that the group was asleep. They then hid in the brush and waited. At sunrise, a salvo of shots thudded into the bedrolls. The braves who poured into the camp ran right into the fire of the twenty-five concealed hunters and beat a hasty retreat back into the forest.

On a solitary scouting expedition somewhat later, between Boonesborough and the Blue Licks, Boone was fired upon near Slate Creek. He dove into a thicket, crossed the creek, and worked his way downstream to a canebreak. He trained his rifle on the spot where he thought his attacker would appear but was dismayed when two braves with rifles came stealthily down the creek. He could easily kill one, but in so doing would make himself a perfect target for the second before he could reload. Luck was with him. For an instant both Indians stepped into the line of his sights. The shot pierced the lead warrior's head and tore into the shoulder of the other, who dropped his gun and ran. Daniel recrossed the creek, took the better of the two rifles, and threw the inferior one into the water before continuing on to the Blue Licks.

Daniel was more fortunate in his encounters with Indians than many

Daniel Boone Escorting Settlers through Cumberland Gap. 1851–1852 painting by George Caleb Bingham. Courtesy of the Washington University Gallery of Art, St. Louis, Missouri.

Simon Kenton. Painting by Louis Morgan. From Samuel W. Price, *The Old Masters of the Bluegrass* (Louisville, 1902). Courtesy of the Filson Historical Society, Louisville, Kentucky.

Above, Karl Bodmer. *Capture of the Daughters of D. Boone and Callaway by the Indians.* 1852. Lithograph, 17 1/16 x 22 1/8". Courtesy of the Washington University Gallery of Art, St. Louis. Transfer from Special Collections, Olin Library, Washington University, 1988. *Below,* The rescue of Jemima Boone and Betsey and Fanny Callaway, kidnapped by Indians in July 1776. From William A. Crafts, *Pioneers in the Settlement of America* (Boston, 1877).

THE
DISCOVERY, SETTLEMENT

And prefent State of

KENTUCKE:

AND

An ESSAY towards the TOPOGRAPHY, and NATURAL HISTORY of that important Country:

To which is added,

An APPENDIX,

CONTAINING,

I. The ADVENTURES of Col. *Daniel Boon,* one of the firſt Settlers, comprehending every important Occurrence in the political Hiſtory of that Province.

II The MINUTES of the *Piankaſhaw* council, held at *Poſt St. Vincents, April* 15, 1784.

III. An ACCOUNT of the *Indian* Nations inhabiting within the Limits of the Thirteen United States, their Manners and Cuſtoms, and Reflections on their Origin.

IV. The STAGES and DISTANCES between *Philadelphia* and the Falls of the *Ohio;* from *Pittſburg* to *Penſacola* and ſeveral other Places. —The Whole illuſtrated by a new and accurate MAP of *Kentucke* and the Country adjoining, drawn from actual Surveys.

By *JOHN FILSON.*

Wilmington, Printed by JAMES ADAMS, 1784.

Title page of John Filson's *Kentucke,* which contained the first published account of Daniel Boone's life. Courtesy of the Filson Historical Society, Louisville, Kentucky.

Fort Boonesborough as it appeared before the siege of September 1778. From George W. Ranck, *Boonesborough* (Louisville, 1901). Courtesy of the Filson Historical Society, Louisville, Kentucky.

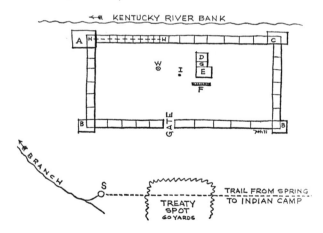

A copy of Judge Moses Boone's sketch of Fort Boonesborough before the siege of 1778. "A—Henderson's Kitchen; B—Two new [two-story] bastions; C—Phelp's house; D—Squire Boone's house; E—Col. Callaway's house; F—The Ball Battery; G—Boone's gun smith shop; H—The ditch or countermine; I—The flag staff; [W]—old well; [S]— Spring—a fresh & a sulphur one[,] near together." Diagram from Neal O. Hammon's "The First Trip to Boonesborough." Courtesy of the Filson Historical Society. Legend clarified from the Draper Manuscript Collection's version of the source of Hammon's sketch (DM 19C12).

Bring me the Scalps:
and the King our Master
will reward you!

Reward for 16 Scalps

Arise Columbia's Sons and forward press,
Your Country's wrongs call loudly for redress;
The savage Indian with his scalping knife
Or tomahawk may seek to take your life.

By bravery aw'd, they'll in a dreadfull fright
Shrink back for refuge to the woods in flight;
Their British leaders then will quickly shake,
And for those wrongs shall restitution make.

Henry Hamilton, British governor of Detroit, known as "The Hair-Buyer," in a Revolutionary propaganda broadside. Inscription on the sign (center): "Reward for 16 Scalps." Inscription above Hamilton (right): "Bring me the Scalps and the King our Master will reward you!" Courtesy of the Museum of Northern Arizona, Earle R. Forrest Collection, MS 143, Neg. 657-A.

Daniel Boone. Painted by John James Audubon sometime after their meeting about 1810. Courtesy of the Kentucky Department of Parks, John James Audubon Museum and Nature Center, Henderson, Kentucky.

Col. Daniel Boone. Stipple engraving by James Otto Lewis in 1820 from a portrait by Chester Harding. Courtesy of the St. Louis Art Museum.

Home of Col. Nathan Boone, c. 1900. Collection of the author.

of the white settlers. In March 1780 William Bryan Jr., one of Boone's relatives, went into the woods for his "stray" horse, following the sound of its bell. Having stolen the horse and tied it up, the warriors waited in ambush for the owner and killed him. Just before Bryan's death, another of Boone's in-laws met his doom at the hands of the Shawnees. Richard Callaway (Jemima Boone's father-in-law) and Pemberton Rawlings, the two trustees of Boonesborough with whom Daniel had earlier refused to serve, no doubt because of Callaway's charges against him, were unexpectedly attacked by a party of Shawnee warriors while constructing a primitive ferry-boat only a mile and a half from the fort on March 8, 1780. Draper recounted the story:

> the colonel [Callaway was] killed on the spot, Lt. Pemberton Rawlings badly wounded, who, after running a quarter of a mile, was overtaken, tomahawked in the back of his neck and scalped. Two Negroes were taken prisoners and never heard of afterwards, while the fifth person of the party safely escaped to the fort. A party consisting of Captain Holder, Bland W. Ballard, and others immediately repaired to the scene of the tragedy, found Colonel Callaway scalped, his head shockingly cut and mangled, and his body stripped and rolled in the mud. Rawlings was conveyed to the fort but lived only a few hours. Two days after, the remains of Callaway and Rawlings were buried in one grave just back of the fort. When Colonel Callaway's scalp was taken to the Indian towns, the peculiarly long and mixed grey appearance of the hair was recognized by Joseph Jackson, then a prisoner who had been captured with Boone's salt-boilers at Blue Licks.

Such deaths were a harbinger of the bloodshed yet to come. Major De Peyster, Hamilton's successor as lieutenant governor of Detroit, planned to attack the Spaniards along the Mississippi and the American settlers in Kentucky simultaneously. De Peyster had sent his best agents to buy the Indians' help with amazingly large quantities of weapons. Two of his bills for "Indian goods" from this period totaled in excess of fifty-five thousand pounds.

The advance guard of an ever growing force of seven hundred Shawnee and Great Lakes Indians had by June 20 reached Ruddle's Station, one of the northernmost Kentucky settlements. The commander of the expedition, Capt. Henry Bird, had marched very slowly from Detroit with two cannons and a detachment of British bombardiers to man them. Against orders and before either piece of artillery had arrived, his Indian troops fired at the settlers who emerged from Ruddle's Station that same morning. At noon the small fort was still defensible, though having just taken two rounds from the newly emplaced light field gun. Then the British six-pounder came up, leaving no hope for the station. One or two well-placed shots by the British regulars who manned the heavy cannon would batter down a large section of the stockade. Ruddle's Station became the first fort in Kentucky ever to surrender. Within a week, Martin's Station became the second. The settlers of two other forts, warned of the Indian army's advance, fled. Their homes were burned to the ground.

Capt. Bird never had firm control over the Indian forces, especially over those of Great Lakes tribes; thus, he could not prevent a number of gory executions among the approximately three hundred helpless prisoners. Probably out of humanitarian motives he refused to continue the expedition and headed his "troops" back to Detroit. The captives became beasts of burden for the Indians, who loaded them down with plunder that often included the prisoners' own goods. For many, Boone said in the "autobiography," it was a death march: "Such as were weak and faint by the way, they tomahawked. The tender women, and helpless children fell victims to their cruelty. This, and the savage treatment they received afterwards, is shocking to humanity, and too barbarous to relate."

George Rogers Clark, joined by Boone, Logan, and other commanders, mounted a retaliatory attack on the Shawnees toward the end of July. The combined force of about eight hundred to eleven hundred men burned Chillicothe and other villages and committed atrocities to repay similar Indian acts. According to Boone in the "autobiography," Clark's army "finished with great success, took seventeen scalps, and burnt the town to ashes, with the loss of seventeen men." Starting back to Kentucky on August 9, the army was harried by pursuing bands of Indians much of the way.

Bird's infamous campaign had not scarred Boonesborough and its immediate satellite settlements. Life seemed reasonably peaceful after the Indian retreat. In October, however, Daniel and his younger brother Edward were returning from a salt-making trip at the Upper Blue Licks and had stopped to graze their horses when a bear suddenly wandered within rifle range. Daniel hurried a shot and followed the animal down the creek while Edward remained with their horses and equipment and resumed leisurely cracking hickory nuts on some stones. Daniel was about to butcher the carcass of the bear, which had collapsed after running only a short distance, when he heard shots ring out from where he had left Edward. Then he heard the baying of a dog that had picked up a scent—his scent. He knew that his brother had been captured or killed and he plunged into a canebrake to try to save himself. He could lose the Indians but not their dog. Having dropped his ramrod, Boone could not reload his rifle, nor could he silence the dog, which easily kept out of his reach. Finally putting some distance between himself and the animal, he grabbed a stalk of cane to serve as a ramrod, loaded his rifle, and killed the dog. He then moved off on a new course through the cane, confident that he could now elude the Indians.

Peter Houston remembered that Daniel returned to Boonesborough "at ten o'clock at night and filled the fort with gloom." Boone raised a party of twenty-six men to pursue the raiders and the next day they found Edward's decapitated body in the woods. The Shawnees may well have mistaken Ned for Daniel and taken his head to prove that he was dead. Daniel and his men buried his brother's remains and tracked the retreating braves north as far as the Ohio before giving up the chase.

Since Boonesborough again had no salt, Daniel soon set out with Peter Houston and perhaps two other men for the Goose Creek salt springs with his kettles. After six days of boiling salt, they had made over a bushel and decided to return to the fort. Houston recorded the events of the next day, November 8:

> The sun was about an hour high and whilst we were discussing, one of our horses lifted his head and looking up the creek, snorted fearfully. "There are Indians near!" whispered Boone. We all sprung to our feet and seized our rifles and got ready for the worst. But Boone told us all to be silent, and keep a sharp look-out. We could see from our hiding place about 120 yards up the creek to a turn it made in the direction the horses kept looking, with every few minutes, a snort. Finally we saw three Indians come into sight from around the bend. Again Boone gave us orders to be silent until he gave the word. The Indians continued to approach us, evidently knowing nothing of our presence. But having approached within about eighty yards of us they discovered the smoke from our fire and halted, all three of them got behind a large tree and began to peer out from behind it.
>
> "Be silent," said Boone "until we see whether there are

more behind." Ten minutes elapsed, I suppose, when, the Indians still peeping from their cover, two on one side and one on the other, when Boone ordered Dodson to draw a bead on the single Indian and for Dickey and I both to aim at "the tall Indian" and he would take the other. We all fired at the word "fire" from Boone. Boone's Indian and ours fell but Dodson's gun failed to go off and his Indian, with a terrific yell, took to the brush. We did not go to the dead Indians. They were both shot through the head for we could see no other part of them and they pitched forward and fell in full view.

Boone, fearing the escaped Indian might return with an overpowering force ordered us to "be quick and strap the kettles together," which we did by taking the bark they were tied on the truckle with[,] by running the bark through the eyes of the kettles. Meantime, Boone had the horses in readiness with the sack of salt across one of their backs. And across this "pack saddle" the kettles were swung and two and two we mounted and off we started for the fort, traveled all night, changing, as we went, the kettles from one horse to the other as they were tired. And frequently we all walked to rest the horses. We reached the fort on the night of November 9. We never visited the Goose Creek Springs again from the fort.

Salt was not the only item in short supply. The influx of new settlers made the lack of clothing and bedding a significant need, and Daniel, Houston, and a few others decided to hunt for "skins," tan the hides, and thus remedy the situation. Deerskins, according to Houston, became "leather trousers and jackets and moccasins . . . principally for men but some of the women were under the necessity of wearing them." Buffalo hides became bed quilts. Supplying the wants of Boonesborough occupied Houston and the others for eight months (until mid-July, 1781), but Daniel was needed elsewhere.

The Virginia legislature divided Kentucky in November 1780 into three counties: Jefferson County, south of the Kentucky River and north and west of the Salt and Green Rivers; Lincoln County, south and east of the Salt and Kentucky Rivers; and Fayette County, north and east of the Kentucky River. Daniel was soon pressed into service in many roles, including sheriff, coroner, and county lieutenant of Fayette County, as well as deputy surveyor, lieutenant-colonel of the militia, and a county representative to the Virginia State Assembly.

In April 1781 he was in Richmond for the meeting of the assembly. The advancing British troops under Cornwallis forced the group to reconvene in May in Charlottesville, where Boone was sworn in as a delegate on the twenty-fourth. Soon, however, a detachment under Col. Banastre Tarleton, a famous Tory partisan, routed the Charlottesville defenders and swarmed into the town with 180 dragoons and seventy mounted infantry. Gov. Thomas Jefferson and Patrick Henry, as well as Benjamin Harrison and John Tyler, whose sons later became presidents, escaped with most of the legislators.

Daniel and three or four others remained behind to load public records into a wagon. He and John (Jack) Jouett mounted their horses and slowly made their way toward the edge of town. The British troopers did not challenge the men, who, in frontier dress, looked like individuals of little consequence. An observer noted that Boone "was dressed in real backwoods stile, he had on a *common jeans suit*, with bucksinin [buckskin] legg[ings] beded vary neatly, his leggins were manufactured by the Indians." They had nearly escaped, when Jouett grew very nervous and addressed Boone as "Captain" or "Colonel" within earshot of a British officer. Thus on June 4, both were seized, brought before Tarleton, questioned, and confined in a coal house.

The two prisoners received a parole for some unexplained reason after Tarleton rejoined Cornwallis at his Elk Hill headquarters. One story said that Boone escaped. Perhaps Daniel employed the same tactics that he had used to convince Governor Hamilton at Detroit of his loyalty to the British. Or perhaps one of Rebecca's Tory relatives who was said to have been in Tarleton's detachment arranged his release. (Like several North Carolina families, the Bryans had split over the cause of the American Revolution; two of Rebecca's uncles were Loyalist militia officers.) What actually happened has never been ascertained, but the events fueled old suspicions over Daniel's sympathies, which for the most part were quite simple. He put the safety and welfare of his family and friends ahead of the politics of nations. While he was far from alone in his caution and moderation, his attempts at relative neutrality numbered among the most difficult endeavors of his life.

If his politics were sometimes hard to judge, it was clear that Daniel always tried to fulfill his obligations. Two documents corroborated Boone's attendance at the final days of the legislative session, which reconvened in Staunton. The first, the Fayette County sheets in the House of Delegates' *Attendance Book* for the May 1781 session, recorded Daniel's twelve days in attendance at Charlottesville and then noted six days in attendance at Staunton. The second, a warrant issued to Boone on June 23, is in the *Vouchers for Old Treasury Warrants of the Virginia Land Office* and reads:

> We the Public Auditors of the Commonwealth of Virginia do certify that Daniel Boon hath delivered to us this [*sic,* the] Treasurers receipt for five thousand six hundred and fifty five pounds and that he the said Boon is entitled to three thousand five hundred and thirty four acres waste or unappropriated lands within this Commonwealth. Given under my hand this 23rd. of June 1781.
>
> H. Randolph
>
> June 23rd 1781 issued warrant for 1500 acres

Thus Daniel participated in the business of the legislature from the eighteenth of June to the twenty-third, the last day the assembly met in Staunton, and apparently also introduced a petition from Fayette County to establish the town of Lexington by an act of the assembly on June 21. He was the only representative of Fayette County then present. The other delegate, Thomas Swearingen, had also been captured by Tarleton, but never rejoined the assembly at Staunton.

By the end of August Daniel was back in Kentucky to meet his new son, Nathan, who was to be his last child. Peter Houston said at this time "Daniel remained with his family and hunted with others to supply meat for the fort, and in meeting immigrants by the way, conducting them on to the fort and seeing to their comfort after their arrival. He was one of the most benevolent and fatherly men I ever knew, and all looked to him as their counselor and guide." On October 20 James Boone recorded in his Bible that "Daniel Came [home to North Carolina] to See us," and in November Boone returned to Virginia for the next legislative session, which he attended sporadically until it ended in January 1782. Sometime after the session, perhaps by February or March, he had again returned to Kentucky.

Although Cornwallis had been forced to surrender in the East in October 1781, neither the Americans nor the British would accept the stalemate in the West. From 1780 on, both sides had suffered from a lack of trained troops, insufficient provisions and armament, and a rugged terrain that forestalled decisive victory or defeat. The frontier had some of its bitterest fighting still ahead of it. Kentucky was to suffer such an increase of fearsome Indian attacks that 1782 was justly called its "year of blood."

Since news of Cornwallis's defeat did not reach Detroit until April 13, the British authorities there prepared throughout the winter to launch another invasion into Kentucky. The raids began as early as February. To make matters worse, the savage Wyandots, who had now made peace with the more eastern tribes, joined the British cause. In March, the same month in which nearly one hundred Delaware Christians were murdered in an American raid across the Ohio River, a band of twenty-five Wyandot warriors passed by Boonesborough without incident, but caught a young girl and a black man, Monk Estill, outside the stockade of Strode's or perhaps Estill's Station (the accounts are contradictory). They killed the girl within full view of the fort and carried the slave off as a prisoner.

The slave's owner, Capt. James Estill, and his twenty-five-man garrison were away at that time on a scouting mission, but on March 22 Estill and his band of perhaps eighteen men caught up to the twenty-five Indian raiders at Little Mountain, the future site of Mount Sterling. Almost evenly matched, the two forces began one of the bloodiest battles for its size in Kentucky's history of native conflict. The vicious, pitched battle lasted two hours and ranged only over a few acres. Monk shouted across the lines to urge on the pioneers and encourage his owner; he also let Captain Estill know how many braves opposed him. As the Wyandots forded Little River Creek to attack, Estill split his men into three groups. When the left flank, under the command of William Miller, gave way and fled, the Wyandots poured in. James Estill was wounded at least three times and then killed. The whites killed an estimated seventeen Wyandots and wounded two or three before escaping with six badly wounded men of their own; seven whites were left dead on the battlefield.

Monk also escaped from the battle using the strength of his five-foot-five-inch, two-hundred-pound frame to carry one of the wounded men twenty-five miles back to Estill's Station. Estill's son freed Monk because of his bravery, making him perhaps the first slave freed in Kentucky. Settling in Boonesborough, he began a business making gunpowder for the community and for Estill's Station and is said to have taught Daniel Boone that process of combining sulfur, charcoal, and saltpeter. Already known for his apple nursery at Boonesborough, Monk also was a skilled woodsman, an excellent shot, and a talented musician. He eventually became a Baptist preacher in Shelbyville, Kentucky.

The norm in Virginia, slavery had moved west into Kentucky as a matter of course. The number of slaves was hard to determine accurately. The 1777 James Cowan census of Fort Harrod lists 19 slaves, 7 of whom were under the age of ten, out of a total population of 198. As the white settlers poured into Kentucky they brought their slaves with them. Daniel Boone was no exception. "In 1792, Boone was assessed with personal property, and also in 1793; he owned horses and negroes." John Filson's book, *The Discovery, Settlement And present State of Kentucke,* when published in 1784, estimated the number of slaves at about 4,000. In 1790, the first national census found 11,830 slaves and 114 freedmen in Kentucky. Within a decade the number of slaves had risen to 41,084, or about 19 percent of the total population; the number continued rising to 24 percent in 1830, but dropped to 19.5 percent in 1860 (224,483 slaves), likely because of both an 1833 law forbidding the importation of slaves into Kentucky for resale and an agricultural system based more on small farms than plantations.

10

~~~

"OUR AFFAIRS BECAME MORE
AND MORE ALARMING"
The Disaster at Blue Licks

Encouraged by their victory at Little Mountain, the native forces continued their offensive. In June 1782 the Indians decisively defeated a force of
approximately five hundred militia from Virginia and Pennsylvania on the
Sandusky River in Ohio. Col. William Crawford, the commander, died
only after a two-hour ordeal of slowly burning at the stake, during which
he was scalped and had burning coals poured on his bleeding head. Simon
Girty, the much feared "white Indian," was said to have watched the spectacle with great enjoyment.

The high point of the Indian onslaught occurred in August. Seventy braves attacked Hoy's Station in what is now Madison County, captured two boys, and started north toward the Ohio at a sluggish pace.
Their diversionary raid, meant to draw the white forces away from Bryan's
Station, the object of the main attack, almost worked. Captain Holder
gathered up what men he could at Hoy's, sent for reinforcements from
all the other stations, and rushed after the Indians. Receiving the news,
Daniel put others in command at Boone's Station and hurried to
Boonesborough to raise a party. Bryan's Station was the scene of similar
activity. Meanwhile, Holder and his seventeen men had ridden into a
trap, and as Daniel noted in the "autobiography," were "defeated, with
the loss of four men killed and one wounded." The whites were forced to
retreat without even catching a glimpse of the prisoners they had hoped
to rescue. And, as Boone then underscored the situation, "Our affairs
became more and more alarming."

Before the main force of over three hundred Indians had left Chillicothe, Simon Girty stirred them with his now famous speech:

> Brothers: The fertile region of Kentucky is the land of cane and clover—spontaneously growing to feed the buffalo, the elk and the deer. There the bear and the beaver are always fat. The Indians from all the tribes have had a right from time immemorial, to hunt and kill unmolested these wild animals, and bring off their skins—to purchase for themselves clothing, to buy blankets for their backs and rum to send down their throats, to drive away the cold and rejoice their hearts after the fatigues of hunting and the toil of war. [Great applause.]
>
> Brothers, the long knives [i.e., Virginians] have overrun your country and usurped your hunting grounds. They have destroyed the cane, trodden down the clover, killed the deer and the buffalo, the beaver and the raccoon. The beaver has been chased from his dam, and forced to leave the country. [Palpable emotion among the hearers.]
>
> Brothers: The intruders on your land exult in the success that has crowned their flagitious acts. They are planting fruit trees and plowing the lands where, not long since, were the canebrake and the clover field. Was there a voice in the tree of forest, or articulate sounds in the gurgling waters, every part of this country would call on you to chase away these ruthless invaders, who are laying it waste. Unless you rise in the majesty of your might and exterminate their whole race, you may bid adieu to the hunting grounds of your fathers—to the delicious flesh of the animals with which they once abounded—and to the skins with which you were once enabled to purchase your clothing and your rum.

Excise the rhetoric of war from Girty's words and what remains is a remarkably fair statement of the Indians' point of view and an eloquent expression of a valid complaint. This renegade white, regarded as the scourge of the frontier by the settlers, knew that the clash between Indians and whites was inherent in their opposing views of the function and use of the wilderness. Girty did much to agitate the tribes to make war on the intruders, perhaps because he recognized that conflict between these two cultures was inevitable; however, he was a complex figure who also had befriended Daniel during his Shawnee captivity, had saved his old friend Simon Kenton from burning at the stake, and had saved more than eighteen other white people, including Henry Baker, John Burkhart, Margaret Handley Erskine, William May, Samuel Murphy, and Thomas Ridout. When he was fourteen, Girty was captured in 1756 along with his three brothers. After three years of captivity he began to serve the American colonies as an interpreter at Fort Pitt, Pennsylvania, and did so for fifteen years until 1774. In 1776 his talents were employed by the Continental Congress, but in 1778 he deserted to the British cause. It was likely that the patriot-turned-loyalist aspect of his life fueled his depictions as an infamous white Indian who was the terror of the American West almost as much as his savage wartime deeds.

Incited by Girty's war speech, the Indians, under the command of British officers—William Caldwell, Alexander McKee, and Matthew Elliott—and of Simon and George Girty, secretly surrounded Bryan's Station on August 15 or 16. Daniel provided a bit more detail in the "autobiography," saying that the "nations of Shawanese, Cherokees, Wyandots, Tawas, Delawares, and several others near Detroit, united in a war against us, and assembled their choicest warriors at old Chelicothe, to go on the expedition, in order to destroy us, and entirely depopulate the country." By sheer luck the men inside the fort were still preparing to march off to the aid of Hoy's Station. The war party would not have the easy prey it expected.

No one knows how the settlers discovered the Indian presence. One unverified story stated that a messenger brought word of the attack just before the Indians' arrival. In any event, the gates stood closed and the men manned the bastions. The settlers had had no time to bring in the cattle or collect water and knew that they could not long withstand a siege under the hot August sun. The Indians, for their part, were unsure of the situation they faced. Was the fort essentially undefended, its men having gone off to the relief of Hoy's Station, or was the twelve-foot-high stockade occupied by forty-four expert shots? They waited. Before dawn a black man was attacked and an Indian scout fell victim to James McBride's rifle. Girty and Caldwell, the main Indian commanders, hoped the settlers would imagine that the dead brave was part of a small raiding party, and continued to wait in ambush for the men of the fort. So intent were they on not revealing their position and number that they let two messengers from the station slip unmolested through their lines.

Tradition or legend held that within the fort the defenders decided that the women would have to go to the spring to get water. It was their normal chore, and perhaps the Indians would not fire if the daily routine was carried out. Hopefully the war party would believe itself still undetected and wait to ambush the men who would soon leave the stockade. There would be no favoritism—all the females in the fort would go. They knelt in prayer, then picked up their buckets and other containers and walked casually to the spring at intervals. Valiantly keeping up cheerful talk in groups, they gathered all the water they could, and, trembling inwardly, began the seemingly endless walk back to the stockade. Once they were safe inside the fort the gates were quickly shut and barred. Thanks to the women, the garrison now had a chance to repel the impending assault.

Girty became impatient as the morning grew late and the gates remained closed. He ordered a small attack on the wall farthest away from the main body of his troops as a decoy, an old trick and one known to the men of Bryan's Station. They had an equally small party from the fort make a great show of flinging open cabin doors, firing, and running after the Indians. Most of the men stood at the loopholes in the stockade with their rifles cocked. Girty thought his plan had worked and ordered the principal attack. By this time the pursuing band of whites had nearly gotten back to the stockade; they soon brought the garrison up to full strength. The men had two or three rifles each and the women kept them loaded. The deadly marksmanship of the frontiersmen soon forced the warriors to give up the attack and take cover.

Girty, a formidable tactician who knew he had little chance of taking the fort before the messengers brought help, prepared to ambush the relief columns instead. The messengers had overtaken Maj. Levi Todd and his thirty riflemen at Boone's Station, where Capt. William Ellis was in command of sixteen or seventeen mounted men. Both forces rushed to the aid of Bryan's Station. As they approached all was quiet—too quiet. The commanders recognized the ambush. They decided that Ellis's cavalry would ride straight through the trap at full speed to try to reach the station and that the foot soldiers would try to get to the compound using the nearby cover of one hundred acres of tall corn. Tradition holds that the dust raised by the galloping horses prevented the Indians from getting a clear shot. All of the horsemen reached the safety of the walls of the fort. The still exposed men on foot were less fortunate—the cornfield also provided the Indians with excellent cover. The men in the fort heard the sounds of the battle gradually fading away, as their would-be rescuers fled back to Lexington, leaving two dead comrades behind.

Realizing that his men probably could not take a fort defended by some sixty rifles, Girty decided to try guile. He yelled out a demand that the garrison surrender, saying he had cannons that would arrive by evening. If they gave up now, they would not be harmed; if they chose to fight, his artillery would smash down the stockade and no quarter would be given. For a moment the settlers, no doubt remembering the fate of Ruddle's and Martin's stations, were silent. Then Aaron Reynolds, reputed to be one of the mightiest of frontier cursers, showered Girty with a volley of insults that broke the tension. There would be no surrender. A few random shots directed at the fort kept the defenders at their posts all night, but by daybreak the Indians were gone. Daniel summed up the human toll in the "autobiography": the attackers suffered "the loss of about thirty killed, and the number of wounded uncertain.—Of the garrison four were killed, and three wounded."

The next day saw reinforcements arrive. The scene that greeted them could only inspire an avenging anger. Everything outside the fort that would burn had been reduced to rubble. All the animals had been killed and the crops destroyed. By noon the men of Bryan's Station, together with the troops from Boonesborough, Harrodsburg, and Lexington, a total force that Peter Houston numbered at 182 men, sallied forth on the trail of the Indians. The commanders had decided not to wait for the four or five hundred additional men coming up from the south under Col. Benjamin Logan. Boone commanded one of the divisions, which contained his son Israel and numerous other relations and totaled forty-five men. John Todd and Stephen Trigg commanded the other divisions. Daniel anticipated close combat and chose an English fowling piece that he seldom used as his weapon. His son Nathan noted that Daniel "loaded each shot with three or four rifle bullets and sixteen or eighteen buckshot."

In an unusual maneuver that made their trail impossible to miss, the Indian force had retreated in one group. The Kentuckians moved swiftly through the wilderness after the war party, covering over thirty miles in twelve hours. Coming upon the Indians' camp of the previous night, Boone counted the fires and revised the estimate of the enemies' strength to at least five hundred Indians. Daniel grew more suspicious with each step he took: the braves were making no attempt to disguise their tracks; in fact, they had blazed trees with their tomahawks.

The whites had made their way to the Licking River near the Lower Blue Licks ford by the following morning. When the scouts found only two Indians on a ridge ahead of them, Todd, the senior officer in command, asked for Boone's advice. Daniel said that the signs he read, of Indians stepping in each others' tracks to conceal their numbers, indicated an ambush. He proposed crossing farther upriver to avoid this possibility, but was overruled. After sighting a few Indians on a hill a mile away, Todd again called upon Daniel's judgment. Boone urged that they wait for Logan and his troops. Even after the scouts returned with the report that all was clear for more than a mile ahead, Boone asserted that the two ravines connecting the hill with the river could easily hide the entire Indian force. Later, Daniel's daughter-in-law Olive Boone said, "Boone used to say that he knew every inch of ground around Blue Licks. He knew the Indians were in ravines ready to ambush them, and that the whites would be whipped like dogs. It grieved him to think into what a hopeless engagement they were about to enter." Todd seemed inclined to heed Boone's warning. Unfortunately Hugh McGary, still smarting from a remark made about his courage when he suggested waiting for Logan at Bryan's Station two days before, was determined to prove himself. He thrust his rifle over his head and spurred his horse into the river, screaming "All who are not damned cowards follow me, and I'll soon show you the Indians." Since Boone had counseled delay, he felt that McGary was questioning his bravery and said, "I can go as far as any man." Daniel then pleaded with Todd to assert his authority, but Todd told him, "Let them go, and we will remain in the rear, and if they are surprised by the Indians the blame will be on McGary and he will have the brunt to bear."

With the troops at a feverish pitch, it was unlikely that Boone or Todd could have stopped them from following McGary's lead. Helpless to stem the tide of men surging into the river, the two commanders plunged into the water themselves and managed to regroup the enthusiastic mob on the opposite shore into three columns. The whites left most of their horses at the river and crested the ridge on foot.

Boone, Todd, Trigg, and McGary were part of a twenty-five-man advance guard that moved down the hill and got within about sixty yards of the suspect ravines before they were caught in a murderous volley. Peter Houston said that "Boone yelled 'Colonel Todd, order a retreat across the river and make your fight there, the Indians are surrounding you.' But before Todd could accomplish anything he and Colonel Trigg both fell amid a shower of bullets from the ravine on the right." Twenty-two were killed. Boone, McGary, and one other survived. In the next three minutes eighteen more fell dead. Boone rejoined his column and managed to drive the enemy back momentarily. He later realized that their retreat was a ruse to draw him and the Fayette militia he commanded into a trap. Moments later, Major McGary rode up and shouted, "Colonel Boone, why are you not retreating? Todd and Trigg's line has given way, and the Indians are all around you." Daniel gathered his men into a body to try to break through the enemy at his rear. Then they and the other Kentuckians ran panic-stricken back toward the river—with a few exceptions, it was every man for himself.

The actual battle lasted only five to fifteen minutes. Boone tried to keep his men together and escape to the west into the forest. He got a horse for his son Israel, who was still recovering from a fever, urged him to escape, and ran to get another mount for himself. A rifle ball whistled past Boone, who spun around to see blood pouring from his son's mouth and his arms outstretched and quaking. Israel had waited for his father.

Bleak information about the Boones reached those survivors who had managed to cross to the opposite shore of the river. In his eyewitness account Peter Houston said, "My self and my brother Robert were in front of Boone and his son and did not miss them until we had recrossed the river, but in a few minutes Boone's nephew, Samuel, crossed, wounded in the leg and told us that Israel Boone had been shot from his horse and that Daniel had dismounted to bring him away before him on his own horse and he expected his uncle had been killed also. But by the time our men yet living had all crossed, we saw a man plunge into the river some seventy-five yards below. He swam across, and it proved to be Daniel Boone. . . ." Houston also recalled Boone's description of the tragic events after Israel was shot:

> I called to our fleeing men for help but they heeded not; where-
> upon I took my boy on my shoulder, and with gun in hand I
> hastened for the bushes on the bluff. Three Indians discovered
> me, and with a yell pursued me into the bushes. A very large
> Indian [a Wyandot] was ten steps in advance of the others and
> with my son on my shoulders, I saw I would be soon overtaken,
> and was forced to abandon my son. I let him to the ground,
> raised my gun and the big Indian fell, then, being familiar with
> the country, I found no trouble in eluding pursuit of the other

Indians and here I am safe, thank God, but it is painful to think that my poor boy has fallen prey to the scalping knife.

Then, according to Houston, "the grand old pioneer wept bitterly."

Most of Daniel's men had been able to recross the Licking at a ford near the mouth of Indian Creek, but many others were not so fortunate. Houston again painted a vivid scene of the brief battle:

The ridge where our men were fired on was almost barren and they were exposed whilst the Indians were protected by trees in front and by bushes in the ravines, and my impression is that but few Indians were killed by the emptying of our guns. Had the Indians rushed to the edge of the brush and timber before they fired they might have killed all the advance, and all that were in the gauntlet. But, as we saw when we returned to bury our dead, a great many of their balls had struck the trees and bushes before they passed out of the hiding places. They evidently, most of them, emptied their guns in the assault, and then began to close in on our men intending to complete their work with spears and tomahawks.

The braves reached the horses left by the riverbank at the same time as the whites and wreaked destruction and havoc on all sides. Boone caught the hopelessness of the settlers' plight in the "autobiography," saying "When we gave way, they pursued us with the utmost eagerness, and in every quarter spread destruction. The river was difficult to cross, and many were killed in the flight, some just entering the river, some in the water, others after crossing in ascending the cliffs."

An act of cool courage by a man named Benjamin Netherland saved a number of Kentuckians from the ranks of the massacred. Netherland rode his horse across the Licking and could have easily continued on to complete safety. Seeing the slaughter occurring on the opposite bank, he dismounted and organized the men fleeing by him into a line, saying "Let's halt boys, and give them a fire." On his command, ten to twenty rifles were fired, and the Indians, many of whom had no rifles, were forced to retreat. Netherland thus gained precious minutes for a number of his comrades to ford the river and escape the scalping knife, a fate that Daniel knew awaited Israel.

Colonel Logan and his troops arrived at Bryan's Station on Monday, August 19, the day of the battle, only to find that Todd had proceeded without them. Logan's force started after them immediately but met the first of the fleeing Blue Licks survivors within a few miles. Logan prepared to repel the attack by the warriors, whom he felt must be right on the heels of the terrified militia. The trickle of survivors continued through the night and then stopped. There was no attack. Houston summed up the battle for the survivors with a terrible simplicity: "Never was there an army better prepared to deal death to their enemies with less harm to themselves than was the army of Indians we met; never was an army in a more helpless condition than ours on this occasion. . . . In an open field, our force with Logan's would have been an over match for them, but with their ambush to protect them they could have vanquished a thousand men." Boone took no comfort in being proved right about the trap.

Meanwhile, the Indians took scalps. Many believed that the victors counted sixty white scalps and sixty-four dead braves and then killed four of their prisoners to even the score, but Boone thought the Indian losses were not that large. An August 28, 1782, letter from Alexander McKee to Major De Peyster puts their loss at eleven or less killed. The Kentuckians lost about seventy-five men. No matter what the numbers, in his "autobiography" Boone tersely stated the horror of the Blue Licks defeat: "Many widows were now made." Over 40 percent of the expedition was killed and nearly every home suffered a loss.

Moving his men up to the Licking, Logan refused to cross, rightly suspecting a second ambush. On August 24 Boone joined Logan's larger force on a second march to the Blue Licks, after he had returned from breaking the news to Rebecca at Boone's Station. The aftermath of the massacre was an almost unbearable sight to behold. Boone said in the "autobiography" that the burial party "found their bodies strewed every where, cut and mangled in a dreadful manner. . . . Some torn and eaten by wild beasts; those in the river eaten by fishes; all in such putrified condition, that no one could be distinguished from another."

Slashed, disfigured corpses littered the landscape; some still had their hands tied. These were the unfortunates taken alive by the Wyandots. Five days of heat had bloated the mangled bodies, and the only remaining means of possible identification were the occasional small remnants of clothing not stripped away by the Indians, wolves, vultures, and the current of the river. The settlers buried the bodies they could find in a common grave.

Boone found Israel's nearly unrecognizable body in the place where he had
to leave his son and brought it back to his station for burial.

Boone saw the whole venture of the settlement of Kentucky on
the brink of collapse. He wrote to Gov. Benjamin Harrison on August
30, 1782, and said, "I have Encouraged the people here in this County
all that I Could, but I Can no longer Encourage my Neighbours nor my
Seff to risque our Lives here at Such Extraordinary hazzards. the Inhabitants of these Counties are very much alarmed at the thoughts of the
Indians Bringing another Campaign into our Country this fall, which if
it Should be the Case will break these Settlements, So I hope your Excellency will take it into Consideration and Send us Some Relief as quick as
possible."

Recriminations over responsibility for the Blue Licks disaster occupied over a month's time. Logan blamed George Rogers Clark for calling
away a hundred men to defend Louisville and western Kentucky and thus
weakening the local militia. Clark stated that the defeat was a direct result
of the officers in charge: "The conduct of those unfortunate Gents was
extremely reprehensible." Neither side ever named Boone as one of the
parties at fault; nevertheless, his inability to convince the others of the
impending ambush disturbed him. He felt responsible for the bloody
defeat and for the death of his son. Boone told Filson that "I cannot
reflect upon this dreadful scene, but sorrow fills my heart." One family
story had it that Daniel had tried to convince the feverish Israel not to
come, while another stated that he shamed the sick boy into coming by
calling him timid. Either way, he had lost one more child and was over-
come with grief.

A second letter of Daniel's from September 11, 1782, again to Governor Harrison, indicated that while life had to go on after the Battle of
Blue Licks, the worries over survival continued unabated:

From a Late R[etur]n of the Publick Stores of this County, [I
fear?] they are almost exhausted[.] The no less Dangerous, than
Precarious Situation of our County Requires An Immediate
supply of Ammunition & Salt—for which purpose I Rely on
your Excellency Goodness in furnishing Mr. And.ᵂ Steele with
Two Hund,ᵈ Weight of Powder & Lead in Proportion a small
Quantity of Gun flints & some writing Paper, & as he has hith-
erto had the Conducting of [such?] [s]tores in this County I

hope that your Excellency will Confirm his Appointme[nt. He] seems well Calculated for such pub[lic t]rust—

As the Dry Beef [in our?] store is of an unsound Quality & not [suit?]able &[,] It may be necessary to Lay up a [new store?] this fall for Emergencie[.] [For this pur?]pose I would Request Twenty [one word missing] [bus]hels of salt as our store is Indebt by the Late fatal Excurtion of the savages—

It is [not for me to?] [give?] you a Detail of [that?] [three or four words missing] as I Expect you have already Rec.^d a perfect account[.] I would only Inform y^r your [*sic*] Excellen^y, that Sixty six of our Brave Kanetuckians fell the matchless Massecraed victoms of their Unprecedented Crueltie, Y^r Excellency, Compliance with the above Request will Oblige Your Assured f[r]iend & Hb.^e Sev^t

Daniel Boone

In the fall, when Clark led a force of one thousand riflemen against the native towns, the dispute over blame finally abated. Benjamin Logan and John Floyd served as his seconds in command, and Boone headed his own detachment. They encountered little resistance. Daniel described the retribution in the "autobiography": "We immediately took possession of Old Chelicothe without opposition, being deserted by its inhabitants. We continued our pursuit through five towns on the Miami rivers, Old Chelicothe, Pecaway, New Chelicothe, Will's Towns, and Chelicothe, burnt them all to ashes, entirely destroyed their corn, and other fruits, and every where spread a scene of desolation in the country. In this expedition we took seven prisoners and five scalps, with the loss of only four men, two of whom were accidentally killed by our own army."

Although Blue Licks was the last major battle of the Revolutionary War, the defeat of the Kentuckians had little influence on the tide of the war. Britain was ready to seek an end to the conflict, and the subsequent retaliatory campaign against the native towns had the intended effect of intimidating the Indian tribes in British employ. As Boone said of the warrior forces in his "autobiography," "Their connections were dissolved, their armies scattered, and a future invasion put entirely out of their power." Victory did not ease the price that had been exacted from the settlers. In concluding the "autobiography," Boone recalled the prophetic words that Dragging Canoe offered at the treaty that established Transylvania and then listed his own trials that had proved the chief's words true: "Brother, says he, we have given you a fine land, but I believe you will have much trouble in settling it.—My footsteps have often been marked with blood, and therefore I can truly subscribe to its original name. Two darling sons, and a brother, have I lost by savage hands, which have also taken from me forty valuable horses, and an abundance of cattle."

Preliminary peace talks opened between the Americans and the British in November 1782. But Indian raids, though much reduced, continued well after the signing of the formal treaty on April 19, 1783. The British stopped supplying the Indians with weapons, but found halting the attacks far more difficult than inspiring them. Sporadic raids continued to victimize emigrants moving down the Ohio on flatboats, hunters and trappers pursuing game in the woods, and settlers farming far from the forts until Gen. "Mad Anthony" Wayne finally defeated the Indians at Fallen Timbers in 1794.

11

"YOUR LAND IS ALL SURVAYD"
Prosperity, Debt, and Retreat

Daniel Boone had one of his closest escapes about the same time as the 1783 Treaty of Paris, which brought the Revolutionary War to a close. He had taken to raising some tobacco as a cash crop to supplement his income and had built a small curing shed. One day when he was on the poles, or rafters, of the shed raising a tier of dried leaves to add more tobacco below, he looked down and discovered four grinning Shawnees. One of them said, "Now, Boone, we got you. You no get away any more. We carry you off to Chillicothe this time. You no cheat us any more." Suspended in the air, far from his cabin, and unarmed, Daniel was in no position to disagree. He struck up a pleasant conversation to gain time and assured the warriors he would enjoy going back to Chillicothe to see his old friends. All the while he was gathering rows of dried tobacco in his hands. He explained that he wanted to finish his work and told them to watch him closely. In an instant he dumped all the tobacco and tobacco dust in their faces, pulled as much more tobacco upon them as he could while jumping down, and ran for his house. Looking back from a distance, he could not resist a chuckle. The braves were still stumbling around rubbing their eyes, all the while swearing at Boone for having tricked them again.

Also sometime probably in 1783, Daniel Boone moved his family to Limestone (now Maysville), Kentucky. The town served as an outfitting station and jumping-off point for Kentucky immigrants coming down the Ohio River. One of the few places on the Kentucky side of the river other than the distant Louisville where boats could find protection from the current for disembarking, Maysville served as a perfect spot for trading, general business, and land speculation. Daniel, never inclined to farming or homesteading, meant to do the best he could at all three. He opened a store and tavern and functioned as a surveyor.

Boone became a deputy surveyor in both Lincoln and Fayette Counties by the end of 1783 and, more because of his reputation as an explorer than a surveyor, drew more than his share of work. It has been calculated that Daniel completed almost 150 surveys of claims in the next three years. Daniel did a great deal of lucrative, albeit dangerous, surveying work for absentee claimants who entrusted him with treasury warrants to purchase land. He received up to half of the acreage he surveyed for them in return for finding good land and guaranteeing a free and clear title to it.

In a letter to Col. Robert Burton of the Transylvania Company on August 28, 1784, Daniel provided a vivid picture of his surveying business:

> Sir I have mised Severel opertunitys of wrighting to you however it is Never to Late to Do good[.] your Land is all Survayd But that of Martin Hamans and that Is to much exsposd to Danger to survay at this time and I shall be obliged to hire aman to go ans Show me Linns improvement as I Donot no his from the Rast and thare is 4 or 5 on that Crick[.] I never Re^d your horse till about 2 Weekes a go But Desired Cearey to Sell him if possible But he Could not[.] then I took him to our Corte and Sat the price of 250 pounds on him but I could Not gat a Single Bid for him tho every Man Liked the horse[.] But money is not to be had at any Rate[.] So I took him home and swopt him for a Mare and Colt for my own use in Less I can Sell hir to a good advantage and Shall advance 25 pounds for you[.] I can a sure you if I had Cash I could by 20 horsis in a week of pepel who want to Lift there plots out of the ofis[.] the Cearseys 2 plots for Setelment and preemtion and farrows are all in the Regesters ofis[.] your Land obtained by tresury warrants the plot is Not yet Returned But will in a few Days[.] I am Sir your Most obedient omble Survant
>
> *Daniel Boone*

For Boone the main danger in his surveying enterprise came not from the still fairly active Indian raiders, whose ways he knew and could defend himself against; instead, the most danger came from his guaranteeing his

clients a clear legal title to the lands he laid out and purchased in their
names. Daniel was a tolerable surveyor and better than most in the inclu-
sion of landmarks. But the surveys of the period were rough at best and
warrants had been issued for more land than existed. A survey made for
himself, dated "Aperel the 22 1785," for a claim on the Kentucky River
illustrated Boone's haphazard technique: "Survayd for Dal Boone 5000
acres begin at Robert Camels NE Corner at at [sic] 2 White ashes and
Buckeyes S 1200 p[oles] to 3 Shuger trees Ealm and walnut E 666 p to 6
Shuger trees and ash N 1200 p to a poplar and beech W 666 p to the
begining." Conflict was inevitable.

More often than not Boone failed to complete the legal steps necessary to insure ownership of land, particularly his own. He seems to have
entered into the surveying business with such relish that he did not take
the time to work through the lengthy process of land registration.

At other times, Daniel simply did not have the money needed to
register his claims. His letter of August 23, 1785, to Col. William Christian highlights both Boone's bustling activities and financial problems:

> Dear Col   the Land Bissness your father Left in my Hands
> is Ch[i]efly Dunn and R[e]ady to be Returned[.] Sum [Some] I
> have Registered and I have at your Requ[e]st pay[e]d by a Later
> [Letter.] payd Sum money for that bisness and Not thinking of
> this opertunity have Not time to Draw up your acoumpt [ac-
> count.] Requst the faver [favor] of you to Send me by the bearer
> James Brigis [Bridges?] ten pound and this Shall be your Resite
> [Receipt] for that Sum and you Will oblyge your omble [humble]
> Sarvent [Servant]
>
> Daniel Boone
>
> NB I have a Number of plots to Regester at the generel Co[u]rt
> and am Scarse [Scarce] of Cash[.] please to oblyge [oblige] me if
> pos[s]ible[.] DB

Daniel's lack of time and money often was matched only by his na-
ivete. He never thought anyone would question the legality of his claims.
He was wrong.

Boone should have learned this lesson earlier. When the commission
on land claims appointed by the governor of Virginia could reassemble in

December 1782, after Indian hostilities had somewhat abated, Peter Houston noted that "Boone's claim to a tract of land, on which he had erected a comfortable house and which he claimed, not by purchase or preemption but by 'right of discovery'" was in dispute, as was another claim he had originally received from "Henderson as a gift for services performed." The commissioners, well aware of Boone's great services in settling and protecting the country, read the law aloud and rendered the only judgment they felt they could: "whilst the case of Boone was one to excite sympathy, yet many were equally unfortunate and that the law was inexorable."

Not all of his land was lost through cross-filings and eventual suits of ejectment, however. Boone frequently sold what he believed to be his land, in good faith, to raise money for further speculation. When his buyers found that he had unknowingly sold them land to which other claimants held the valid title, they sued him for damages (as could victorious plaintiffs in suits of ejectment), and what land he truly owned he had to sell to repay his debts. Not until his last years was he finally able to state that he owed money to no man.

History testified to the truth of Daniel's legendary honesty, but other traits of his character and personality were often romanticized. While many accounts related Boone's love of hunting and stressed his desire for isolation in continually seeking new wilderness to the west, leading a solitary life was never his aim. His moves generally stemmed from an economic necessity. Hunting and trapping paid far better than farming and, to be successful at either, he had to follow the game. Both his love of hunting and a bit of his social side were well documented in a little-known visit to Peter Houston and his new bride of one month in October 1786. Peter fondly recounted the three-week stay of Daniel, Rebecca, and part of their family:

> Boone having found me with logs ready to put up a malt house[,]
> he engineered that and saw it completed and the two big kettles
> set that the bull had drawn from North Carolina, and which we
> had left at Houston Station where we had used them in tanning. We took several hunts whilst he was with us, and on one
> occasion we went to Stoner Creek in search of wild turkeys and
> having killed three, he two of them, he took me to a spring
> running out of one of the banks of Stoner Creek to slake our
> thirst, and when he arrived, he looked at the gurgling water
> for a moment as if deterred from drinking, but presently said,

"Peter, here is a spring that John Findley and I and my brother Squire often visited during our first visit to Kentucky."

We drank and sat down to rest and he related many reminiscences of his first visit to Kentucky. The conversation led to moral questions, and these to questions of religion. His family were what was called Friends and I was, then, a Presbyterian and we got into a sharp discussion of the relative merits of our creeds. And the dispute became so sharp that Boone, after a short silence in a reflecting mood looked at me and said, "Peter I never knew any good to come of religious disputes and I want to make an agreement with you that we will never dispute again on the subject of religion." I agreed to it and we shouldered our turkeys and moved off pleasantly together for home. And when we arrived he insisted that he could "beat anybody picking and dressing turkeys" and not a soul would he let take a part in dressing those turkeys. And then he said he would show my wife how to cook one for supper. He tied a piece of bark to the neck and hung it before the fire and called for a pewter plate (all the kind the colonies used then) to set under it to catch the gravy. And with a pewter spoon he continued to dip the gravy and pour it over the turkey and at the same time keeping the turkey turning round and round until it was thoroughly roasted. And at supper, it appeared that he not only knew how to cook a turkey, but to eat it as well.

According to Houston, Daniel then "returned to Boone's Station, determined to make an appeal to the legislature to reinstate him with his old home upon which he settled his family when he first arrived to Kentucky." While no official mention of the appeal or action taken upon it was recorded, Houston did also note that Boone "was appointed about the 15th of November, 1786, with four others to go to Limestone (now Maysville) to form a treaty with the western Indian chiefs for exchange of prisoners." The agreement was eventually signed in August 1787.

During this time Daniel also fared better as a tavern proprietor and businessman than as a land speculator and surveyor. He carried on a lively trade not only with the many settlers on the move to the interior of Kentucky, but also with the government by supplying the needs of the Indian prisoners taken in the area. One of his first bills sent to the state of Virginia, dated October 15, 1786, indicated the cordial treatment that the Indians received. Boone asked payment of three pounds for the "19 galons of Whiskey Delivered to the Indins priseners on there first arrival at Limeston." By mid-1787 the large volume of business in feeding the captured Indians led him to create a special account ledger, which he entitled "Daniel Boones Indan Book."

Several tribes were also quite energetic in taking prisoners. Estimates of the Kentucky settlers either captured or killed from 1783 to 1790 ran as high as fifteen hundred. In 1784 Boone began writing a telling contingency clause into his contractual agreements: "I will Bee accountable for any money put into his hands inless kild by Indians." In a letter written August 16, 1785, to Gov. Patrick Henry, Daniel reported the killing of two men at Squire Boone's settlement and flatly stated that "in Short an Inden Warr is Exspcted." The war never materialized but the harassing raids continued. One of the largest took place on May 23, 1786, when a party of two hundred warriors attacked flatboats on the Ohio near its confluence with the Kentucky River.

When George Rogers Clark and Benjamin Logan each headed a column in a retaliatory attack against the Indians, Clark targeted the tribes along the Wabash, while Logan, accompanied by Boone, directed his force against Shawnee towns on the Miami. Part of the mission was to take prisoners to exchange for white captives. Late on the night of September 29 and into the wee hours of the following day, Logan's troops crossed the river. They took the Indians by surprise, many of the braves having already left to fight Clark. As the Shawnees fled before the advancing column, Boone spotted some dogs running and told his party that following the dogs would lead them to the enemy. Pursuing and finally overtaking the braves, Boone recognized a familiar face in a band of fleeing Shawnees and told his companions to beware of that warrior: "Mind that fellow—I know him—it's Big Jim, who killed my son in Powell's Valley." Wounded by rifle fire, Big Jim, Boone's "friend" who thirteen years earlier had tortured his eldest son, James, to death, turned and fired as the white pursuers closed the gap. Big Jim killed one man and killed or wounded another before he himself was killed. About nineteen other warriors fell victim to the settlers' rifles and over seventy prisoners were taken.

Among those who surrendered were the old chief Moluntha and his squaw. Moluntha appeared not to fear capture, and with good reason. He had been working with American officials for some time, trying to free or exchange captive whites. At the white camp the chief soon was confronted by Maj. Hugh McGary, who for four years had been labeled as the man responsible for the Blue Licks massacre. McGary demanded to know if Moluntha remembered the battle. The chief, who in all likelihood did not understand the question and had not been present at Blue Licks, answered yes, he did recall it. The irrational McGary cursed Moluntha and split his head open with two quick blows of a small ax. Before he could be restrained, he turned his vengeance on Moluntha's wife, cutting off three of her fingers with the next swipe of his ax. Although Boone and others were outraged at this senseless act, McGary's punishment was less than severe. He was reprimanded and stripped of his commission by a court-martial.

Sometimes the prisoner exchange moved too slowly to suit Daniel Boone. At one point he rescued a small girl named Chloe Flinn from the Indians and cared for her for over a year before locating her family. In March 1787 the Indians released a boy upon Boone's word that one of their braves would also be freed. By abusing official procedures Boone probably saved the boy from months of captivity. When upbraided for his conduct by an officer, Daniel angrily wrote, "I am hire With my hands full of Bisness and No athority and if I am Not indulged in What I Do for the best it Is Not worth my While to put my Self to all this trubel." No more was said of the matter.

As a token of good faith, preliminary peace negotiations began in April 1787 with the return of four white prisoners. Nine more captives were exchanged late in the same month. Boone fed them all, whites and Indians. On August 20, more than nine months after Daniel and others were appointed as negotiators, the new Indian leaders—Captain Johnny, Wolf, and others—met with Boone, Logan, Levi Todd, Kenton, and a few more white leaders at Limestone (now officially renamed Maysville) and successfully drew up a formal treaty. After the all-night celebration feast, Boone's son Daniel Morgan Boone went hunting with the Shawnee chief Blue Jacket (a true native, not, as legend had it, a white Indian named Marmaduke van Sweringen) as a symbol of the new peace.

Boone's "Indan Book" account entry for August 22 might have reflected this occasion, but seemed instead to note only staples—beef, salt, corn, and bacon. Even the "4 galons Whiskey" and "2 galons Brandy" were not unusual. The most interesting item was "2 yd Caleco for burel [burial] of the Dad [dead]" charged at sixteen shillings. No mention, however, was made of who was laid to rest. Benjamin Logan endorsed the charges on the same page, writing, "The within mentioned Artickels was nessasary for the

Indians & I think the Accounts is just." Payment was slow. The governor did not place the bill before the Council of Virginia until October 22, and the council ordered that it be settled "out of the Contingent fund: to be charged to the United States."

Unfortunately, no matter how good the celebration might have been, the treaty proved less than effective. The Indians who signed the agreement represented only five of the villages within striking distance of Maysville. Those groups who had not signed the document continued to send out war parties.

But even the inhabitants of friendly villages sometimes broke the peace. Blue Jacket, the friend of Daniel's son, was to cause the elder Boone a great deal of embarrassment. In the spring of 1788 Blue Jacket was caught after stealing eight to ten horses from Strode's Station. He was brought to Maysville, which had made Boone and Kenton two of its trustees the preceding year, and was placed in Daniel's custody. Boone had recently come back to Kentucky with his wife, Rebecca, his son Nathan, and two other sons after a trip to North Carolina and Pennsylvania to visit his family. This was not the type of homecoming welcome he appreciated. Daniel did the only thing he could. He regretfully had the chief bound and locked in the sturdiest cabin in the settlement to await trial. But someone, no one knew who, left a knife sticking in one of the logs of the cabin, either by accident or deliberately. With it, Blue Jacket managed to cut his bonds and escape; Maysville residents cast a number of suspicious sideways glances at Boone.

The journey back to Pennsylvania had been in part a business trip. Boone and the worker he employed had dug twelve to fifteen tons of ginseng to place on the market in Philadelphia for sale to American druggists and for shipment to China. Son-in-law Philip Goe and daughter Rebecca managed his tavern and warehouse business at Maysville in Boone's absence. The upriver journey began badly; three miles before Point Pleasant the current swamped Daniel's keelboat. The boat was bailed out and refloated, but the wet ginseng required re-drying and lost half its value. Within a week or two the Boones resumed their trip up the Ohio and reached Redstone (now Brownsville, Pennsylvania) without further incident. There the ginseng was packed on horses and transported to Daniel's old friend Col. Thomas Hart, in Hagerstown, Maryland. Hart would be responsible for seeing that the ginseng reached Philadelphia. With the shipment in good hands, the family pushed on to Boone's old neighborhood and birthplace in Berks County, Pennsylvania. The young Nathan Boone recalled that while in Hagerstown his father purchased "a stock of goods for the frontier trade" and "also decided to take up residence at Point Pleasant and not return to Maysville as he had originally intended when he left there."

Somewhat to his own amazement, by this time Daniel Boone had become famous. The "autobiography" of the pioneer, "The Adventures of Col. *Daniel Boon . . .*" had been published in 1784 as a thirty-four-page appendix to John Filson's *The Discovery, Settlement And present State of Kentucke.* Filson's work was not a financial success, but it brought Boone international prominence. The work was translated and reprinted in France and Germany within a year of its publication. By 1785 the "Adventures" had been extracted from Filson's book and printed in America in an edited form that omitted many of Filson's overly ornamented oratorical phrases and passages. The 1785 edition de-emphasized Daniel's portrayal as a somewhat verbose eighteenth-century philosopher ironically capable of waxing eloquent over both the beauties of nature and the joys of civilization; instead, it characterized him as more of a hunter, explorer, and Indian fighter. His story became, in fact, more appealing to the average American citizen—the quickened pace of the "autobiography" focused the reader's attention upon action rather than words.

Fame neither lessened his desire to hunt nor marked an end to his adventures. In the fall of 1789 Daniel and his son, Daniel Morgan Boone, became separated on a deer hunt not far from the mouth of the Kanawha River on the Ohio side. Two of three Indians who had taken Daniel Morgan by surprise fired upon him. A swift and skillful runner, he evaded and outdistanced his pursuers after a chase of a half mile. His father, however, now in their camp and hearing the shots but not knowing what had happened, hid in the nearby woods and waited. To Daniel's great relief, his son came into the camp unhurt. They quickly packed up the few deerskins and the portion of meat that they had taken in their two-day hunt and crossed to the southern bank of the Ohio and back into Kentucky. Boone rightly decided that hunting north of the Ohio River was too dangerous for the time being.

A newfound affluence also now made Daniel Boone one of the wealthiest men in Kentucky. During his residence in Maysville he had purchased three slaves. Legal suits against him proceeded slowly, not yet making any substantial dent in the nearly one hundred thousand acres of land he had under claim. It was the most prosperous period in his life.

Why, then, did he follow through on his decision and move to Point Pleasant in Kanawha County, Virginia, sometime in 1789 or 1790? Was it merely business, or his old case of the "itching foot" flaring up again, or were the mounting number of lawsuits lodged against him taking a greater, more personal toll? His young friend Peter Houston seemed to support the latter view when he bitterly said that the reason for the migration of Daniel and Rebecca, the people he considered his "Kentucky father" and his "Kentucky mother," was the ingratitude of "their adopted state," an ingratitude that surely was linked to Daniel's increasing land trouble.

Before leaving Kentucky and moving to Point Pleasant, Daniel made the rounds of his friends to say goodbye. Peter Houston, whose family Boone visited, accompanied his "Kentucky father" to visit Thomas Starks, another old North Carolina friend, for a day. Houston noted that they delayed their return several hours more than they had intended:

> so interested did we become in the hair-lifting stories of Boone that it must have been long after midnight before we had lighted our torch and started. The cane was thick and high with a narrow path cut from house to house. . . . We had reached within a quarter of a mile of home when we were startled by the hideous scream of a panther. (I should have said at the proper time that Starks had given us a ham of fresh deer for our dinners the next day when he and his wife were to be with us.) The panther had scented the ham of deer and was in pursuit of it.
>
> We hastened but the wall of cane on either side soon knocked our torch to pieces and we were left with nothing but walls of cane to guide us. Thrice the scream was heard[,] the last time very near us whilst we were yet two hundred yards from the house[,] when Boone said, "Peter we will have to leave our meat or we shall soon be overtaken," and down he threw it. We heard no more of the panther; he had found what he was after. As soon as we reached the house I ran to my kennel and let out Nip and Tuck, two ferocious Spaniel dogs for hunting. They had heard the panther and were howling at a fearful rate to get after it. I gave them the direction and off they went. Boone and I and his son Nathan, who had sprung out of bed, awaiting the result. It was well nigh a half hour before we heard the dogs bay.
>
> "There," said I, "they have treed him."
>
> "Well," said Boone "let us get our guns and tinder box and go after him." . . . I remonstrated against going a mile

through the cane at that late hour to kill the panther. But Boone said, "no panther shall run me and rob me of my dinner without value received. If you do not want to go I will go alone." So I yielded. Nathan was anxious to go with us but his mother forbade it. It was near an hour before we completed our struggle through the cane and reached the dogs, who kept us posted as to their location by their yelps. The tree was a leaning oak. We halted some thirty yards from the tree and Boone said "light your shavings behind me so that I can see his eyes plainly." The light was struck and the fiery eyes of the panther were visible to Boone. He leveled his gun, fired and down came one of the largest panthers my eyes ever beheld, though Boone said "I have killed many such." No sport was left for Nip and Tuck: Boone, without being able to use the sights on his gun, had struck the panther almost squarely between the eyes.

His visiting done, Boone again went on the move. In May 1789 he was on the Monongahela with a drove of horses for sale. He sent sons Daniel Morgan and Jesse with horses for sale to Thomas Hart, his merchant friend in Hagerstown, and continued his shipments of ginseng as well, becoming a well-known face on the river. Two months later he wrote to a business client that he expected to be in Philadelphia that winter. But his sons lost a large number of the horses and Hart reported that the price brought by ginseng had fallen so far that Boone actually had lost money on the last shipment. What money was realized was applied to the balance due Hart for the trading goods he previously had supplied.

As badly as business was going, the settlers still held Daniel in high esteem. In October the Kanawha residents recognized his talents in a popular petition that asked that he be appointed lieutenant colonel of the county militia. The county court quickly recommended the petition for approval, but the official commission did not arrive until April 1791. A description of how Daniel Boone, now in his mid-fifties, appeared to one of his new Kanawha neighbors yielded a pleasing picture of the man: "His large head, full chest, square shoulders, and stout form are still impressed upon my mind. He was (I think) about five feet ten inches in height, and his weight say 175. He was solid in mind as well as in body, never frivolous, thoughtless, or agitated; but was always quiet, meditative, and impressive, unpretentious, kind, and friendly in his manner." Nathan Boone confirmed the greater part of this description of his father, but put his height at five feet eight inches and amplified the physical description, noting that his "hair was moderately black, eyes blue, and he had fair skin." And Peter Houston added of Daniel "that at the end of a hand spike he could lift more than any man I ever saw. At a log-rolling and house-raisings he was always leader and director."

In his third term as a representative Boone seems to have been a silent delegate to the 1791 Virginia Assembly, which met from October through December. Although serving on two committees, one on religion and the other on propositions and licenses, he evidently did little more than vote. He did, however, give guidance for the defense of the county through the proper allocation of military personnel—the "Privets" and "sypes or scutes" [spies or scouts] whom, he insisted, must be local men who knew the woods and waters well. Still the businessman, on December 13, 1791, Daniel offered to take ammunition to Redstone (Brownsville, Pa.) in return for the contract to supply provisions to his county's militia. While in Richmond he phrased the matter in a letter to the governor as follows:

> Sir as sum purson Must Carry out the armantstion [ammunition] to Red Stone if your Exclency should have thought me a proper purson I Would undertake it on Conditions I have the apintment to vitel the Company at Kanhowway so that I Could take Down the flowre as I paste the place. I am your Excelencys most obedent omble servant,
>
> Dal Boone

Five days later the contract was awarded to him. Surviving receipts testify to his delivery of lead, flints, and powder to various military outposts, but it was slow going; the cargo weighed over a ton. It took Daniel until April to complete his deliveries.

On his way home, Daniel, Rebecca, and their son Daniel Morgan stopped in Augusta County, Virginia, to visit his boyhood friend Henry Miller. Back in Point Pleasant, business problems continued as Boone proved to be less than successful as a supply officer. In 1792 and 1793 Capt. Hugh Caperton and Col. William Clendenin complained in writing that on one occasion Boone refused to deliver provisions and that on another he agreed to delivery but neither he nor the consignment ever arrived. Boone likely had a running argument with Caperton, and in one instance, because Daniel was a man of few words, he just grabbed his rifle and left camp for a number of days. Questioned about his actions when the scouts who had run out of rations found him down the Ohio River, he would only say, "Captain Caperton did not do to his liking." Others must have echoed his sentiments, for a court-martial soon relieved Caperton of his command. Daniel's dispute with Caperton largely soured Boone on such business ventures and may have encouraged him to close his Point Pleasant store the next year.

Daniel's position in 1785 was paradoxical. Although essentially unsuccessful in his businesses as a merchant and speculator in land, he found himself internationally famous as a hero thanks to Filson's publication of his "autobiographical" adventures. Further, and somewhat ironically, it was of no matter that Daniel could hold his own in any fight on the frontier, for he began to face enemies he was ill-equipped to combat—lawyers. The suits of ejectment trickled in at first, but by 1798 the constant barrage had left him essentially landless. The fearless Shel-tow-ee found himself rendered helpless by a confusing jumble of legal jargon and technicalities.

Similarly, as a guileless man, Daniel was sometimes bilked by smooth-talking con artists and certainly no stranger to financial loss. He once secured a five-hundred-pound bond for one Ebenezer Platt and loaned the man a horse and equipment for a trip to Louisville. It turned out that Platt had been an inmate at Newgate Prison in England. His route to Louisville was less than direct, his next known whereabouts being New Orleans. Boone never seemed able to realize that treating a man honestly did not guarantee being treated honestly in return. He took a one-thousand-pound bond for land from Gilbert Imlay, who later sailed for England and became the lover of Mary Wollstonecraft, the mother of Mary Shelley. Before his departure Imlay sold the land he had never paid for and in 1786 wrote Boone an apologetic note claiming he could not redeem the debt. Remembered as the author of *A Topographical Description of the Western Territory of North America,* Imlay added Filson's narrative to its second edition in 1793, perhaps to ease his conscience a bit, but more likely to increase its sales.

Daniel was not alone in his losses. Imagine the reaction of the inhabitants of Bryan's Station, who, after having survived both a siege and the battle of Blue Licks, were confronted in 1784 with a Virginian who was now the legal owner of the station. It was the first time that he had been in Kentucky.

Understandably embittered by his experiences, not only did Boone lose his land and become submerged in debt through lawsuits, but he fell from public esteem. The honored pioneer became perhaps the most hated man in Kentucky. Because of his vast knowledge of the land and his great activity in surveying, he often testified as an "expert" witness in the count-less lawsuits over "shingled" claims in which he had no other involvement. Each case had to have a loser, a party who felt cheated. Boone made so many enemies that even his honesty was impugned. He was called a liar and accused of being a "chimney corner" surveyor, one who sat by his chimney and set down property boundaries from memory, or worse, from imagination. He suffered through threats of assassination and felt that trav-eling in Kentucky was more dangerous for him now than it was during the Indian wars. For these reasons Daniel decided to distance himself as much as he could from the machinery of the law and vowed never to defend himself in any suit against land he had under claim. He gave the one tract of land he possessed that had not been cross-filed to his nephew Col. John Grant, with the simple instructions to use it to repay anyone with a valid claim against him.

In the fall of 1794, once more lured on by the amount of game on the north side of the Ohio River, Daniel took his youngest son, Nathan, now thirteen years old, on a hunt some ten or twelve miles above Point Pleasant. Nathan remembered his initiation into the ways of the wilderness:

> my father didn't leave me at camp anymore. He took me with him and two or three times pointed out deer, then showed me how to manage to get off shots. I was not to move or attempt to steal up on the deer when his head was up chewing and he was looking around, but to do so when his head was down feeding and could not so well see me. Following this advice, I killed one or two other deer during this hunt. While we were together, my father shot a bear, and one or two others when he was alone the first day. From these two or three bear we saved all the meat, and of the ten or fifteen deer we saved the best hindquarters.
>
> On the fifth night, about midnight, I had been asleep for some time. But my father, Daniel Boone, heard a chopping or hacking some distance above and across the river. He awakened me and told me he thought the noise was made by Indians, as he thought it was made by their hatchets. He concluded that the Indians had probably seen the fire at our camp and were

making a raft to cross. We carried meat and skins to our canoe, which was twenty-five yards from camp, and returned to our fire again. The night was clear and frosty and a little foggy, so we remained at our fire with our blankets for some little time. After the chopping ceased we then went to our canoe; there we stayed some ten minutes until we heard the Indians paddling in the water. At that time we pushed off, and Father ordered me to roll his blanket around myself and lie down in the canoe. He sat in the stern, put the paddle carefully in the water, and then gave a push. We went forward noiselessly and were soon in the main current, which washed us down the river.

On the way Father put his head over the canoe and close to the water and said he thought he could catch a glimpse of the Indians. He had looked between the surface of the water and the fog, which did not quite reach to the water. Soon we were beyond harm. We reached Point Pleasant by daylight and learned that Daniel M. Boone and Matthias Van Bibber had each lost a horse that night. Daniel M. Boone raised a small party of men and pursued them but found the Indians had made their raft and crossed the river, as my father had supposed. They discovered evidence that the Indians had divided into two groups; one had left with the stolen horses, and the other had gone across the river to attack our camp.

Nathan continued, underscoring the ongoing problems: "Nearly the entire time I lived at Point Pleasant there were Indian troubles. The Indians would frequently get upon the high ridge behind the town, just above Crooked Creek. There they would erect blinds and spy out what they could discover." At every alarm, the people "would leave their dwellings in town and take refuge in the fort. This fleeing to the fort occurred almost every year and sometimes several times a year. When our spies discovered that the Indians had left the country, the people would return to their houses. We usually stayed in the fort a week or ten days." During these alarms, according to Nathan, the Boones would stay in the second story of the blockhouse adjoining the house of Capt. John Van Bibber.

Although Daniel Boone encouraged others, such as his acquaintance Nathaniel Pope of the Society of Friends, to seek land in the Ohio country, stating that the beauty of the lands near its rivers (the Scioto and the Big and Little Miami in particular) equaled that of Kentucky, he contented himself with a more local move. By 1795—the year in which Gen. "Mad Anthony" Wayne finally forced the Indians in the Northwest Territory to sign the Treaty of Greenville, after their 1794 defeat at Fallen Timbers— Boone had resettled his family at Brushy Fork near the Blue Licks on a tract of unimproved land owned by his son Daniel Morgan Boone. A bit less in demand now for his skill in treating gunshot wounds, he hunted and farmed for the next few years, clearing ten acres and raising two crops in 1796 and 1797. Game was scarce and rheumatism at times made the simplest task an ordeal.

Daniel heard early in 1796 that the Wilderness Road was to be widened to accommodate travel by wagons. Kentucky had become the fifteenth state in 1792, and Isaac Shelby, an old acquaintance from the Boonesborough days during the Revolution, was its first governor. As Daniel put pen to paper on February 11, 1796, he had hopes of recouping some of his losses. He wrote to Shelby:

> Sir—After my best Respts to your Excelancy and family I wish to inform you that I have sum intention Of undertaking this New Rode that is to be cut through the Wilderness and I think my Self intitled to the ofer of the Bisness as I first Marked out that Rode in March 1775 and Never rec'd anything for my trubel and Sepose I am no Statesman I am a Woodsman and think My Self as Capable of Marking and Cutting that Rode, as any other man Sir if you think with Me I would thank you to wright me a Line by the post the first oportuneaty and he will lodge it at Mr. John Milers on Hinkston fork as I wish to know Wheer and when it is to be Latt [let] So that I may attend at the time I am Deer Sir
>
> your very omble servent Daniel Boone

Shelby's reply either did not survive or was never made. In any case, Daniel Boone was not given the opportunity of "Cutting that Rode." Instead Shelby commissioned James Knox and Joseph Crockett to improve the road from Crab Orchard to the Cumberland Gap. In October 1796 they announced the opening of the road over which "wagons loaded with a ton weight, may pass with ease, with four good horses."

Daniel had good reason to try to get the road contract: he needed

cash. In one instance an uncollected debt of three hundred pounds in-
curred by Boone and his nephew John Grant on November 12, 1791, and
due on April 1, 1793, was pursued in court. To make sure that they appeared at the courthouse, the Campbell County sheriff received on September 6, 1796, the following order: "You are hereby Commanded to take
Daniel Boon and John Grant if they be found within your Bailewick and
them safely keep so that you have their Bodies before the Justices of our
Court on the 1st Monday in October next to answer John Ware assignee of
Hugh French of a Plea of Debt for Three hundred pounds[,] Damage
£50." The case dragged on into the August term of 1798, when the debt
was settled and the "Plea withdrawn." Whether the debt was paid outright
by Daniel or John Grant, or whether Grant sold the one unencumbered
piece of land that Daniel had entrusted to him for just such a purpose, was
unclear.

In October 1796, the same month that Boone was to appear in court
in the matter of this debt, Daniel was given a deputy surveyor's commission from General Lee of Mason County. The position allowed him to
bolster, however temporarily, his sagging financial fortunes. He completed
his work in time for a fall bear hunt with Nathan up the Big Sandy River.

This time the hunting was good and trouble free. By the end of the
year the men killed thirty to forty bears that had not yet gone into hiberna-
tion. They saved the skins, smoked the meat, and in the spring made a
canoe and sent other men to carry the meat down the river to Maysville.
Daniel and Nathan rode home to discover that bear oil was more valuable
than meat. Nathan noted that because of the demand from tanners "the oil
brought a dollar a gallon and a bear's carcass would yield from ten to twenty
gallons." A bearskin usually brought a hunter two dollars, but could bring
as much as five. Encouraged by this hunt and the increased cumulative
value of each bear taken, the Boones returned to the same region in the fall
of 1797 for further commercial hunting and killed 156 bears.

12

eso.so

"I WANT MORE ELBOW-ROOM"
Bound for Missouri

Some dreams never die. Although sixty-three and rheumatic, Boone kept faith in his dream of owning land. His dream, the same dream his grandfather George had when he left England for Pennsylvania, also passed on to his children. Like his great-grandfather, Daniel's son Daniel Morgan Boone went ahead to investigate the possibilities of a new "promised land." As early as 1795 Daniel Morgan had hunted and explored the region along the Mississippi and the upper waters of the Tombigbee River, but had not found that country to his liking, and was eager to undertake another journey. In the fall of 1797 Daniel Morgan decided to investigate the prospects in Missouri. His father heartily endorsed the venture and instructed his son to call on the Spanish governor to inquire about the terms that would be granted to new settlers. Interestingly, one of Daniel Morgan's initial companions was Col. James Smith, whose captivity narrative and adventures, when published in 1799, would rival Daniel's "autobiography" in popularity. Smith and Joseph Scholl, Daniel Morgan's brother-in-law, however, turned back in Illinois. Daniel Morgan pressed on, examined the Femme Osage region in the St. Charles district of Missouri, and then, following his father's instructions, called on Don Zenon Trudeau, the Spanish lieutenant governor.

Given both the lack of settler-defenders in this territory and the conflict that started between Spain and England in 1796, it was no wonder that Trudeau wished to encourage American settlement. Knowing full well that where Daniel Boone went many others would eagerly follow, in a letter of January 24, 1798, Trudeau happily promised handsome grants of land to the old pioneer and those who accompanied him. Daniel Morgan hurried back to Kentucky to explain the proposition to his father and to describe the region's abundant game and fertile soil. He returned to Missouri in the fall of 1798 and made one more trip back to Kentucky to confer with his father the following year, by which time the younger Boone had already settled in St. Charles County, Missouri.

Daniel, again like his grandfather, had grown cautious with age. His best land was gone, but in 1797 he still held title to over twenty-seven thousand acres of second- and third-rate land and still worked as a surveyor. On December 5 he penned a receipt to H. Lee for the fee received for "an 1000 acre Survey made for Charles Yancy." In the fall of 1798 Daniel moved from Brushy Fork onto his son Nathan's land near the mouth of the Little Sandy River. Perhaps the irony of two events in 1798 helped him to make the decision to migrate once more. That year, when a county of Kentucky was named in his honor, the sheriffs of Mason and Clark Counties sold over ten thousand acres of his land for back taxes.

If that indignity was not enough motivation to move west, the continuing disputes over lands that Daniel had surveyed for others added immeasurably to his desire to leave. A March 19, 1799, deposition taken in Mason County recorded his discomfort in trying to settle a boundary dispute between two adjacent surveys he had made. To the question of one owner who asked "Is this the spot intended in the entry for my beginning[?]" Boone testified, "It is as near as I Could gu[es]s when I mead [made] the entry and at all events includ[e]s the land I aludst [alluded] to when I made the Entry." Also, Daniel responded to the other owner's question concerning the omission of a spring from his entry by admitting that "when I came to make the Survey I found there was a mistack [mistake] in the entry and I could not include the spring and comply with the cals [calls, i.e., the points in a surveyor's description] of the entry." With all the parties assembled on the site of the surveys, the commissioners were able to settle the dispute the same day. Such thorny legal entanglements, however, were clearly not the way in which Daniel wished to occupy his time if he could avoid it.

By the time Boone left Kentucky in September 1799, the paradise of hunters had become a paradise for lawyers. Lexington was now a bustling commercial center with an upper class that fashioned itself after the Tidewater gentry and English aristocracy, even importing a passion for horse racing, a sport that some would argue was perfected in the bluegrass state. The *Kentucky Gazette* recorded on October 12, 1793, that the townspeople were concerned over "jockeys racing their horses through the streets" and on October 21 that the trustees of the city asked for the authority to regulate this dangerous activity. Receiving a mandate, they issued orders confining racing to "the lower end of the Commons (west Water street) where stud horses can be shown." Another sure indicator of the transformation of Lexington was that the city now boasted several dancing masters ready to polish frontier roughness into gentility. It was not surprising that Daniel looked beyond Kentucky and again to the West, to better hunting and new land.

His contemporary George Washington died later that same year, but Boone, two months shy of his sixty-fifth birthday, again pulled up stakes and moved west. James Fenimore Cooper used this event to forge another link between Boone and the main character of his Leatherstocking Tales. At the beginning of *The Prairie,* the author describes a "resolute forester" who migrated to Missouri in later life. In a footnote, Cooper identifies the figure as "Colonel Boon, the patriarch of Kentucky," who at the close of the eighteenth century emigrated for much the same reasons as Leatherstocking. Boone left "because he found a population of ten to the square mile, inconveniently crowded."

Daniel fashioned a five-foot-wide, sixty-foot-long dugout canoe out of a huge tulip poplar to carry most of the family and household goods as well as sons Daniel Morgan and Nathan, their mother, and several other relatives and companions. He clearly took a bit more of civilization with him than Cooper's spartan Leatherstocking. Boone drove their stock along the overland route himself, accompanied by a young man named George Buchanan and a slave named Sam. Like the Pied Piper of western migration that he was, along the way Daniel drew other relatives, friends, and their families and goods to him and to his journey. Jemima's husband, Flanders Callaway, joined, as did Forest Hancock, Isaac Van Bibber, and William Hays Sr. and Jr., among others. Daniel's brother Squire, similarly ridden with debt and tired of a decade of failed settlements (near the present Vicksburg, Mississippi, and in New Orleans, Florida, and Pennsylvania) and now back in Kentucky, also gladly joined the new adventure. Trudeau had correctly anticipated Daniel's power to draw settlers to Missouri.

Legend has it that on this journey, while stopped at Cincinnati, Daniel was asked why he was leaving Kentucky. "Too crowded" was the famous reply, "too crowded—I want more elbow-room."

In October 1799, Boone and his party and those traveling by boat (likely down the Ohio and then up the Mississippi)reached St. Louis.

Trudeau and his successor as lieutenant governor, Carlos D. Delassus, welcomed the bedraggled old pioneer with full military honors. Agreeing with Trudeau, who stressed the importance of keeping the agreements made with Boone, Delassus went so far as to put Daniel in charge of portioning out the land grants to his followers and selecting the site of each parcel. The blank concession papers for land given to Boone were backdated to correspond to the date of Trudeau's January 24, 1798, letter to insure the validity of the claims after the expected transfer of territorial jurisdiction from Spain to France.

Daniel directed the operation mainly from the home of his son Daniel Morgan in the Femme Osage district sixty miles west of St. Louis. Each settler received from four hundred to six hundred arpents of land depending on whether the man was single or married, with an additional forty arpents for each family member or servant. (Each arpent equaled .85 acres.)

Boone, as the leader of the settlers, was rewarded with one thousand arpents anywhere in the district, giving him quite a choice. The Femme Osage comprised everything north of the Missouri River and west of the Mississippi and had no given western boundary. The tract that he selected was mostly bottomland that abutted his son's estate upon the north. Daniel erected a small log cabin but, perhaps for convenience, made the mistake of constructing it on his son's property. By February 1800 Daniel and Rebecca had built a sugar camp on the land of their other son, Nathan, and produced some three to four hundred pounds of maple sugar over several weeks.

Perhaps because he was a Spanish official in Spanish territory, and thus protected from the large number of Kentucky lawsuits over land that involved him directly or indirectly, and perhaps because the lure of the gains possible through land speculation always captivated him, Daniel soon led his family into a new land scheme. On the banks of the Missouri River about five miles below the present town of Augusta, they plotted out a settlement called Missouriton, or "Daniel Boone's Palatinate," and hoped to attract wealthy Virginians as citizens. The town prospered briefly, but a shift in the course of the river eventually carried away a large part of its surveyed land. Daniel consoled himself with the excellent prospects of trapping and hunting.

Lieutenant Governor Delassus made him the "syndic," or magistrate, of Femme Osage on July 11, 1800. Daniel already exerted much power, for he had continued to serve as the disburser of land to all new settlers.

Now he was also the judge, jury, sheriff, and commandant of the district. In effect he was the *patron* or Spanish *don* of the territory. As the Lewis and Clark expedition proceeded up the Missouri, Meriwether Lewis noted Boone's influence on the people in and around St. Charles, stating that they "yeald passive obedience to the will of their temporal master, the Commandant." Although the Louisiana Territory passed from Spanish to French hands in October 1800, all these lands never drew any attention from the French authorities. Spain and her officers, including Daniel Boone, continued to govern.

Daniel managed to indulge his favorite endeavor of hunting despite his many obligations as syndic. His first few trips were for enjoyment, but the ventures could be commercially profitable as well. Markets in St. Louis paid forty cents per pound for deerskins and did not demand that the hides be grained. Not having to scrape off the hair gave the riflemen additional time to hunt and increased the weight of their skins. The beaver were so plentiful during the winter of 1800–1801 that Daniel was able to pay off some of his debt to a French merchant in St. Louis. Greatly encouraged by this lucrative harvest of game, Daniel joined his sons in commercial hunting sometime late in the next summer, again meeting with good success.

The next trapping season, as related by Nathan, however, was a near disaster for Boone:

> In October 1802, my father, Daniel Boone, accompanied by Derry [a black slave in his early twenties who liked to go trapping with Daniel], took his grandson, William Hays, Jr., and joined Flanders Callaway and his son James for a fall and winter's hunt along the Niango River. There they separated, with the Callaways making one party; my father, Hays, and Derry another. They trapped on the Big Niango and Pomme de Terre but stayed a few miles apart. One day while Hays was absent trapping and Father had just ridden away from camp to look at traps, a party of eight or ten Osages came running toward the camp yelling and shooting off their guns. Derry took to his heels and hid. My father saw that the Indians were firing into the air, no doubt trying to frighten him and Derry away so they could take the goods from their camp.
>
> My father rode back to camp, and the Indians pulled him

from his horse and took his capeau coat [a coat with a hood]. However, they were not openly hostile, so he called Derry back to camp. Derry managed to secrete a chunk of lead and Boone had a supply of powder concealed. The Indians took their furs, Father's capeau coat, the powder in his horn, etc. They also had Derry cook a meal for them. Afterwards Father and Derry had enough hidden ammunition left to kill meat, so they remained trapping until spring. They finally came home with about two hundred beaver skins.

After the raid by the Osages, Daniel and Derry moved camp to a cave on the bank of the Grand River. After a lucky snowfall that covered their tracks, they were penned in the cave for twenty days because another band of Osage warriors had pitched their hunting camp in the same area. If that stress was not enough, Daniel had to finish the season seriously injured after one of his beaver traps snapped shut on his hand and he had to go back to camp for help to pry open the steel jaws. He used his share of the pelts to pay off part of the seemingly never-ending Kentucky debts. As a final blow, his rheumatism flared up for the next few winters and elimi-nated any trapping activity. Rheumatism also likely soon caused him to give up his heavier blacksmithing activities, allowing him only to make and repair traps and guns for his family and a few neighbors.

Bad luck and illness did not dampen Boone's spirit for long. He en-joyed his first years in Missouri more than any other time since his first hunt in Kentucky more than thirty years earlier. He and his fellow settlers adjusted well to their new life under Spanish rule. A problem might have developed over religion, since each new immigrant technically had to be a Catholic. While public policy was stringently adhered to, Trudeau and Delassus kept their word that any religion might be practiced in private. Each incoming settler faced questions to determine his or her religion that almost all Christians, whether they were Catholic or not, could answer in the affirmative. After listening to the expected replies to such queries as "Do you believe in God Almighty?" the examiners proclaimed each Bap-tist or Methodist a good Catholic. Similar lenience marked the official behavior toward visiting Protestant preachers. No notice was taken of them until their tour of ministry was nearly complete. Then a warning was de-livered demanding that they leave the district in three days or be arrested. All complied, only to return on the next tour and be ordered out of the country again when they were ready to leave. Matters went so well with the new immigrants in the next few years that the Spanish authorities offered Boone ten thousand arpents if he would induce a hundred additional American families to settle west of the Mississippi. Boone's name still exerted a magic drawing power upon pioneers. The people came and Daniel got his land.

As syndic, Boone held court near his small cabin under what came to be known as the "Justice Tree." Not unexpectedly, this court was rather dramatically different from any court Boone had ever encountered. He was the judge and jury and even supervised the implementation of the sentence—usually a whipping with the strokes "well laid on." A guilty offender could be tried, sentenced, punished, and released into society as a reputable citizen within an hour or two. The court reflected its magistrate: honest, fearless, and straight from the shoulder. Daniel observed no rules of evidence, saying that he only wished to know the truth. His less-than-subtle justice often was a good match for the crime. Some surviving legal documents show that the district over which he ruled was far from peaceful:

> June 30th, 1804
>
> This Day Came before me Justice of the Peace for the District of the Femmeosage, Francis Woods[,] Peter Smith & John Manley and made oath that on the 29th of June of said Month at the house of David Bryan a Certain James Meek and the Bearer hereof Bery Vinzant had some differance Which Came to blows and in the scuffle the said James Meek bit of[f] a piece of Bery Vinzants Left Ear, further the Deponent sayeth not[.] Given under my hand and seal the day and Date above written
>
> Daniel Boone [seal]

Those appearing before Boone's bench did not object to his rough-and-ready approach. When one offender whom Daniel had sentenced to a number of lashes was asked how he fared, he replied "First rate. Whipped and cleared." Boone's contemporaries stated that the old frontiersman had never before seemed so satisfied with his actions or displayed such dignity as he did in his magistrate's role.

Family tragedy interrupted Daniel's happiness. His old friend and the husband of his daughter Susannah, William Hays Sr., was killed by James Davis, Hays's son-in-law, in front of Daniel's grandson. Hays had become a heavy drinker and gained notoriety within the family for his raging temper and for beating Susannah. After she died in 1800, he grew even worse. The grandson, Daniel Boone Davis, provided the details for the December 1804 event. There had been bad blood between Hays and James Davis, and Hays told him never to come to his farm again. Davis returned, however, to try to borrow a horse that he needed to bring supplies back from St. Charles. Hays got his rifle and cocked it; Davis ducked behind a tree with his gun, but Hays brought his rifle to bear and dared Davis to fire. Davis's ball struck Hays in the chest and gave him a mortal wound. As syndic, Daniel ordered the arrest of James Davis, officiated over the preliminary hearing, and bound him over to stand trial in St. Charles. As the concerned patriarch of the family who knew the history behind the killing, he brought Davis to St. Charles, posted the three-thousand-dollar bail bond, and testified as to William Hays's actions and temper at the trial. James Davis was eventually acquitted of the charge of murder.

Boone's family troubles continued. Son Nathan, who had been trapping along the Kansas River with a companion, was first raided by the Osages and then by Kansa tribesmen; the raiders took all the proceeds of the hunt and all their equipment, leaving them with only one gun—no coats, blankets, or protection from the winter storms. They barely survived, were rescued, placed on litters, and brought home to Missouri on Christmas Eve, 1804. Nathan's wife, Olive, later teased him, saying "It was the first Christmas he had spent at home since our marriage, and I had to thank the Indians for that."

Land problems loomed large throughout this period as well. On April 30, 1803, about the time that Daniel Boone learned of his daughter Lavinia's death the previous year in Kentucky, the United States and France signed a treaty that would have a great impact on his future. On March 9 of the following year Spain officially transferred Louisiana to France, and the next day France transferred it to the United States. President Thomas Jefferson had completed the Louisiana Purchase, buying the territory from which all or part of thirteen new states would be formed for 15 million dollars, or approximately three cents per acre.

The Spanish government in Missouri was not immediately replaced by the United States. And when the American officials did arrive, they came with instructions from Jefferson to make as few changes as possible. Boone therefore continued as syndic for some time after the Louisiana Purchase. Even years after his commission had expired, people with civil disputes would come to the "Justice Tree" and submit themselves to Boone's judgments, which they considered binding.

All of the inhabitants of Missouri were most concerned with whether or not the change in government would affect their ownership of land. The United States Land Commission did not reach Missouri until months after the purchase, and the volume of cases to be examined caused a lengthy backlog in the hearings. Testimony on Boone's claims was not taken until February 13, 1806. Although he had kept all the papers that verified his grants and there had been no cross-filings on his claims, Daniel had not learned enough prudence from his Kentucky experiences. Relying upon Delassus's word that as syndic he need not conform to the standard validation practices required by Spanish law, he had not bothered to clear ten acres annually on each of his two tracts until one-tenth of the entire acreage had been improved, nor had he filed the necessary papers in New Orleans to obtain the Spanish governor's approval of a permanent title. Delassus had told him that it was customary to exempt officials from this lengthy process. But that was a Spanish, not an American, custom. Daniel had not even built his cabin on his own land. He had no way of demonstrating conclusive legal ownership of his property.

On December 1, 1809, the commission's recommendation that Boone's "claim ought not to be confirmed" was officially adopted; however, having known the verdict would be unfavorable for some time, Daniel had already turned to influential friends in high places who would try to right this injustice. Judge John Coburn, a former land commissioner, continued to champion Boone's cause, and likely wrote the petition presented to Congress for the old pioneer. An indication of how much Daniel relied on Coburn is evident in a letter written to the judge on October 5, 1809.

Deer Sir

The Later [letter] I Rc^d [Received] from you Respe[c]ting Squire Boones Surtivate [Certificate?] Was Long Coming to hand and my Not beeing able to go to St Lewis I Dunn the Bisness before Col Keebby and sent it on by Lewis Bryan in Closed in a Later to your Self and one to Squire Boone Derecting him to Deliver it to you him Self[.] these Laters Could Not Rech [Reach] you before you Left home[.] if that Willnot Dow [will not do] pless [please] Wright to me at St Charles and I will Make out another and send it to you before Courte adjornes as

I have the form you Sent me[.] I am well in h[e]alth But Deep in Markury [Mercury] and Not able to Come Down[.] I Shall Say Nothing about our petistion [petition] but Le[a]ve it all to your Self

I am Deer is [sir] youres
Daniel Boone

Daniel was putting on a good face about his health. Being "Deep in Markury" meant that he was trying to lessen his severe rheumatic pain by treating himself with calomel, or mercurous chloride.

Another friend, Col. Return Jonathan Meigs, the former commander of St. Charles County from 1804 to 1806, was now in the Eleventh Congress and on the Public Lands Committee. Equally determined to see that Boone received some benefit from his years of service to his country, he returned a favorable report on Boone's petition.

Daniel led the normal life of a wilderness hunter while waiting for action on his request to Congress for some compensation for his lands. He had a few close escapes from the Osage Indians, but the old trapper had forgotten none of the tricks that had enabled him to keep his scalp for three-quarters of a century.

About this time in late 1805 and early 1806, Daniel's old friend Simon Kenton came to visit him in Missouri and stayed for about a week. Nathan Boone recalled that "The old pioneers seemed to enjoy themselves finely in recounting their old Kentucky troubles and hardships." Daniel had somber news to tell his friend as they reminisced—Boone's daughter Rebecca died probably of consumption in 1805 and her husband, Philip Goe, drank himself to death. Daniel Morgan Boone returned to Kentucky and brought back five of the seven Goe children, who would be added to the brood of twelve that he and his wife Sarah would have. Of all the elder Boone's four daughters, only his precious Jemima was still alive.

While Boone knew from experience how to deal with such sorrow, his sense of personal loss surely was not lessened by his land troubles. The measure of Daniel's bitterness over his treatment in Kentucky could not be underestimated. When Gen. Green Clay wrote to him on May 4, 1806, from Madison County, Kentucky, acknowledging how badly the old frontiersman had been used and asking for Boone to return to help to resolve two claims, Daniel flatly refused despite Clay's generous offer of lifetime support, part interest in the land, and stock, cash, or slaves. Nathan remembered his father's verbal response to the letter: "He said that when he left Kentucky, he did it with the intention of never stepping his feet upon Kentucky soil again; and if he was compelled to lose his head on the block or revisit Kentucky, he would not hesitate to choose the former."

Daniel went on his last winter beaver hunt probably in the fall of 1808 with the same two who accompanied him in 1802, William Hays Jr. and Derry, but with worse results. Attacked by twenty or thirty Indians, they "wheeled their horses and escaped but had to cut loose their traps and the few skins and furs they had taken." Also, according to Nathan Boone, Daniel "later became ill and, fearing he might not recover, gave instructions to Hays and Derry to bury him between two certain trees near camp." It may be that Boone, who had been carried home for Christmas by Nathan and Daniel Morgan after falling up to his neck into the icy Missouri River on an 1805 winter hunt, had never fully recovered from the bone-chilling plunge and was anticipating the worst.

13

ONE LAST HUNT
The Final Decade

Perhaps these events and thoughts about his own mortality caused Daniel to emphasize his softer side. Sometime about 1809, Daniel and Rebecca took a room in St. Charles. They had heard that their young grandson James, who had been sent to school there by his father, Nathan, was homesick; they went there to make a home for him. The move also allowed the ailing Daniel to receive a doctor's care.

Daniel also finally mellowed a bit in his feelings about Kentucky. Sometime about 1810 he was in Kentucky making his way to the Indiana shore of the Ohio River to visit with his brother Squire when the now-famous meeting took place between Boone and John James Audubon, who later painted a portrait of Boone. The ornithologist, then in his mid-twenties, had already begun to capture the beauty of America's birds in his drawings. Boone took an immediate liking to his new companion; Audubon reciprocated the feeling and recorded the following example of premier marksmanship on the part of his new seventy-six-year-old friend:

> *Barking off squirrels* is delightful sport, and in my opinion requires a greater degree of accuracy than any other. I first witnessed this manner of procurring squirrels whilst near the town of Frankfort. The performer was the celebrated Daniel Boon. We walked out together, and followed the rocky margins of the Kentucky River until we reached a piece of flat land thickly covered with black walnuts, oaks and hickories. As the general mast was a good one that year, squirrels were seen gambolling on every tree around us. My companion, a stout, hale, and ath-

letic man, dressed in a homespun hunting-shirt, bare-legged and moccasined, carried a long and heavy rifle, which, as he was loading it, he said had proved efficient in all his former undertakings, and which he hoped would not fail on this occasion, as he felt proud to show me his skill. The gun was wiped, the powder measured, the ball patched with a six-hundred-thread linen, and the charge sent home with a hickory rod. We moved not a step from the place, for the squirrels were so numerous that it was unnecessary to go after them. Boon pointed to one of these animals which had observed us, and was crouched on a branch about fifty paces distant, and bade me mark well the spot where the ball should hit. He raised his piece gradually, until the *bead* (that being the name given by the Kentuckians to the *sight)* of the barrel was brought to a line with the spot which he intended to hit. The whip-like report resounded through the woods and along the hills in repeated echoes. Judge of my surprise, when I perceived that the ball had hit the piece of bark immediately beneath the squirrel, and shivered it into splinters, the concussion produced by which had killed the animal and sent it whirling through the air, as if it had been blown up by the explosion of a powder magazine. Boon kept up his firing, and before many hours had elapsed, we had procured as many squirrels as we wished; for you must know, that to load a rifle requires only a moment, and that if it is wiped once after each shot, it will do duty for hours. Since that first interview with our veteran Boon, I have seen many other individuals perform the same feat.

Daniel also told Audubon another fine tale during the night that they spent together. He stated that Boone "related to me the following account of his powers of memory, which I lay before you, kind reader, in his own words, hoping that the simplicity of his style may prove interesting to you." The reader must exercise some caution in accepting "Boone's" account told "in his own words." It is an ironic truism of the Boone biographies that the narratives taken from Boone's "own mouth" seem to have received the most "improvement." Audubon, like Filson, probably kept the core of Boone's story but polished the rhetoric of the pioneer a bit too obviously and allowed his own perceptions of Indians and their conflicts with whites to color or substitute for Daniel's views:

"I was once," said he, "on a hunting expedition on the banks of the Green River, when the lower parts of this State (Kentucky) were still in the hands of nature, and none but the sons of the soil were looked upon as its lawful proprietors. We Virginians had for some time been waging a war of intrusion upon them, and I, amongst the rest, rambled through the woods in pursuit of their race, as I now would follow the tracks of any ravenous animal. The Indians outwitted me one dark night, and I was as unexpectedly as suddenly made a prisoner by them. The trick had been managed with great skill; for no sooner had I extinguished the fire of my camp, and laid me down to rest, in full security, as I thought, than I felt myself seized by an indistinguishable number of hands, and was immediately pinioned, as if about to be led to the scaffold for execution. To have attempted to be refractory, would have proved useless and dangerous to my life; and I suffered myself to be removed from my camp to theirs, a few miles distant, without uttering even a word of complaint. You are aware, I dare say, that to act in this manner was the best policy, as you understand that by so doing, I proved to the Indians at once, that I was born and bred as fearless of death as any of themselves.

"When we reached the camp, great rejoicings were exhibited. Two squaws and a few papooses appeared particularly delighted at the sight of me, and I was assured, by very unequivocal gestures and words, that on the morrow, the mortal enemy of the Red-skins would cease to live. I never opened my lips, but was busy contriving some scheme which might enable me to give the rascals the slip before dawn. The women immediately fell a searching about my huntingshirt for whatever they might think valuable, and, fortunately for me, soon found my flask filled with *Monongahela* (that is, reader, strong whisky). A terrible grin was exhibited on their murderous countenances, while my heart throbbed with joy at the anticipation of their intoxication. The crew immediately began to beat their bellies and sing, as they passed the bottle from mouth to mouth. How often did I wish the flask ten times its size, and filled with aquafortis! I observed that the squaws drank more freely than the warriors, and again my spirits were about to be depressed, when the report of a gun was heard at a distance. The Indians all jumped on their feet. The singing and drinking were both brought to a stand, and I saw, with inexpressible joy, the men walk off to some distance and talk to the squaws. I knew that they were consulting about me, and I foresaw that in a few moments the warriors would go to discover the cause of the gun having been fired so near their camp. I expected that the squaws would be left to guard me. Well, Sir, it was just so. They returned; the men took up their guns, and walked away. The squaws sat down again, and in less than five minutes had my bottle up to their dirty mouths, gurgling down their throats the remains of the whisky.

"With what pleasure did I see them becoming more and more drunk, until the liquor took such hold of them that it was quite impossible for these women to be of any service. They tumbled down, rolled about, and began to snore: when I having no other chance of freeing myself from the cords that fastened me, rolled over and over towards the fire, and, after a short time, burned them asunder. I rose to my feet, stretched my stiffened sinews, snatched up my rifle, and, for once in my life, spared that of Indians. I now recollect how desirous I once or twice felt to lay open the skulls of the wretches with my tomahawk; but when I again thought upon killing beings unprepared and unable to defend themselves, it looked like murder without need, and I gave up the idea.

"But, Sir, I felt determined to mark the spot, and walking to a thrifty ash sapling, I cut out of it three large chips, and ran off. I soon reached the river, soon crossed it, and threw myself deep into the cane-brakes, imitating the tracks of an Indian with my feet, so that no chance might be left for those from whom I had escaped to overtake me.

"It is now nearly twenty years since this happened, and more than five since I left the Whites' settlements, which I might probably never have visited again, had I not been called on as a witness in a lawsuit that was pending in Kentucky, and which I really believe would never have been settled, had I not come forward, and established the beginning of a certain boundary line. This is the story, Sir.

"Mr—— moved from Old Virginia into Kentucky, and having a large tract granted to him in the new State, laid claim to a certain parcel of land adjoining Green River, and as chance would have it, took for one of his corners the very Ash tree on which I had made my mark, and finished his survey of some thousands of acres, beginning, as it is expressed in the deed, 'at an Ash marked by three distinct notches of the tomahawk of a white man.'

"The tree had grown much, and the bark had covered the marks; but somehow or other, Mr—— heard from someone all that I have already said to you, and thinking that I might remember the spot alluded to in the deed, but which was no longer discoverable, wrote for me to come and try at least to find the place or the tree. His letter mentioned that all my expenses should be paid, and not caring much about . . . going back to Kentucky, I started and met Mr——. After some conversation, the affair with the Indians came to my recollection. I considered for a while, and began to think that after all I could find the very spot, as well as the tree, if it was yet standing.

"Mr—— and I mounted our horses, and off we went to the Green River Bottoms. After some difficulties, for you must be aware, Sir, that great changes have taken place in those woods, I found at last the spot where I had crossed the river, and waiting for the moon to rise, made for the course in which I thought the Ash tree grew. On approaching the place, I felt as if the Indians were there still, and as if I was still a prisoner among them. Mr—— and I camped near what I conceived the spot, and waited until the return of day.

"At the rising of the sun, I was on foot, and after a good deal of musing, thought that an Ash tree then in sight must be the very one on which I had made my mark. I felt as if there could be no doubt of it, and mentioned my thought to Mr ——. 'Well, Colonel Boon,' said he, 'if you think so, I hope it may prove true, but we must have some witnesses; do you stay here about, and I will go and bring some of the settlers whom I know.' I agreed. Mr—— trotted off, and I, to pass the time, rambled about to see if a deer was still living in the land. But ah! Sir, what a wonderful difference thirty years makes in the country!

Why, at the time when I was caught by the Indians, you would not have walked out in any direction for more than a mile without shooting a buck or a bear. There were then thousands of buffaloes on the hills in Kentucky; the land looked as if it never would become poor; and to hunt in those days was a pleasure indeed. But when I was left to myself on the banks of the Green River, I dare say for the last time in my life, a few *signs* only of deer were to be seen, and, as to a deer itself, I saw none.

"Mr—— returned, accompanied by three gentlemen. They looked upon me as if I had been WASHINGTON himself, and walked to the Ash tree, which I now called my own, as if in quest of a long lost treasure. I took an axe from one of them, and cut a few chips off the bark. Still no signs were to be seen. So I cut again until I thought it was time to be cautious, and I scraped and worked away with my butcher knife, until I *did* come to where my tomahawk had left an impression in the wood. We now went regularly to work, and scraped at the tree with care, until three hacks as plain as any three notches ever were, could be seen. Mr—— and the other gentlemen were astonished, and, I must allow, I was as much surprised as pleased myself. I made affidavit of this remarkable occurrence in presence of these gentlemen. Mr—— gained his cause. I left Green River for ever and came to where we now are; and, Sir, I wish you a good night."

Boone, in a somewhat similar story, reportedly settled a land dispute by stating that he previously had hidden an empty whiskey bottle in the tree upon which the case hinged. Some chopping and scraping at the tree in question soon revealed the bottle, now encased in wood. It should also be noted that the first part of Boone's composite tale documented a fourth, and previously unrecorded, Indian captivity and that the latter part described the great changes that had taken place in this part of Kentucky in the last thirty years. No longer a hunter's paradise, Daniel found only "a few *signs* of deer" where there was once a seemingly endless supply of deer, bear, and buffalo.

British-inspired Indian attacks upon Missouri were the norm by 1811. When Daniel Boone learned of the formal declaration of war in 1812, he was among the first volunteers for the army. He was indignant when he was refused enlistment because he was too old for combat; he was only seventy-eight. Although not actively engaged in the fighting, Daniel served when and where he could, as a sentry and frontier doctor. Indian alarms at the Femme Osage settlement continued from 1811 into 1815. During this period Daniel, Rebecca, and Nathan and his family twice had to flee in the dead of night to the picketing surrounding both the neighborhood fort and the home of Daniel Morgan Boone, some four miles distant from Nathan's house.

The Indians were ingenious in many of their methods. Nathan remembered that they "would often have a dried deer skin with small holes plentifully inserted along the edge by which to fasten it on a hoop to use as a canoe. In these little boats they would put a gun and budget [leather pack] and swim behind, pushing it over the stream. When dry, they would use it as a blanket at night."

Early in 1813 Daniel and Rebecca moved temporarily from Nathan's house to Flanders Callaway's, roughly twelve miles away, to aid in sugar making. After about a month, Rebecca fell ill and rode the four miles from the sugar camp back to Callaway's house. Sick for a few weeks, Daniel's uncomplaining wife of fifty-six years died on March 18 at the age of seventy-four. It was, according to his granddaughter, Susanna Callaway, "the Saddest affliction of his life." Matters were not to improve. Soon exaggerated estimates of the size of an attacking Indian force reached the ears of Flanders Callaway and made him decide to abandon his farm. Daniel and Flanders decided to move to Daniel Morgan Boone's fort in the Femme Osage settlement. They went by land, and Callaway loaded Boone's manuscript autobiography, which Daniel had dictated to his grandson, John B. Callaway, into a canoe along with other household goods for transport by water. The vessel struck a snag and overturned. The only sustained description of the frontiersman's life that really was in his "own words" was lost forever. At Daniel's age, dictation proved such a tedious chore that he gave up the idea of reconstructing the work for a time.

The book-length poem *The Mountain Muse,* written by Rebecca's nephew Daniel Bryan, was published in 1813, almost as if to rub salt in this wound. Bryan's attempt to produce an American epic based on Boone's life and adventures, *The Mountain Muse* was intended to be similar in scope to Milton's *Paradise Lost.* Poetically, it was a steady disaster. Daniel sincerely regretted that Bryan was a relative, for he felt that he "could not sue him for slander." In the understated irony typical of his dry humor, he added that such works "ought to be left until the person was put in the ground."

Daniel was deluding himself if he thought that no further problems could possibly occur in this one year. His friend Judge John Coburn had continued his efforts on Boone's behalf and presented a memorial before the Kentucky General Assembly. They passed a resolution urging the congressional delegation from Kentucky to press those in the national government to take up Daniel's case. The result was a formal petition placed before Congress that documented Boone's decades of service, his personal tragedies, and financial losses and compared his present reduced state and poverty to the wealth of Kentucky. Perhaps the most telling part of the appeal was the statement that Boone, who had opened the west to millions of settlers, did not now own a plot of land on which he could be buried.

On the day before Christmas, the Congressional Committee on Public Lands brought in another report favorable to substantiating Boone's ten-thousand-arpent claim, but for some unknown reason Mr. Edward Hempstead, the nonvoting delegate from the Missouri Territory, stated that he knew Boone desired only his original grant of one thousand arpents. Assuming that the representative expressed Daniel's wishes, the sponsors changed the act accordingly. When Boone learned the provisions of the special bill, signed by President Madison on February 10, 1814, he became furious. He said that he was no beggar and no pauper, and he threatened to write a letter to the Speaker of the House refusing the gift. Fortunately, Congress was not in session and Daniel's family had time enough to persuade him to keep the land.

Fifteen months later, he had to sell the entire tract to appease the creditors from Kentucky who had hurried to Missouri to collect their debts after reading of the government's grant. The last man to present a claim against Daniel Boone was the husband of an orphan girl, perhaps Chloe Flinn, who had received a gift of land from the generous old pioneer. It now turned out that someone had a previous or better claim to the land. The husband demanded compensation and refused to stop badgering Boone even when he was told that there was no money left. According to Nathan Boone, his father, "vexed at the greedy, unfeeling disposition the fellow manifested, finally told him in a quiet way, that he thought he had come a great distance to suck a bull, & he reckoned he would have to go home dry."

Other old problems reappeared for Boone. Although most of Missouri, indeed most of the trans-Appalachian frontier, was still relatively untouched by white settlement in 1810, the very next year saw the dawn of a new era as the steamboat *New Orleans* made the first steam-powered trip from Pittsburgh to St. Louis and then to New Orleans. Further, Missouri, like Kentucky before it, was irresistible to settlers. In his 1812 memorial to the legislature of Kentucky, Boone said that "those fertile plains were unequaled on our earth, and laid the fairest claim to the description of the garden of God." It was now just as easy to describe Missouri in Edenic terms due to the fertility of the land, abundance of vegetation, numerous rivers, and a seemingly limitless supply of large game, fowl, and fish. Such descriptions, together with the end of the War of 1812 and a sense of lessened conflict with Indian tribes, helped to usher in the beginning of a great migration.

In this next large step toward fulfilling Jefferson's dream of a transcontinental United States, more and more Americans chose once again to follow the pattern set by Daniel Boone. Many followed the path of the first generation of trans-Appalachian pioneers along Boone's now widened Wilderness Road through the Cumberland Gap, and many continued to come down the Ohio and then the Mississippi by flatboat. Their dreams were all the same—the desire to own land and to create a better life for themselves and their children—and they eagerly set out in Boone's footsteps to participate in what would become one of the defining parts of the American experience, the ongoing migration to the West.

Timothy Flint, an early observer and writer about this West and a future biographer of Daniel Boone, accurately captured the feeling of the times and the people who were on the move when he noted that

> From some cause, it happens that in the western and southern states, a tract of country gets a name, as being more desirable than any other. The imaginations of the multitudes that converse upon the subject, get kindled, and the plains of Mamre in old time, or the hills of the land of promise, were not more fertile in milk and honey, than are the fashionable points of immigration. During the first, second, and third years of my residence here [1816–1819], the whole current of immigration set towards this country, Boon's Lick, so called, from Boon's having discovered and worked the salines in that tract. Boon's

Lick was the common centre of hopes, and the common point of union for the people. Ask one of them whither he was moving, and the answer was, "To Boon's Lick, to be sure."

Boone's Lick, near the Missouri River, was mainly a venture of Nathan and Daniel Morgan Boone. Daniel never had much to do with it, perhaps because of his own history of salt boiling and more likely because of how little salt those waters actually held, and his sons actually sold their interest in the salt works around 1810.

John Mason Peck, an itinerant Baptist minister and another future biographer of Boone, echoed and amplified Flint's points. He said that in 1810 people first began to move

> westward and planted themselves in the Boone's Lick country, then reported as the *el dorado* of all new countries. Off from the river bottoms the land was undulating, the prairies small, the soil rich, and the timber in variety and of a fine quality. Deer, bears, elk, and other game were in abundance, and furnished provisions, and, in many instances, clothing, until the people could raise crops.
>
> There were in all about one hundred and fifty families that came into the Boone's Lick country in 1810–11, when the Indian war stopped further immigration till 1815 or 1816. . . . Then the "new-comers," like a mountain torrent, poured into the country faster than it was possible to provide corn for breadstuff. Some families came in the spring of 1815; but in winter, spring, summer, and autumn of 1816, they came in an avalanche. It seemed as though Kentucky and Tennessee were breaking up and moving to the "Far West." Caravan after caravan passed over the prairies of Illinois, crossing the "great river" at St. Louis, all bound to the Boone's Lick. The stream of immigration had not lessened in 1817. Many families came from Virginia, the Carolinas, and Georgia, and not a few from the Middle States, while a sprinkling found their way to the extreme west from Yankeedom and Yorkdom.

Peck also made clear the reason for this deluge of humanity: "Following in the wake of this exodus to the middle section of Missouri was a terrific excitement about getting land." The pressures of settlement were drastically increasing. In 1810 the Missouri population was 19,783. By 1820 it would triple to 66,586, with nearly 20,000 people in the newly organized Howard County, which contained the region of Boone's Lick. And, although Boone would not live to see it, the population reached 140,455 in 1830.

Not surprisingly, Daniel Boone was soon on the move again. He traveled a good deal for a man his age, both before and especially after the War of 1812. More settlers meant less game. He reached Kansas and some think perhaps even Yellowstone, for he intended to explore the Rocky Mountains. William Hays Jr. said that he, Boone, and a small party of others made it to the Yellowstone country. Writing from Los Angeles on January 18, 1889, his son Wade recorded that "Daniel Boone & My Father and others Made a trip to the Yellow Stone on the he[a]d waters of the Missouri River[and] was in that country about two winters after Furrs[.] Daniel Boone had a vary great idea of the Pacific Co[a]st[.] he described it vary acurate from som[e] Reason[,] I supose from talking with Indians[.] I had an acquaintanns [named Graham] that com to this Co[a]st Many years before gold was found and he told me that Boone was the cause of his coming to this Co[a]st . . . he toled me that he never would of started had Boone ont [sic, not] urgid [sic, urged] him to com and told him that this was the finest climate in the world[.]" Daniel always seemed to have his eye on that better land to the west.

Boone also may have traveled east back to Berks County, Pennsylvania. A receipt of his to Jacob Van Reed Hunter issued in Reading for "three dollars in full for wagon hire" recently surfaced at auction. Its proposed date, however, of February 21, 1814, is difficult to discern and may instead be 184[?]. Two other Daniel Boones were in Pennsylvania in the 1840s, one in Berks County, but the signature closely resembles that of the old pioneer. However, it seems unlikely that Daniel would be hiring out wagons in Pennsylvania at this point in his life, and family stories note that he was in Missouri to receive the rush of people coming to collect debts from him as soon as the news of the February 10, 1814, congressional grant of land became known.

Occasional Indian raids continued upon the outlying farms in the Femme Osage, but false alarms outnumbered attacks. No matter what the case, Daniel was still at the ready to defend, track, scout, or serve as surgeon.

By April 1816 Boone had hired Indian Phillips, a noted woodsman, to accompany him on a new hunt. Nathan Boone outlined the route:

> The two started up the Missouri in a canoe, reached the mouth of the Grand River, and proceeded up the Grand or Iowa River about eight or ten miles, as far as Coal Banks. They hoped to find beaver there, but the Indian and French trappers had pretty much cleaned them out. They went back to the Missouri again and traveled up some twenty miles above Ft. Leavenworth, which had just been established. Then my father became sick, and so he returned to Ft. Leavenworth and remained there a few days. While at the fort he became acquainted with Captain Bennett Riley of the army, who was then in command. He recovered sufficiently to return home, and Phillips returned with him.

It was on this trip that officers at Fort Osage near the site of the present Kansas City reported that Boone spent two weeks with them sometime in 1816 before leaving "for the River Platt, some distance above." The Platte River would have served as a likely route for an explorer on his way to the Yellowstone country.

If Daniel did not reach all of these places, his dreams still lived on and motivated his descendants. His son Daniel Morgan Boone is reported to have been one of the first settlers of Kansas in 1827. His grandson Albert Gallatin Boone, an early settler of Colorado, explored the Rocky Mountains and served prominently in negotiations of treaties with the western tribes. Kit Carson, Fremont's famous scout on his transcontinental trek, also was a distant relation of Daniel's; coincidentally, President Grant appointed Carson, along with Albert Gallatin Boone, to negotiate the Indian treaty that ceded San Juan County, Colorado, to the United States.

Another trip Daniel made in 1816 was to the house of Dr. John Jones, the husband of one of his granddaughters. He had a double purpose: medical treatment for scrofula and a final attempt at dictating the story of his life, at least up to his migration to Missouri. Jones intended to prepare the work for publication with the resulting profits to go to Daniel. This second narrative was never completed and the manuscript was lost after Dr. Jones's sudden death around 1842. Daniel never did have his say.

A letter from this period has survived, however. It tends to verify that in later years Boone thought a good deal about religion, even if he never formally joined a particular church.

october the 19th 1816

Deer Sister

With pleasuer I Rcd a Later from your sun Samuel Boone who informs me that you are yett Liveing and in good health Considering your age I wright to you to Latt you know I have Not forgot you and to inform you of my own Situation Sence the Death of your Sister Rabacah I leve with flanders Calaway But am at present at my sun Nathans and in tolarabel halth you Can gass at my feilings by your own as we are So Near one age I Need Not write you of our satuation as Samuel Bradley or James grimes Can inform you of Every Surcomstance Relating to our famaly and how we Leve in this World and what Chance we Shall have in the next we know Not for my part I am as ignerant as a Child all the Relegan I have to Love and fear god beleve in Jeses Christ Don all the good to my Nighbour and my self that I Can and Do as Little harm as I Can help and trust on gods marcy for the Rest and I beleve god neve made a man of my prisepel to be Lost and I flater my Self Deer sister that you are well on your way in Cristianaty gave my Love to all your Childran and all my frends fearwell my Deer sister

Daniel Boone

Mrs. Sarah Boone

NB I Rcd a Later yesterday from sister Hanah peninton by hir grand sun Dal Ringe She and all hir Childran are Well at present

DB

The Bible provided Daniel with his favorite reading in his later years, much as history had in his middle age. Although inclined somewhat toward Presbyterianism in his old age, for him religion was always a private affair, and he disliked the bickering and competition that all too frequently marked the various Christian sects.

One account stated that 1816 was also the year of Daniel Boone's last hunt. In a letter Stephen Hempstead recalled sighting Boone, his son-in-law Flanders Callaway, and Boone's slave, Derry Coburn, near St. Louis about 1817 returning from a fall hunt.

> I remember of seeing a canoe coming with [?]ing over the Cargo[,]a sure sign of her coming from the upper Missouri[,] and [I] went down to the landing to see who they were. The canoe was covered with Bearskins and she landed first the stern and the steersman got out and then the bowsman rowed her around and they landed, this was done to enable them to land and not disturb the cargo, the whole middle being full and covered. Mr. [Flanders] Callaway and the Negro rowed in front and Colo[nel] Boone steared in the River, the value of their furs and skins I cannot state but it was considerable[.] I know also it was their constant practice to go by themselves or with two Negro[es] every winter to hunt even long after all their friends were very much opposed to it and Colo[nel] B[oone] I should suppose then to be Eighty years of age or upwards. . . .

Hempstead's sighting may also have occurred in 1811 rather than 1817 (the date is hard to make out in the manuscript). Whatever the year, they were headed for St. Louis, where their beaver would bring a better price.

Nathan, however, said that his father also went hunting with James Boone, his grandson, in late November 1817, further adding, "My father said he was as naturally inclined each fall to go hunting and trapping as the farmer is in spring to set about putting in his crops." On this trip Daniel seemed to gain strength when in his beloved wilderness and was exhilarated to be camping out once again. The glare of their campfire on the newly fallen snow caused a wild duck to land beside the fire, neatly serving itself up for a meal, and James caught it easily. Daniel "seemed to feel himself in his ancient element," according to Nathan, and after "the evening meal he told stories of his 'olden times' adventures" to James. Nathan continued, saying

> The pair had the duck for breakfast the next morning and continued on their way. The weather had become cold and blustery, so they had to stop and make a fire for Father to warm himself. They went only eight miles that day and stopped at a

house of entertainment at Camp Branch, a noted camping place
for travelers. The next day they went twenty-two miles to Loutre
Lick. The weather had moderated a little but was still cold, and
all but two miles of that day's travel was on the exposed prairie.
The cold had affected my father's aged frame, and he found he
could proceed no further since he could not bear the exposure.

The numbing effects of the elements had once again taken their toll.
Too cold to go on, Daniel abandoned the hunt and remained at his granddaughter Van Bibber's cabin at Loutre Lick, where he became seriously ill.
Receiving word of his deteriorating condition, Nathan assumed the worst
and ordered a coffin to be made. He was a bit premature. Arriving at the
Van Bibber home, he found that Daniel had been treated by a passing
doctor and was well on the way to recovery. When Boone saw the coffin
his son had ordered for him, he said it was too rough and uncouth and
proceeded to have a better one fashioned out of cherry according to his
directions. The first coffin was used to bury a relative. The second one,
much to the fright of the small grandchildren, was stored in the cabin loft
by Daniel until it was needed.

It took until summer until Boone was strong enough to make another journey to Kentucky. It was on this trip, or perhaps the earlier one on
which he met Audubon, that Boone finally paid off all his creditors. Doing
so had taken more than thirty years, but at last the stigma of debt was
removed. He had no records or accounts; he paid whatever each man said
was due him. Tradition has it that when Daniel returned to his home in
Missouri he had fifty cents left in his pocket.

Chester Harding, an American portrait painter of some note, made a
trip from St. Louis in June 1820 to capture the old pioneer's likeness on
canvas. Harding, the best teller of the tale, noted that Boone was a hard
man to find and not well known by his neighbors. The statement was a bit
far-fetched, but it added interest to the story.

In June of this year I made a trip of one hundred miles for the
purpose of painting the portrait of old Colonel Daniel Boone. I
had much trouble finding him. He was living, some miles from
the main road, in one of the cabins of an old block-house which
was built for the settlers against the incursions of the Indians. I
found that the nearer I got to his dwelling, the less was known

of him. When within two miles of his house, I asked a man to tell me where Colonel Boone lived. He said he did not know any such man. "Why, yes, you do," said his wife. "It is that white-headed old man who lives on the bottom, near the river." A good illustration of the proverb, that a prophet is not without honor save in his own country.

I found the object of my search engaged in cooking his dinner. He was lying in his bunk, near the fire, and had a long strip of venison wound around his ramrod, and was busy turning it before a brisk blaze, and using salt and pepper to season his meat. I at once told him the object of my visit. I found that he hardly knew what I meant. I explained the matter to him and he agreed to sit. He was ninety years old, and rather infirm; his memory of passing events was much impaired, yet he would amuse me every day by his anecdotes of his earlier life. I asked him one day, just after his description of one of his long hunts, if he never got lost, having no compass. "No," he said, "I can't say as ever I was lost, but I was *bewildered* once for three days."

Daniel's humor was dry to the last.

The family liked Harding's portrait. Their only complaint was that they wished the artist had depicted him with the plump cheeks that had graced his face in more robust days. Daniel had been ill off and on after the aborted 1817 hunting trip. His hearing and eyesight had begun to fail and, although mild-mannered, he would avoid the anticipated prying questions of visiting strangers by grabbing his cane and walking away from Nathan's house.

Still at the home of Flanders Callaway for the summer of 1820, but feeling his condition had improved, Daniel wished to be taken back to Nathan's home. As always, the old pioneer took charge. Nathan said, "He directed me to get a couple of long poles and fasten them to a couple of horses with a bed swung across, as wounded men were carried on campaigns in the Indian country. This sling was swung over the horses' backs, one horse several feet before the other, with a blanket placed across the poles. I obeyed his instructions and got the litter ready, when Dr. Jones came in and said he must not be transported. The doctor decided he was too feeble and might die on the way. The trip was then postponed two or three weeks."

Nathan finally took his father home in a carriage. Daniel rallied, played with his grandchildren, slept well, and upon arising said that if he felt this well tomorrow that he would ride on horseback around the farm. The fever, however, recurred that night, and whether the illness was brought on by the rich treats his grandchildren pressed upon him or by an overindulgence of sweet potatoes, as some thought, mattered little. Daniel's description of an "acute burning sensation, such as he had never before felt, in his breast" indicated a heart attack. He was again attended by Dr. Jones, but refused medication. Daniel said that this was the last time he would be sick and he was not afraid to die. Lucid until the end, he managed to hold on to life until his daughter Jemima could reach his bedside. Daniel expired ten minutes later, just before sunrise on September 26, 1820.

Fittingly, Nathan Boone brought his father's story to an end, noting that Daniel's "body was conveyed to Flanders [and Jemima Boone] Callaway's home at Charette, and there the funeral took place. There were no military or Masonic honors, the latter of which he was a member, as there were then but very few in that region of the country. The Reverend James Craig of the Baptist denomination, my son-in-law, delivered the funeral discourse. There was a very large funeral, and the remains were buried beside those of his wife, a mile below Charette Creek and on the elevated second bank of the Missouri, a mile from the river."

14

"THE SONS OF DANIEL BOONE"
A Hero's Legend and Legacy

One of the first public tributes to Boone came about because of a hurried joint commercial venture between Chester Harding and James Otto Lewis, a part-time actor and engraver in St. Louis, who hoped to capitalize on Boone's fame. Harding furnished a portrait for Lewis to engrave and sell. The advertisement that ran in the *Missouri Gazette* on October 11, 1820, played in part upon Boone's fading from the pantheon of American heroes and read as follows:

PROPOSALS
by
HARDING & LEWIS
For Publishing by Subscription, an
Engraving of the venerable
Col. DANIEL BOONE

. . . To transmit to the posterity of a country, the actions and features of those who fought and bled in her cause, is a duty too sacred and useful to neglect. While the memory of the heroic deeds of the early adventures is passing away, this work will be means of rescuing from oblivion the features of ONE who took the most active part in sustaining the early settlements of the Western Country; whose fortitude and patriotism is so well worthy of imitation and calculated to call forth the finest feelings of the heart.

CONDITIONS

The size of the print will be 15 inches by 10, engraved full length from a characteristic and correct painting, and printed on paper of the first quality.

The price to subscribers will be $3 payable on delivery. Subscriptions will be received by

James O. Lewis
Engraver S. Louis

The power and appeal of Boone as an emblematic man, one who was a true representative of American ideals and dreams, established him as a valuable public property from the first publication of Filson's *Kentucke* in 1784 and continued on long after his death. Even beyond the grave such forces were at work, making it seem that Daniel Boone still could not control his "itching foot." Another journey awaited Daniel and Rebecca. After a strong appeal by the Kentucky legislature in 1845, the people of Missouri agreed to have the remains of the Boones moved to Frankfort, where they would be reinterred and provided, it was promised, with a fitting monument. The ceremony featured speeches, a full-dress military parade, members of the orders of Masons and Odd Fellows in full regalia, a "procession of more than a mile in length" to accompany the "hearse, decorated with evergreens and flowers, and drawn by four white horses," a salute with rifles and swords, and taps—almost all the earmarks of the civilized life that Daniel had often tried so hard to avoid. No irony was intended, of course, only the greatest honor. Still, one must wonder what the pioneer really would have thought of all this pomp. And might not a knowing half-smile have crossed his face when in 1880 the Kentucky politicians finally got around to erecting the promised monument, only thirty-five years late?

Born the year that Daniel died and himself dead before the erection of the monument, Theodore O'Hara (1820–1867), an oftentimes soldier and the first notable Kentucky poet, captured much of the romance and true significance of Boone's life in the last two verses of his undated poem "The Old Pioneer, Daniel Boone" as he meditated about Daniel's grave and how it was perhaps fitting that no monument marked its location:

A dirge for the brave old pioneer!
His pilgrimage is done;

He hunts no more the grizzly bear,
    About the setting sun.
Weary at last of chase and life
    He laid him here to rest,
Nor recks [reckons] he now what sport or strife
    Would tempt him further West.

A dirge for the brave old pioneer!
    The patriarch of his tribe!
He sleeps, no pompous pile marks where,
    No lines his deeds describe;
They raised no stone above him here,
    Nor carved his deathless name—
An empire is his sepulcher,
    His epitaph is Fame.

Daniel's fame expanded rapidly after his death and he became an icon for the American nation. Just as Filson had rendered Boone's "autobiography" through his own political lens and with considerable hope for the commercial success for his book and land dealings, others continued to produce their versions of the pioneer's life for their own specific and often contradictory purposes. Glancing briefly at only the period before the Civil War and omitting the significant number of renditions of his life in the modern media of the last hundred years (including five prime-time television seasons from 1966 to 1970 of Fess Parker playing the lead in *Daniel Boone,* a historical disaster for baby-boomers who still confuse Boone with Crockett because Parker had become a star making Walt Disney's Davy Crockett a household name in the mid-1950s), it becomes clear how malleable a public property Daniel has become.

In 1823, John Trumbull's 1785 Americanization of Filson's Boone, which edited out the most bombastic sections of Filson's rhetoric, was expanded and extended for the period after 1782 by C. Wilder, who cast Boone in the role of a white Indian by plagiarizing large sections from a book entitled *An Account of the Remarkable Occurrences in the Life and Travels of Col. James Smith* (1799) and having his "Boone" parrot Smith's words. Also in 1823, the poet Byron included seven verses about Boone in his long poem *Don Juan.* For Byron, Boone was an ideal example of Rousseau's natural man whose life in the wilderness gave him spiritual purity, serenity, freedom, simplicity, and good health. Byron also promoted the colonel to a general, an honor corrected in the American reprints of the excerpt. John A. McClung gave voice to a savage Boone in his *Sketches of Western Adventure* (1832) by providing his readers a Boone who pined away for the "thrilling excitement of savage warfare" after Kentucky had become too thickly settled. Timothy Flint penned the first full-length biography of the pioneer the next year. His *Biographical Memoir of Daniel Boone,* a best-seller that went through fourteen editions by 1868, trumpeted the concept of Manifest Destiny by interpreting Daniel's life in the wilderness as part of the initial stage in the working-out of a grand Providential plan that would culminate in the triumph of civilization and civilized life: "In the order of things, . . . it was necessary that men like Finley and Boone, and their companions, should precede in the wilderness, to prepare the way for the multitudes who would soon follow." William Gilmore Simms, the most popular southern novelist of the day, presented the public with Boone the "knight errant," a heroic exemplar of the virtues of the southern aristocracy, in an 1845 issue of a magazine that he edited. Yet, this knight, this noble lover of natural beauty, also paralleled James Fenimore Cooper's Hawkeye as a man who could out-Indian the Indians and who, according to Simms, "was a hunter of men too, upon occasion." Perhaps the most idiosyncratic biography of the pioneer was authored by John Mason Peck, who in 1847 revealed Boone not as a hunter, pioneer, or Indian-fighter, but more as the ideal Christian, family man, farmer, and pious teetotaler, everything perhaps that this Baptist minister thought Daniel should be. McClung's savage Boone was reanimated in an 1852 Crockett almanac, a series that did much to popularize the tall-tale frontier hero. Termed "The Great Lion and Father of Adventures of the Back Woods," Boone defeated an Indian attack upon his cabin by decapitating two braves with his sword, which he then used to sever his daughter's hair in such a way that the remaining warriors who were trying to drag her away "fell full length into the fire."

By the 1850s, Filson's narrative and those of subsequent biographers and writers of fiction had become so ingrained in American culture that Daniel's likeness, as depicted in illustrations, pictures, engravings, and paintings, became a key visual symbol of the country's belief in Manifest Destiny. After viewing an exhibition in New York in 1852, the art critic Henry T. Tuckerman proclaimed Boone "the Columbus of the woods," equating his trek through the Cumberland Gap with Columbus's discovery of a new world as two key events in a westward movement that would forever alter the continent. Such evidence abounded for Americans eager to support a growing nationalism. Jefferson's Louisiana Purchase of 1803, the annexation of Texas in 1845, the conquest of the Southwest and California in the Mexican War (1846–1848), and even "Seward's Folly," the purchase of Alaska in 1867, were all events that testified to the power of belief in Manifest Destiny and the near-irresistible lure of vast tracts of land.

But no matter what the manipulations, alterations, fictions, and political agendas of the visual images and narratives that have been and will be brought to bear upon Daniel Boone to make him the founding father of westward expansion, there is an irreducible and genuinely admirable core of meaning to his life. Similarly, while he certainly left much history and considerable legend behind him, a study of the man is incomplete without some consideration as well of the larger significance of his contributions to a westering America. The physical contributions—the trails blazed, the battles fought, the forts and communities established—already have been documented. Yet there are far wider implications in the benefits to exploration and settlement of his actual deeds. From his "discovery" of Kentucky in 1769 in his thirty-fifth year until decades past his death in 1820, through manifold political and socioeconomic changes in America, Boone remained a valuable constant. He epitomized the American way of life, the patterns that the Revolutionary War was fought to preserve, and the virtues deemed most important by the nation's first citizens.

Thousands upon thousands followed his westward journeys, moving east across the Appalachians and the Mississippi to wherever a man and his family might improve their lot. Life was, or at least could be, better to the west. Oftentimes they were possessed with nearly religious zeal for the trek; they had in mind the same belief that allowed a Methodist preacher of the time to bring his sermon on the happiness of heaven to a climax by stating, "my brethren, to say all in one word, heaven is a Kentuck of a place."

For them and for their descendants, Boone was, and perhaps still is, the embodiment of the representative man, the national ideal of frontier independence and virtue. In a country whose history has been dominated by continuing migration, the majority of early Americans believed themselves to be pioneers to some extent and, as such, identified with Boone as their hero. He was indeed like them—neither wealthy nor powerful—and saw himself as a common man whose success or failure rested upon his own efforts and deeds and not upon an accident of birth.

Boone also mirrored one very central American concern—the conflict of civilization and the wilderness—in much the same way. Which was the ideal state? On the one hand Boone was the pioneer, a man happy to do his part to help civilize the frontier and to praise these improvements. But on the other hand, as a hunter and man of nature, Boone was appalled at the encroachments of civilization and he retreated before its corrupting influence to insure his own happiness. These contradictory impulses are still with us. Farms and forests, factories and parks, energy economics and ecology—all are pairs of opposites that are integral though unreconciled parts of the American self-image that Boone represents.

Boone as the "spirit of America" is an intangible that cannot be separated from the man and his endeavors. But his varied careers—explorer, adventurer, wagoner, husband, father, farmer, surveyor, land speculator, conservationist, hunter, military commander, spy, scout, sheriff, coroner, tavern proprietor, elected representative, and Spanish magistrate—were mere occupations, just so many categories that tell little of the essential unity of Daniel Boone. A man equally pragmatic and romantic, his achievements and fame live on for Americans in this dual role of pioneer and preserver because—imagined, desired, or enacted—this is the dual role of the American people, as well.

As the historian Richard Slotkin convincingly demonstrated thirty years ago, Daniel "became the most significant, most emotionally compelling myth-hero of the early republic" and the careers of later frontier heroes were often seen as versions of or variations upon Boone's own life. Perhaps most important, and building upon his impact as a hero, Boone still functions both as an ideal and as a representative man, a model worthy of emulation. It is not widely known, but Dan Beard, the founder of the Boy Scouts of America, a group that has turned and is turning millions of young Americans into trailblazers, woodsmen, and good citizens, stated that he based his conception of this organization upon the following premise: "A society of scouts to be identified with the greatest of all Scouts, Daniel Boone, and to be known as the Sons of Daniel Boone."

NOTES

Although most of the sources of the references below are indicated by the last name of the author, other works from which quotations are frequently taken are identified by short titles or abbreviations. Full citations can be found in the narrative or selected works sections of the bibliography.

Among the most frequently cited short references are:

Bakeless   John Bakeless's *Daniel Boone: Master of the Wilderness*

DM   Material from the Draper Manuscript Collection (the number and letter(s) immediately following DM indicate the volume; the page range appears next; and parentheses enclose the page number of any inserted pages)

Filson   John Filson's *The Discovery, Settlement And present State of Kentucke: . . . To which is added. . . . I. The Adventures of Col.* Daniel Boon. . . .

Houston   *A Sketch of the Life and Character of Daniel Boone: A Memoir by Peter Houston,* ed. Ted Franklin Belue

Life of Boone   Lyman Copeland Draper's *The Life of Daniel Boone,* ed. Ted Franklin Belue; see also pages 197–98 on my use of Draper

My Father   *My Father, Daniel Boone: The Draper Interviews with Nathan Boone,* ed. Neal O. Hammon

1. "Let the Girls Do the Spelling": The Boyhood of Daniel Boone

2 "They did not" Bakeless 5.
" "a Certificate of" Bakeless 6.
3 "the whole truth . . . prepared?" *Life of Boone* 110.
4 "ever unpracticed in" DM 22C14(1) and Bakeless 10.
" "herdsman's club" *Life of Boone* 111.
" "to the north" *Life of Boone* 112.
" "it's all right" Douglass 18.
5 "for early morning . . . it was a [emphasis mine]" *Life of Boone* 114.
6 "darned gun . . . a *dear* shot [emphasis mine]" *Life of Boone* 114.
" "If thee has not" *Life of Boone* 113.
7 "about 20 men" *Pennsylvania Archives* 1:218.
" "worldling" McCarthy 36.

7 "himself in a Fault" DM 1C24 and Faragher, *Daniel Boone,* 24.
8 "The Soil is" Byrd 300.
"   "Publick House at" Wall, Martin, and Boone 2, 4.
9 "if it has come" *Life of Boone* 128.

2. Soldier, Suitor, Hunter, Explorer

12 "After taking Fort Duquesne" Bancroft 4:184.
13 "The only Danger" Franklin 119.
14 "little courage or . . . to drill them" Bancroft 4:185.
"   "to level every molehill" Bancroft 4:186.
"   "with colors flying" *Life of Boone* 129.
"   "the perfection of" Bancroft 4:187.
15 "Waggoners took each" Franklin 120.
"   "About sun down" Smith 9.
"   "was tied naked" *Life of Boone* 132.
"   "burned to death" Smith 9.
"   "to employ strong" *Life of Boone* 113.
"   "very mild and" Faragher, *Daniel Boone,* 43, 369.
"   "five feet eight" *Life of Boone* 141.
16 "to try her temper" *Life of Boone* 140.
"   "fire-hunt . . . shined" Flint, *Biographical Memoir of Daniel Boone,* 26–29; *Life of Boone* 160n. a; and Faragher, *Daniel Boone,* 44, 370.
"   "You are like" DM 16C57 and 6S17(1).
17 "a neck piece" *Life of Boone* 148.
18 "I thought it" *Life of Boone* 148.
"   "from his father" Bakeless 31 and Wall, Martin, and Boone 4, citing Rowan County *Minutes,* book 3. The original grant to Squire Boone is noted in book 3:164.
"   "D. Boon cilled" *Life of Boone* 158.
19 "He looked so" DM 2C53. The information came from Thomas Norman.
21 "she gave him" *Life of Boone* 176.
23 "a small shaving" *Life of Boone* 185.
24 "little girl" *Life of Boone* 188.
"   "as quick . . . of a gun" *Life of Boone* 190.
25 "was a man . . . such great cronies" *My Father* 18, 17.
"   "ketched in a" DM 6S6.

3. "In Quest of the Country of Kentucke"

28 "of the Tombigbee" *Life of Boone* 198
"   "Ah, Wide-Mouth" *Life of Boone* 198.
29 "in quest of" Filson 51-52
"   "passed over Stone" *Life of Boone* 208.
30 "Nature was here" Filson 52.
31 "the time of" Filson 52.

31 "Now, brothers, go" *Life of Boone* 216.
"   *"Steal horse, eh?" Life of Boone* 217.
32 "Notwithstanding the unfortunate" Filson 53.
33 "cottage" *Life of Boone* 238.
"   "Thus situated, many" Filson 53.
"   Lay of[f] a" Rowan County *Minutes* 3:171. See also Wall, Martin, and Boone 5.
"   on the first day" Filson 54.
"   I continued this" Filson 55.
34 "while I was" *Life of Boone* 244.
"   "D.B.—1770" *Life of Boone* 245.
35 "I was happy" Filson 56.
"   "His life was" Simms, *"Daniel Boon,"* 229–30.
37 *"Fifteen hundred skins" Life of Boone* 263.
38 "six or eight" *Life of Boone* 266.
"   "robbed of all" *Life of Boone* 268.
39 "you have danced" DM 16C81(1).
"   "the story of" DM 16C81(2).

4. Henderson's "Infamous Company of Land Pyrates": Transylvania

40 "the French Lick" *Life of Boone* 284.
"   "2 quarts of Rum" DM 11DD8.
43 "this unhappy affair" Filson 57.
44 "the Murder of . . . every ones mouth" DM 3QQ40.
"   "no questions were" *Life of Boone* 299.
"   "Captain Russell, from" *Virginia Gazette,* March 17, 1774, 2. Also in *Life of Boone*
    300.
"   "no room to doubt" *Life of Boone* 300–301.
45 "two faithful woodsmen" *Life of Boone* 305.
"   "I have engaged" *Life of Boone* 306.
"   "If they are alive" *Life of Boone* 307.
46 "Shtop, Gabtain, and" *Life of Boone* 307.
"   "Schoot her, Gabtain!" *Life of Boone* 308.
"   "an awkward Dutchman" DM 6S85 and *My Father* 42.
"   "a half-acre in-lot" *Life of Boone* 308.
"   "Alarmed by finding" *Life of Boone* 309.
47 "the surveyors were" Hammon, "John Filson's Error," 463, quoting "Boofman's
    Heirs v. James Hickman, Fayette County Complete Book A," 604–42, Fayette
    County Courthouse, Lexington, Kentucky.
"   "what induced me" *Life of Boone* 310.
"   "pray let Boone" *Life of Boone* 311.
"   "Sept. 22d. Lieut. Boone" *Life of Boone* 313.
"   "a petition signed" *Life of Boone* 320.
49 "There is something" Aron, *How the West Was Lost,* 62 and Lester 41.
"   "an Asylum to" Aron, *How the West Was Lost,* 62, quoting "A Proclamation by
    Gov. Martin against Richard Henderson and the Transylvania Purchase, Feb-

ruary 10, 1775," in North Carolina, *The Colonial Records of North Carolina*, 9:1124.

49 "If some effectual . . . the Indian country" Aron, *How the West Was Lost* 62 quoting Gov. Martin to the Earl of Dartmouth, November 12, 1775, in North Carolina, *Colonial Records,* 10:324.

50 "Henderson the famous . . . of land Pyrates" Henderson, "Richard Henderson and the Occupation of Kentucky," 351.

" "Pray, is Dick Henderson" Henderson, "Richard Henderson," 351.

" "Proposals for the Encouragement" North Carolina, *Colonial Records,* 9:1129–30.

" "Furnace or other . . . number of sheep" North Carolina, *Colonial Records,* 9:1129–30.

51 "was solicited by" Filson 59.

" "filled a house" *Life of Boone* 333.

" "only ten waggons" *Life of Boone* 363n. q.

" "Henderson and company" *Life of Boone* 333.

" "The Great Grant" *Life of Boone* 333.

52 "the value of" *Life of Boone* 333.

" "The Path Deed" *Life of Boone* 333.

" "Brother, we have" *Life of Boone* 333.

" "a black cloud" *Life of Boone* 332, 523n. 4.

5. Cutting the Wilderness Road

53 "I . . . undertook to" Filson 59.

" "On leaving that river [Rock-castle] . . . in the woods" Walker, "Narrative of an Adventure in Kentucky in the Year 1775," 152 and *Life of Boone* 336.

54 "But let me" Walker, "Narrative," 154. See also his *Memoirs,* 54, for a slightly different version of this tribute.

" "On March the 28th . . . be the case " *Life of Boone* 339.

55 "April satd first . . . Some turns back" Kilpatrick 367.

56 "was carried in" Walker, "Narrative," 153 and *Life of Boone* 340.

" "On entering the" Walker, "Narrative," 153 and *Life of Boone* 340.

" "On the fourth" *Life of Boone* 340.

" "Met about forty" Henderson, "Richard Henderson," 354.

57 "It was beyond" *Life of Boone* 342.

" "struck whilst the" *Life of Boone* 343.

" "Satterday 15th clear . . . volley of guns" Kilpatrick 368–69. Bracketed clarifications are from Hammon, "The First Trip to Boonesborough," 250.

58 "excellent beef in" *Life of Boone* 344.

" "On Viewing the fort . . . or *vice versa*" Ranck 172. See also Hammon, "The First Trip," 259–60.

59 "every body seemed" Walter Clark, 15.

" "tuesday 25th in . . . Clearing for corn—" Kilpatrick 369.

60 "modesty . . . very strict watch" Walter Clark 17.

" "Many men were" Walter Clark 20–21.

" "a set of" Walter Clark 22.

" "divine elm" *Life of Boone* 365.

60 "church, state-house" Walter Clark 22.
"   "without giving offence" *Life of Boone* 366.
61 *"a bill to" Life of Boone* 367–68.
"   "a committee to" *Life of Boone* 367–68.
"   "Livery of Seizin" *Life of Boone* 369.
"   "for improving the . . . preserving the game" *Life of Boone* 368.
"   "to preserve the . . . in good order" *Life of Boone* 370.
"   "I feel pleased . . . number of savages" Faragher, *Daniel Boone,* 122, 380, citing Daniel Boone to Charles Telfridge, May 19, 1775, Boone Bicentennial Commission Records, 61W11, Special Collections, University of Kentucky, Lexington.
"   "We are informed" *Life of Boone* 382.
62 "The country might . . . who visit it" *Life of Boone* 382–83.
"   "the first white" Filson 60.
63 "for the signal" *Life of Boone* 387.
"   "to be considered . . . into their protection" *Life of Boone* 388.
"   "by no means" *Life of Boone* 387.
"   "that Transylvania will" *Life of Boone* 388.
64 "any person who . . . countries in America" *Life of Boone* 389.

6. Revolution and Rescue on the Frontier

65 "had been fired" *Life of Boone* 391.
66 "seemed determined to" Filson 60.
"   "if any of" *Life of Boone* 391.
"   "Capt. James Harrod" *Life of Boone* 409.
67 "appointed commissioners in" *Life of Boone* 411.
"   "are not likely" DM 45J101–101(1).
"   "have plundered, burnt" DM 45J101(1).
68 *"cane-stab" Life of Boone* 411.
69 "the *Yellow Boys*" *Life of Boone* 412.
"   "We have done" *Life of Boone* 413.
"   "the captives were" *Life of Boone* 414.
70 "tired . . . themselves along" *Life of Boone* 414.
72 "through the country" *Life of Boone* 428n. 31.
"   "that he was" *Life of Boone* 418.
73 "The girls were" *My Father* 50.
"   "That's Daddy!" *Life of Boone* 419.
"   "For God's sake" *Life of Boone* 420.
"   "thank Almighty Providence . . . Cry for joy" DM 21C29.
74 "We sent them . . . almost naked" *Life of Boone* 419.
"   "I fired at" *Life of Boone* 420.
"   "the Indians were" DM 30C48–49.
"   "as magistrate under" *Life of Boone* 423.
75 "attacked several forts" Filson 60.
"   "The D——l [Devil] to . . . too, to hell" Floyd to Preston, May 27, 1776, DM 33S296–97.
76 "six shilling per . . . ten pence" *Life of Boone* 424.

76 "These accounts remain" *Life of Boone* 393.
77 "signal services" *Life of Boone* 387.
78 "the year of" *Life of Boone* 435.
"   "We are surrounded" *Life of Boone* 435.
"   "No, they haven't" *Life of Boone* 438.
79 "Boys, we are" *Life of Boone* 440.
"   "Well, Simon, you" *Life of Boone* 441.
80 "Boone was badly . . . up in forts" *Life of Boone* 446.
"   "New Commission of" Virginia Council of State, *Journals of the Council of the State of Virginia,* 1:424.
"   "the superiority of" Filson 62.
"   "Our affairs began" Filson 62.
"   "we passed through" Filson 62.
"   "I think it" *Life of Boone* 450.
81 "If planted . . . *seven barrels!*" *Life of Boone* 450.
"   "The people in" DM 57J13.

7. Shel-tow-ee, Son of Blackfish

83 "From this event" Thwaites and Kellogg, *Frontier Defense on the Upper Ohio, 1777–1778,* 189.
"   "your Petitioners are" Robertson 43.
84 "a party of" Filson 63.
"   "How d'do, Captain" *Life of Boone* 463.
85 *"Pe-me-mo Lick"* *Life of Boone* 463.
"   "Don't fire!—If" *Life of Boone* 464.
86 *"Brothers!—* What I . . . smile upon you" *Life of Boone* 465 and DM 11C62(6–7).
87 "O Captain Boone" *Life of Boone* 466 and DM 6S109.
"   "vel-ly good so-jer" *Life of Boone* 467.
"   "The same evening . . . against each other" *My Father* 56.
"   "an uncomfortable journey" Filson 63.
"   "received as good" Filson 63–64.
"   "worse than all . . . their long fast" *Life of Boone* 469.
88 "The hair of . . . feast and smoking" Peck, *Life of Daniel Boone,* 47–48.
89 "During our travels" Filson 64.
"   "it was a" *Life of Boone* 471.
"   "You are too . . . them of it" *Life of Boone* 471 and DM 6S113.
"   "These Shawanese delivered" Thwaites and Kellogg, *Frontier Defense,* 283.
"   "By Boone's account" Thwaites and Kellogg, *Frontier Defense,* 283–84.
90 "a horse, saddle . . . silver trinkets" *Life of Boone* 472.
"   "was a long" Filson 64.
"   "take a dance" DM 12CC76 and Belue, "Terror in the Canelands," 26.
91 "was a *little*" DM 12CC76.
"   "did the Indians" *Life of Boone* 481.
"   "I became a son . . . made everything acceptable" Filson 65.
92 "Grandfather Boone said" Belue, "Terror," 8–9n. 16.
"   "had been obliged" Belue, "Terror," 8–9n. 16.

92 "used afterwards to" *Life of Boone* 481.
"   "You need not" *My Father* 62.
"   "alarmed to see . . . the first opportunity" Filson 66.
"   "I am going" *Life of Boone* 479.
93 "scalded" DM 6S125.
"   "after a journey" Filson 66.

8 Patriot or Traitor?: Boonesborough Besieged

94 "found a poor" DM 12CC67.
95 "He [Mr. Hancock] informed us" *Life of Boone* 497.
"   "the Indians had" Filson 66–67.
"   "A smart fight . . . all their baggage. . . ." Filson 67.
96 "My son, what . . . you every assistance" *Life of Boone* 500–501.
"   "taken to Detroit . . . the same rank" *Life of Boone* 501.
"   "There, you see" *Life of Boone* 501.
97 "he would never . . . with the rest" *Life of Boone* 501.
"   "represented Detriot and . . . children to ride" *Life of Boone* 502.
"   "It was now" Filson 68.
98 "sounded grateful in" Filson 69.
"   "to fire at" *Life of Boone* 505.
99 "forever bury the" *Life of Boone* 505.
"   "that entirely alters" *Life of Boone* 506.
99 "long hands" *Life of Boone* 506.
"   "Go!" *Life of Boone* 506.
"   "inflicted a lesser" *Life of Boone* 507.
100 "although surrounded by" Filson 69.
"   "The first day" *My Father* 68.
102 "Pompey nee-poo," *Life of Boone* 512.
"   "pulling up his" *Life of Boone* 516.
"   "not to throw" *Life of Boone* 513.
"   "What are you . . . sons of bitches!" *Life of Boone* 513 and DM 6S143.
103 "the fleshy part" DM 6S142.
"   "a wooden cannon" *Life of Boone* 514.
"   "from a pint" *Life of Boone* 515.
104 "made the Dreadfullest" DM 57J27.
"   procured a quantity" *Life of Boone* 518.
"   "picked up one hundred" Filson 70.
"   "During this dreadful" Filson 70.
105 "i. That Boone had . . . of the garrison" *Life of Boone* 520.
"   "Boon was in" Trabue 63.
"   "Capt. Daniel Boon . . . to fool them" Trabue 63–64.
106 "nothing worthy of" Filson 70.
107 "The history of" Filson 73.

9. From Pauper to Legislator

108 "this country as" Bodley, *George Rogers Clark*, 109, citing as his sources the Archives, Virginia State Library, Richmond and *Illinois Historical Collections* 8:97.

109 ". . . on the morning . . . of the horses" *Houston* 16–17.

110 "All slept in" *Houston* 17–18.

" "on the Waters" Editor's preface, *The Register of the Kentucky Historical Society* 21 (1923): 82.

" "It is with" Richard Henderson to Robert Burton, September 29, 1779, from a transcription in the North Carolina State Archives (PC377.1) noting that the original is in the possession of E.V. Howell.

111 "Pressly Anderson was" DM 11CC55.

" "forty pounds for" Hening 52 from "An act for establishing a Land office, and ascertaining the terms and manner of granting waste and unappropriated lands," 50–65.

" "It was my" *My Father* 71.

" "was left destitute" Bakeless 245.

112 "I feel for . . . at the time" Bakeless 245–46 citing his slightly different transcription of Thomas Hart's letter than the version published in the *Presbyterian Historical Society Journal* 14 (1930–31): 343. The letter is held in the Rev. John Dabney Shane Manuscript Collection at the Presbyterian Historical Society, Philadelphia.

113 "the colonel [Callaway was] killed . . . at Blue Licks" *Life of Boone* 558.

114 "Such as were" Filson 72.

" "finished with great" Filson 72.

115 "at ten o'clock" *Houston* 19.

" "The sun was . . . from the fort" *Houston* 20–21.

116 "leather trousers and" *Houston* 21.

117 "was dressed in" DM 10NN101.

118 "We the Public . . . for 1500 acres" Wyllie 5.

" "Daniel remained with" *Houston* 22.

" "Daniel Came [home . . .]" from "Family Records" in the James Boone diary, North Carolina State Archives (PC343.1).

120 "In 1792, Boone" Laidley 11.

10. "Our Affairs Became More and More Alarming": The Disaster at Blue Licks

121 "defeated, with the" Filson 74.

" "Our affairs became" Filson 74.

122 "Brothers: The fertile . . . and your rum" Bradford 119–21, as edited by Bakeless 273–74. Bracketed comments are in Bakeless's version.

123 "nations of Shawanese" Filson 74–75.

125 "the loss of" Filson 75.

" "loaded each shot" *My Father* 76.

126 "Boone used to" *My Father* 79.

" "All who are" DM 6S152–53.

126 "I can go" *My Father* 76.
"   "Let them go" *Houston* 25.
"   "Boone yelled 'Colonel . . .'" *Houston* 25.
127 "Colonel Boone, why" *My Father* 76.
"   "My self and . . . pioneer wept bitterly" *Houston* 26.
128 "The ridge where . . . spears and tomahawks" *Houston* 26.
"   "When we gave" Filson 77.
"   "Let's halt boys" *My Father* 76.
129 "Never was there" *Houston* 27.
"   "Many widows were" Filson 77.
"   "found their bodies" Filson 77–78.
130 "I have Encouraged" Bakeless 308.
"   "The conduct of" Bodley, *George Rogers Clark,* 219 and Virginia, *Calendar of Virginia State Papers,* 3:345.
"   "I cannot reflect" Filson 77.
"   "From a Late . . . Daniel Boone" Lofaro, "Tracking Daniel Boone," 331–32. My transcription is of a letter (HM 39952) from the collections of the Huntington Library.
131 "We immediately took" Filson 78.
"   "Their connections were" Filson 79.
132 "Brother, says he" Filson 80.

11. "Your Land Is All Survayd": Prosperity, Debt, and Retreat

133 "Now, Boone, we" Peck 102–3.
134 "Sir I have . . . *Daniel Boone*" Daniel Boone to Robert Burton, August 28, 1784, from a transcription in the North Carolina State Archives (PC377.1) noting that the original is in the possession of E.V. Howell.
135 "Aperel the 22 1785 . . . to the begining" DM 26C44.
"   "Dear Col   the Land . . . [.] DB" Daniel Boone to Col. William Christian, August 23, 1785, Manuscript Collection of the St. Louis Mercantile Library Association, University of Missouri, St. Louis, Mo.
136 "Boone's claim to . . . law was inexorable" *Houston* 28.
"   "Boone having found . . . it as well" *Houston* 30–31.
137 "returned to Boone's" *Houston* 31.
"   "was appointed about" *Houston* 32.
138 "19 galons of" Bushnell 3.
"   "I will Bee" Daniel Boone to Jacob Cohen, April 28, 1784, Daniel Boone Papers, Archibald Henderson Collection, University of North Carolina, Chapel Hill, North Carolina.
"   "in Short an" DB to Patrick Henry, DM 32C81A.
"   "Mind that fellow" *My Father* 8.
139 "I am hire" DM 26C176.
"   "4 galons Whiskey . . . Accounts is just" Bushnell 7. The photograph of the August 22 page reproduced before page 1 of the article allows the present correction of Bushnell's transcription.

140 "out of the" Virginia Council of State, *Journals,* 4:159.
141 "a stock of . . . he left there" *My Father* 84.
142 "Kentucky father . . . their adopted state" *Houston* 35.
" "so interested did . . . between the eyes" *Houston* 33–34. The following paren-
  thetical discussion of the tinderbox comprises all the material omitted from the
  quoted passage: "'(The tinder box was a small box in which the settlers burned
  cotton cloth to tinders—nearly ashes—and fit a top over it to shut out moisture.
  And when a fire was wanted thin dry shavings were prepared, the top of the box
  removed and by the friction of a flint and piece of steel sparks were thrown upon
  the tinder which took fire and the shavings were ignited. Sometimes powder,
  when plentiful, was used for tinder.)"
143 "His large head" Thwaites, *Daniel Boone,* 213.
144 "hair was moderately" *My Father* 140.
" "that at the end" *Houston* 36.
" "Privets" and "sypes or scutes" Virginia, *Calendar,* 5:410 and *Boone Pioneer Echoes,* Jan. 1981, 5.
" "Sir as sum . . . Dal Boone" DM 14C105.
145 "Captain Caperton did" Laidley 11.
146 "my father didn't . . . attack our camp" *My Father* 98–99.
147 "Nearly the entire . . . or ten days" *My Father* 99.
148 "Sir--After my . . . Daniel Boone" Bakeless 339.
" "wagons loaded with" Hammon, "Early Roads into Kentucky," 124 (Hammon
  cites Kincaid, *The Wilderness Road,* 191).
149 "You are hereby . . . Plea withdrawn" "Bond of DB and John Grant," Manuscript Collection of the Kentucky Historical Society.
" "the oil brought" *My Father* 102.

12. "I Want More Elbow-Room": Bound for Missouri

151 "an 1000 acre" Manuscript ChC1.120 from the collections of the Boston Public
  Library, Boston, Massachusetts.
" "Is this the spot . . . of the entry" Deposition of Daniel Boone (Ayer MS 96), The
  Edward F. Ayer Collection, The Newberry Library, Chicago, Illinois.
152 "jockeys racing their . . . can be shown" Staples 96.
" "resolute forester" Cooper 10.
" "Colonel Boon, the . . . inconveniently crowded" Cooper 10 n.
" "Too crowded . . . elbow-room" DM 15C4(2).
154 "yeald passive obedience" Meriwether Lewis, May 20, 1804, in Lewis and Clark,
  Original Journals of the Lewis and Clark Expedition, 1804–1806, 1:24, and Bakeless
  372.
" "In October 1802 . . . hundred beaver skins" *My Father* 120.
155 "Do you believe" Bryan and Rose 170.
156 "well laid on" Burnett 343 and Bakeless 373.
" "June 30th, 1804 . . . Daniel Boone [seal]" DM 15C65.
" "First rate. Whipped" Burnett 343 and Bakeless 373.
157 "It was the" *My Father* 124.

158 "claim ought not" Bakeless 378.
"   "Deer Sir / The Later . . . Daniel Boone" Manuscript collection of the Kentucky
       Historical Society, Frankfort, Kentucky.
159 "The old pioneers" *My Father* 47.
160 "He said that" *My Father* 110–11.
"   "wheeled their horses . . . trees near camp" *My Father* 127.

13. One Last Hunt: The Final Decade

161 "*Barking off squirrels* . . . the same feat" Audubon, *Delineations of American Scen-
       ery and Character*, 60–61.
162 "related to me . . . a good night" Audubon, *Ornithological Biography*, 1:503–6.
167 "would often have" *My Father* 133.
"   "the Saddest affliction" DM 21C45(2–3).
"   "could not sue . . . in the ground" DM 7C43(3).
168 "vexed at the" DM 6S252; see also *My Father* 117.
169 "those fertile plains" *Life of Boone* 101.
"   "From some cause . . . 'to be sure'" Flint, *Recollections of the Last Ten Years,* 202–3.
170 "westward and planted . . . Yankeedom and Yorkdom" Peck, *Forty Years of Pio-
       neer Life,* 135, 146.
"   "Following in the" Peck, *Forty Years of Pioneer Life,* 147.
171 "Daniel Boone &" Manuscript 130, Wade Hays Family History, Seaver Center
       for Western History Research, Natural History Museum of Los Angeles County,
       Los Angeles, Calif.
"   "three dollars in" Ebay auction # 1097319884 by Mission Gallery, 320 Wash-
       ington Street, San Diego, CA 92103 and author's correspondence with the gal-
       lery on June 10, 2002.
172 "The two started . . . returned with him" *My Father* 136.
"   "for the River" *Niles' Weekly Register* 14 (May 16, 1818): 208 and Bakeless 391.
173 "october the 19th 1816 . . . DB" DM 27C88.
174 "I remember of . . . age or upwards " DM 16C78(2). For a slightly different
       transcription, see *Houston* 69n. 79.
"   "My father said . . . bear the exposure" *My Father* 137.
175 "In June of . . . for three days" Harding 35–36.
176 "He directed me" *My Father* 138.
177 "acute burning sensation" *My Father* 139.
"   "body was conveyed" *My Father* 139.

14. "The Sons of Daniel Boone": A Hero's Legend and Legacy

178 "PROPOSALS / by / HARDING . . . Engraver S. Louis" Amyx 154–55.
179 "procession of more . . . four white horses" Manuscript reminiscence of J.W.
       Venable, May 4, 1855, from the collections of the Houghton Library, Harvard
       University.
"   "A dirge for . . . epitaph is fame" O'Hara 58–59.

181 "thrilling excitement of" McClung 91.
"   "In the order" Flint, *Biographical Memoir,* 37–38.
"   "knight errant" Simms 226
"   "was a hunter" Simms 226
"   "The Great Lion" *Crockett Almanac* (Philadelphia: 1852), [5].
"   "fell full length" *Crockett Almanac* (Philadelphia: 1852), [5].
"   "the Columbus of" Sweeney ix.
182 "my brethren, to" Flint, *Recollections,* 64.
183 "became the most" Slotkin, *Regeneration through Violence,* 21.
"   "A society of" Beard 353.

A BIBLIOGRAPHIC NOTE
AND BIBLIOGRAPHY

The primary and secondary materials pertinent to the life of Daniel Boone are so voluminous that even a partial listing would swell this volume far beyond its present size. In this selected bibliography, therefore, I make no attempt to be comprehensive. I refer the reader to William Harvey Miner's *Daniel Boone: Contribution toward a Bibliography of Writings concerning Daniel Boone* (1901; reprint, New York: B. Franklin, 1970) for pre-1900 references, and to the bibliography in Willard Rouse Jillson's *The Boone Narrative* (Louisville, Ky.: Standard Printing, 1932). More recent bibliographies concerning pre–Civil War works on Boone can be found in Richard Slotkin's "Emergence of a Myth: John Filson's 'Daniel Boone Narrative' and the Literature of the Indian Wars, 1638–1848" (Ph.D. diss., Brown University, 1967); and Michael A. Lofaro's "The Genesis of the Biographical Image of Daniel Boone" (Ph.D. diss., University of Maryland, 1975). The catalogs of almost all large libraries and other usual bibliographic sources, both online and otherwise, will yield a generous list of post-1930 works on the pioneer, but there is a genuine need for a comprehensive bibliography.

Although several general works dealing with the Kentucky frontier are mentioned in this book, the interested reader is again directed to more detailed surveys of available literature. J. Winston Coleman's *A Bibliography of Kentucky History* (Lexington, Ky.: Univ. of Kentucky Press, 1949), Willard Rouse Jillson's *Books on Kentucky Books and Writers: A Bibliography, 1784–1950* (Frankfort, Ky.: Roberts Printing, 1951), and Jacqueline Bull's annual compilation of "Writings on Kentucky History" for the years 1948 through 1962, which was published irregularly in *The Register of the Kentucky Historical Society,* with the last list appearing in April 1968, should all prove useful in this regard. A separate imprint also was issued by the Kentucky Historical Society for the earlier bibliographies: *Writings on Kentucky History, 1848–1955* (Lexington, Ky.: n.p., 1949–1957), compiled by Jacqueline Bull and Frances L.S. Dugan.

After over two hundred years and numerous biographies of Daniel Boone, it would be folly to pretend that the majority of events and episodes here recounted are startlingly new. But a biographer, consciously or unconsciously, creates a particular image of his subject through the selection of data. To maintain the closest possible ties to primary source material, I have drawn heavily upon such documents, both in quotation and paraphrase. This is especially true of the Draper Manuscript Collection of the State Historical Society of Wisconsin. Credit for much of the "new" material presented in this study, therefore, belongs to Dr. Lyman Copeland Draper, the superb nineteenth-century investigative historian of the trans-Appalachian West.

The results of Draper's more than fifty years of research and collecting fill 486 volumes, which are now divided into fifty series, each with its own alphabetical designation. His "Life of Boone," which covers the frontiersman's life through 1778, is the acknowledged authoritative work on the subject and a constant sourcebook for this text on Boone's first forty-five years. Draper never completed his book, but his partial biography of Boone is now available; see Lyman Copeland Draper, *The Life of Daniel Boone,* ed. Ted Franklin Belue (Mechanicsburg, Penn.: Stackpole, 1998). I cite this edition in my quotes rather than the original manuscripts as a convenience to the reader, but retain my own readings of passages in which small differences occur. (The same methodology is followed with the Peter Houston and Nathan Boone extracts from the Draper manuscript collection cited below.

Likewise edited by Belue, Peter Houston's *A Sketch of the Life and Character of Daniel Boone* (Mechanicsburg, Penn., 1997) reveals his friendship with the frontiersman from 1779, when Houston was eighteen, to 1799, when Boone left for Missouri, and yields new information about that span of years. Approximately forty additional volumes of Draper's manuscripts and notes relating directly to Boone's career also help to reconstruct the story of the second half of the pioneer's life.

Of the Draper volumes' fifty series, I most frequently consulted the following:

B   Draper's "Life of Boone" (5 vols.)

C   Boone MSS. (32 vols.)

S   Draper's Notes (33 vols. Volume 6S contains Draper's 1851 interviews in Missouri with a number of Boone's relatives. The large section dealing with the information given by Nathan Boone and his wife is quite important and is now available in an excellent edition by Neal O. Hammon. *My Father, Daniel Boone: The Draper Interviews with Nathan Boone* (Lexington, Ky.: Univ. Press of Kentucky, 1999). It makes a wealth of important information easily accessible for the first time.)

CC   Kentucky MSS. (30 vols.)

Series J, the George Rogers Clark manuscript (65 vols.), and series QQ, the Preston Papers (6 vols.), yield a good deal of material, and a number of items are scattered throughout the collection.

The best biography of Boone published to date, John Mack Faragher's *Daniel Boone: The Life and Legend of an American Pioneer* (New York: Holt, 1992), is particularly helpful in establishing the contexts of Boone's life. The best of the older biographies is John Bakeless's *Daniel Boone: Master of the Wilderness* (1939; reprint, Harrisburg, Penn.: Stackpole, 1965). Bakeless was the first biographer to make full use of the Draper Manuscript Collection. His work is especially valuable for the post-1778 period because of its adept organization of far-ranging source materials.

Other biographies of particular interest include John Filson's *The Discovery, Settlement And present State of Kentucke: . . . To which is added . . . I. The Adventures of Col.* Daniel Boon . . . (1784; reprint, Fairfield, Wash.: Galleon Press, 2001), the first "autobiography"; John Trumbull's very popular condensed edition of Filson's work, *The Adventures of Colonel Daniel Boon* . . . (1786; reprint, New York: Garland, 1978); C. Wilder's printing of the *Life and Adventures of Colonel Daniel Boon* . . . (1823;

reprint, New York: n.p., 1916), which added a "Continuation of the Life of Colonel Boon" to the Trumbull text; Timothy Flint's *Biographical Memoir of Daniel Boone* (1833; reprint, New Haven, Conn.: College and University Press, 1967) (a runaway best-seller of its day partly because of a number of romantic fabrications, but one that cannot be dismissed out of hand because of Flint's interviews with Boone); John Mason Peck's *Life of Daniel Boone, the Pioneer of Kentucky*, published first in *The Library of American Biography*, 2d ser., vol. 13, ed. Jared Sparks (Boston: Little Brown, 1847) and reprinted in *The Makers of American History* (New York: The University Society, 1904) (a minister's idealized view of the frontiersman, but again one based upon personal interviews); and Reuben Gold Thwaites's *Daniel Boone* (New York: Appleton, 1902), a work drawn in part from the Draper Manuscript Collection. This list is far from complete. Daniel Boone has been and still is a figure that stirs the interest of innumerable biographers.

The magnificent amount of available source material is due in large measure to the diligence of the local historians, especially of Kentucky, but also of North Carolina, Missouri, and Pennsylvania. Two journals, *The Register of the Kentucky Historical Society* and *The Filson Club History Quarterly*, amply repay even the most casual perusal. The many volumes published by the Filson Club from 1884 to the present provide a large additional fund of information. Other valuable collections include the material on Boone in the *Missouri Historical Review* (especially the articles on Boone's life in Missouri by William S. Bryan); the *Mississippi Valley Historical Review*, which is now *The Journal of American History; American Archives; American State Papers; Calendar of Virginia State Papers; Journals of the Council of the State of Virginia, The State Records of North Carolina; Pennsylvania Archives;* and the *Pennsylvania Magazine of History and Biography.*

Bibliography of Works Cited and of Interest to the Life of Daniel Boone

Those marked with an asterisk are discussed or mentioned in the previous bibliographic note.

Abbott, John S.C. *Daniel Boone, Pioneer of Kentucky.* New York: Dodd & Mead, 1872.

Alvord, Clarence W. "Daniel Boone." *American Mercury* 8 (June 1926): 266–70.

———. *The Mississippi Valley in British Politics.* 2 vols. Cleveland: Arthur H. Clark, 1917.

Amyx, Clifford. "The Authentic Image of Daniel Boone." *Missouri Historical Review* 82 (1988): 153–64.

Aron, Stephen. *How the West Was Lost: The Transformation of Kentucky from Daniel Boone to Henry Clay.* Baltimore: Johns Hopkins Univ. Press, 1996.

———. "The Legacy of Daniel Boone: Three Generations of Boones and the History of Indian-White Relations." *The Register of the Kentucky Historical Society* 95 (1997): 219–35.

Audubon, John James. *Delineations of American Scenery and Character,* 1926. Reprint, New York: Arno, 1970.

———. *Ornithological Biography.* 5 vols. Edinburgh: A. Black, 1831–1839.

Audubon, Maria R. *Audubon and His Journals.* 2 vols. 1897. Reprint, New York: Dover, 1960.

*Bakeless, John. *Daniel Boone: Master of the Wilderness.* 1939. Reprint, Harrisburg, Penn.: Stackpole, 1965.

Bancroft, George. *The History of the United States from the Discovery of the American Continent.* 10 vols. Boston: Little Brown, 1834–1875.

Beard, Dan. *Hardly a Man Is Now Alive: The Autobiography of Dan Beard.* New York: Doubleday, 1939.

Beckner, Lucien. "John Findley: The First Pathfinder of Kentucky." *The Filson Club History Quarterly* 1, no. 3 (1927): 111–22.

Belue, Ted Franklin. "Did Daniel Boone Kill Pompey, the Black Shawnee, at the 1778 Siege of Boonesborough?" *The Filson Club History Quarterly* 67 (1993): 5–22.

———. "Terror in the Canelands: The Fate of Daniel Boone's Salt Boilers." *The Filson Club History Quarterly* 68 (1994): 3–34.

Bodley, Temple. *George Rogers Clark: His Life and Public Services.* New York: Houghton Mifflin, 1926.

———. *History of Kentucky.* 4 vols. Chicago: S.J. Clarke, 1928.

Bogart, William H. *Daniel Boone and the Hunters of Kentucky.* New York: Miller, Orton, 1857.

Boone, James. "Family Records" in his diary. North Carolina State Archives (PC 343.1).

Boone Pioneer Echoes. (Various issues published by the Boone Family Research Association, Kansas City, Missouri.)

Bradford, John. *John Bradford's Historical &c. Notes on Kentucky, from the Western Miscellany.* Compiled by G.W. Stipp. 1827. Reprint. San Francisco: Grabhorn Press, 1932.

Brown, William Dodd, ed. "The Capture of Daniel Boone's Saltmakers: Fresh Perspectives from Primary Sources." *The Register of the Kentucky Historical Society* 83 (1985): 1–19.

Bruce, Henry Addington. *Daniel Boone and the Wilderness Road.* New York: Macmillan, 1910.

Bryan, Daniel. *The Mountain Muse: Comprising the Adventures of Daniel Boone; and the Powers of Virtuous and Refined Beauty.* Harrisonburg, Va.: Davidson & Bourne, 1813.

Bryan, William S. and Robert Rose. *A History of the Pioneer Families of Missouri.* St. Louis: Bryan, Brand, 1876.

Burnett, Peter H. *Recollections and Opinions of an Old Pioneer.* New York: Appleton, 1880.

Bushnell, David I., Jr. "Daniel Boone at Limestone, 1786–1787." *Virginia Magazine of History and Biography* 25 (Jan. 1917): 1–11.

Byrd, William. *William Byrd's Histories of the Dividing Line betwixt Virginia and North Carolina.* Edited by William K. Boyd. 1929. Reprint with additions, New York: Dover, 1967.

Byron, Lord George Gordon. *Byron's Don Juan: A Variorum Edition.* Edited by T.G. Steffan and Willis W. Pratt, 3: 143–45. Austin, Tex.: Univ. of Texas Press, 1957.

Clark, Jerry E. *The Shawnee.* Lexington, Ky.: Univ. Press of Kentucky, 1977.

Clark, Thomas D. *Frontier America: The Story of the Westward Movement.* New York: Scribner's, 1959.

———. *A History of Kentucky.* New York: Prentice-Hall, 1937.

———. *Kentucky, Land of Contrast.* New York: Harper & Row, 1968.

———. *Simon Kenton, Kentucky Scout.* New York: Farrar & Rinehart, 1943.

Clark, Walter. *The Colony of Transylvania*. Raleigh, N.C.: E.M. Uzzell, 1903. Contains the "Journal" of Richard Henderson. See "Henderson, Richard" below.

Cook, Roy Bird. "Daniel Boone in the Kanawha Valley." *Boone Pioneer Echoes* (Boone Family Research Association) 23, no.1 (Jan. 1981): 1, 3–7.

Cooper, James Fenimore. *The Prairie: A Tale*. 1827. Reprint, Albany, N.Y.: SUNY Press, 1985.

Douglass, William Boone. "The Ancestry and Boyhood of Daniel Boone." *Kentucky School Journal* 13 (1934): 13–19, 63.

*Draper, Lyman Copeland. *The Life of Daniel Boone*. Edited by Ted Franklin Belue. Mechanicsburg, Penn.: Stackpole, 1998.

*———. Manuscript Collection. State Historical Society of Wisconsin, Madison, Wisc.

Durrett, Reuben T. *John Filson, the First Historian of Kentucky*. Louisville, Ky.: The Filson Club, 1884.

———. *Manuscript Collection*. Joseph Regenstein Library, University of Chicago.

———, ed. *Bryant's Station*. Louisville, Ky.: J.P. Morton, 1897.

Elliott, Lawrence. *The Long Hunter: A New Life of Daniel Boone*. New York: Reader's Digest Press, 1976.

*Faragher, John Mack. *Daniel Boone: The Life and Legend of an American Pioneer*. New York: Holt, 1992.

———. "They May Say What They Please: Daniel Boone and the Evidence." *The Register of the Kentucky Historical Society* 88 (1990): 373–93.

*Filson, John. *The Discovery, Settlement And present State of Kentucke: . . . To which is added . . . I. The Adventures of Col*. Daniel Boon . . . 1784. Reprint, Fairfield, Wash.: Galleon Press, 2001.

Fitzgerald, John. *A Peaceable Pilgrimage: Quaker Migration and the Creation of Leesburg, Ohio, Highland County, and Southwestern Ohio, 1775–1820*. Leesburg, Ohio: Frederick Press, 2002.

*Flint, Timothy. *Biographical Memoir of Daniel Boone*. 1833. Reprint, New Haven, Conn.: College and University Press, 1967.

———. *Indian Wars of the West*. Cincinnati: E.H. Flint, 1833.

———. *Recollections of the Last Ten Years, Passed in Occasional Residences and Journeyings in the Valley of the Mississippi*. 1826. Reprint, New York: Da Capo Press, 1968.

Franklin, Benjamin. *Benjamin Franklin's Autobiography*. Edited by J.A. Leo Lemay and Paul M. Zall. New York: Norton, 1986.

French, Benjamin Franklin. *Biographia Americana; or a Historical and Critical Account of the Lives, Actions, and Writings of the Most Distinguished Persons in North America; . . .* New York: D. Mallory, 1825.

Fretwell, Mark E. "Daniel Boone in Florida." *Escribano* 12, no.3 (1975): 100–111.

Friend, Craig T., ed. *The Buzzel About Kentuck: Settling the Promised Land*. Lexington, Ky.: Univ. Press of Kentucky, 1999.

Hall, James. *Legends of the West*. Philadelphia: H. Hall, 1832.

———. *Sketches of History, Life, and Manners in the West*. Cincinnati: Hubbard and Edwards,1834.

Hammon, Neal O. "Early Roads into Kentucky." *The Register of the Kentucky Historical Society* 68 (1970): 91–131.

————. "The First Trip to Boonesborough." *The Filson Club History Quarterly* 45 (1971): 249–63.

————. "John Filson's Error." *The Filson Club History Quarterly* 59 (1985): 462–63.

————. "Land Acquisition on the Kentucky Frontier." *The Register of the Kentucky Historical Society* 78 (1980): 297–321.

————. "The Legend of Daniel Boone's Cabin." *The Filson Club History Quarterly* 48 (1974): 241–52.

————. "Pioneers in Kentucky, 1773–1775." *The Filson Club History Quarterly* 55 (1981): 268–83.

Harding, Chester. *My Egotistigraphy.* Cambridge, Mass.: John Wilson Press, 1866.

Harrison, Lowell H., and James C. Klotter. *A New History of Kentucky.* Lexington, Ky.: Univ. Press of Kentucky, 1997.

Henderson, A. Gwynn. "Dispelling the Myth: Seventeenth- and Eighteenth-Century Indian Life in Kentucky." *The Register of the Kentucky Historical Society* 90 (1992): 1–25.

Henderson, Archibald. Daniel Boone Papers, North Carolina Collection and Southern Historical Collection, University of North Carolina, Chapel Hill.

————. "Richard Henderson and the Occupation of Kentucky, 1775." *Mississippi Valley Historical Review* 1 (1914): 341–63.

————. *The Transylvania Company and the Founding of Henderson, Ky.* Henderson, Ky.: n.p., 1929.

Henderson, Richard. "Journal of Richard Henderson Relating to the Transylvania Colony" in Walter Clark, *The Colony of Transylvania,* 12-31.

Hendricks, Walter H. "Daniel Boone as a Virginian." *Bulletin of the Historical Society of Washington County, Virginia* 24 (1987): 1–8.

Hening, William W. *The Statutes at Large; Being a Collection of All the Laws of Virginia, from the First Session of the Legislature in the year 1619.* Vol. 10. Richmond, Va.: George Cochran, 1822.

Herrick, Francis Hobart. *Audubon the Naturalist: A History of His Life and Time.* 1917. Reprint, New York: Dover, 1968.

*Houston, Peter. *A Sketch of the Life and Character of Daniel Boone.* Edited by Ted Franklin Belue. Mechanicsburg, Penn., 1997.

Hurt, R. Douglas. *Nathan Boone and the American Frontier.* Columbia, Mo.: Univ. of Missouri Press, 1998.

Imlay, Gilbert. *A Topographical Description of the Western Territory of North America. . . .* London: J. Debrett, 1793; Dublin: William Jones, 1793; New York: Samuel Campbell, 1793; London: J. Debrett, 1797. A reprint of the 1797 edition has been published (New York: Johnson Reprint Corp., 1968).

Irvin, Helen Deiss. *Women in Kentucky.* Lexington, Ky.: Univ. Press of Kentucky, 1979.

*Jillson, Willard Rouse. *The Boone Narrative.* Louisville, Ky.: Standard Printing, 1932.

————. *Filson's Kentucke. . . .* Louisville, Ky.: J.P. Morton, 1930.

————. *The Kentucky Land Grants.* Louisville, Ky.: Standard Printing, 1925.

————. *Old Kentucky Entries and Deeds.* Louisville, Ky.: Standard Printing, 1926.

————. *Pioneer Kentucky.* Frankfort, Ky.: State Journal, 1934.

————. *Tales of the Dark and Bloody Ground.* Louisville, Ky.: C.T. Dearing, 1930.

Kellogg, Louise P., ed. *Frontier Advance on the Upper Ohio, 1778–1779.* Madison, Wisc.: The Society, 1916.

————. *Frontier Retreat on the Upper Ohio, 1779–1781.* Madison, Wisc.: The Society, 1917.

Kenton, Edna. *Simon Kenton: His Life and Period, 1755–1836.* Garden City, N.Y.: Doubleday, 1930.

Kilpatrick, Lewis H. "The Journal of William Calk, Kentucky Pioneer." *Mississippi Valley Historical Review* 7 (1920–1921): 363–67.

Kincaid, Robert Lee. *The Wilderness Road.* Indianapolis, Ind.: Bobbs-Merrill, 1947.

Laidley, W.S. "Daniel Boone in the Kanawha Valley." *The Register of the Kentucky Historical Society* 2 (1913): 9–12.

Lester, William S. *The Transylvania Company.* Spencer, Ind.: S.R. Guard, 1935.

Lewis, Meriwether, and William Clark. *Original Journals of the Lewis and Clark Expedition, 1804–1806.* Edited by Reuben Gold Thwaites. 8 vols. 1904–1905. Reprint, New York: Antiquarian Press, 1959. See also *The Journals of the Lewis and Clark Expedition.* Edited by Gary E. Moulton. 13 vols. Lincoln: Univ. of Nebraska Press, 1983–2002.

Lewis, Virgil A. *History of the Battle of Point Pleasant.* Charleston, W. Va.: Tribune Printing, 1909.

Lipton, Leah. "Chester Harding and the Life Portraits of Daniel Boone." *American Art Journal* 16, no. 3 (1984): 4–19.

————. *A Truthful Likeness: Chester Harding and His Portraits.* Pp. 42, 55–59. Washington, D.C.: National Portrait Gallery, 1985.

Lofaro, Michael A. "The Eighteenth-Century 'Autobiographies' of Daniel Boone." *The Register of the Kentucky Historical Society* 76 (1978): 85–97.

————. "From Boone to Crockett: The Beginnings of Frontier Humor." *Mississippi Folklore Register* 14 (1980): 57–74.

*————. "The Genesis of the Biographical Image of Daniel Boone." Ph.D. diss., University of Maryland, 1975.

————. *The Life and Adventures of Daniel Boone.* Lexington, Ky., 1978. Reprinted with slight additions, 1986.

————. "Tracking Daniel Boone: The Changing Frontier in American Life." *The Register of the Kentucky Historical Society* 82 (1984): 321–33.

Lucas, Marion. "African Americans on the Kentucky Frontier." *The Register of the Kentucky Historical Society* 95 (1997): 121–34.

Marshall, Humphrey. *The History of Kentucky.* Frankfort, Ky.: n.p., 1812.

McCarthy, Koren P. "Daniel Boone: The Formative Years." *Pennsylvania Heritage* 11 (1985): 34–37.

McClung, John A. *Sketches of Western Adventure: Containing an Account of the Most Interesting Incidents Connected with the Settlement of the West. . . .* Maysville, Ky.: L. Collins, 1832.

Metcalf, Samuel L. *A Collection of Some of the Most Interesting Narratives of Indian Warfare in the West.* Lexington, Ky.: W.G. Hunt, 1821.

*Miner, William Harvey. *Daniel Boone: Contribution toward a Bibliography of Writings concerning Daniel Boone.* 1901. Reprint, New York: B. Franklin, 1970.

Moize, Elizabeth A. "Daniel Boone: First Hero of the Frontier." *National Geographic* 168 (1985): 812–41.

Moore, Arthur K. *The Frontier Mind: A Cultural Analysis of the Kentucky Frontiersman.* Lexington, Ky.: Univ. of Kentucky Press, 1957.

*My Father, Daniel Boone: The Draper Interviews with Nathan Boone. Edited by Neal O. Hammon. Lexington, Ky.: Univ. Press of Kentucky, 1999.

Nickell, Joe and John F. Fischer. "Daniel Boone Fakelore." The Filson Club History Quarterly 62 (1988): 442–66.

North Carolina. The Colonial Records of North Carolina. Vol. IX: 1771–1775. Edited by William L. Saunders. Raleigh, N.C.: Josephus Daniels, Printer to the State, 1890.

O'Hara, Theodore. "The Old Pioneer, Daniel Boone." In Theodore O'Hara: Poet-Soldier of the Old South, by Nathaniel Cheairs Hughes and Thomas Clayton Wire, 58–59. Knoxville, Tenn.: Univ. of Tennessee Press, 1998.

Peck, John Mason. Forty Years of Pioneer Life: Memoir of John Mason Peck, D.D. 1864. Reprint, Carbondale, Ill.: Southern Illinois Univ. Press, 1965.

*———. Life of Daniel Boone, the Pioneer of Kentucky. 1847. Reprinted in The Makers of American History. New York: The University Society, 1904.

Pennsylvania Archives, 1st series (Philadelphia, 1852), I.

Phillips, Paul C. "American Opinions Regarding the West, 1778–1783." Proceedings of the Mississippi Valley Historical Association for the Year 1913–1914 7 (1914): [286]-305.

Ranck, George W. Boonesborough: Its Founding, Pioneer Struggles, Indian Experiences, Transylvania Days, and Revolutionary Annals. Louisville, Ky.: John P. Morton, 1901.

Rice, Otis K. Frontier Kentucky. Lexington, Ky.: Univ. Press of Kentucky, 1975.

Robertson, James Rood, ed. Petitions of the Early Inhabitants of Kentucky to the General Assembly of Virginia, 1769–1792. Louisville, Ky.: John P. Morton, 1914.

Rohrbough, Malcolm J. "The Art of Nostalgia: Bingham, Boone, and the Developing West." Gateway Heritage 11, no.2 (1990): 4–19.

———. The Land Office Business: The Settlement and Administration of American Public Lands, 1789–1837. New York: Oxford Univ. Press, 1968.

———. The Trans-Appalachian Frontier: People, Societies, and Institutions, 1775–1850. New York: Oxford Univ. Press, 1978.

Rowan County, North Carolina. Minutes, Court of Pleas and Quarter Sessions, 1753–1868. Book 3 (1768–1772). Raleigh, North Carolina Department of Archives and History.

Seelye, John. "Captives, Captains, Cowboys, Indians: Frames of Reference and the American West." American Literary History 7 (1995): 304–19.

Simms, William Gilmore. "Daniel Boon; The First Hunter of Kentucky." Southern and Western Magazine and Review 1 (April 1845): 225–42.

———. Views and Reviews in American Literature, History and Fiction. New York: Wiley and Putnam, 1845. Reprints the "Daniel Boon" article listed above.

*Slotkin, Richard. "Emergence of a Myth: John Filson's 'Daniel Boone Narrative' and the Literature of the Indian Wars, 1638–1848." Ph.D. diss., Brown University, 1967.

———. Regeneration through Violence: The Mythology of the American Frontier, 1600–1860. Middletown, Conn.: Wesleyan Univ. Press, 1973.

Smith, Henry Nash. Virgin Land: The American West as Symbol and Myth. 1950. Reprint, Cambridge, Mass.: Harvard Univ. Press, 1970.

Smith, James. An Account of the Remarkable Occurrences in the Life and Travels of Col. James Smith during His Captivity with the Indians. 1799. Reprint, New York: Garland, 1979.

Speed, Thomas. *The Wilderness Road.* Louisville, Ky.: J.P. Morton, 1886.
Spraker, Ella Hazel A. *The Boone Family.* Rutland, Vt.: Tuttle, 1922.
St. Louis Mercantile Library Association, Manuscript Collection, University of Missouri, St. Louis, Mo.
Staples, Charles R. *The History of Pioneer Lexington, 1779–1806.* 1939. Reprint, Lexington, Ky.: Univ. Press of Kentucky, 1996.
Stoudt, John Joseph. "Daniel and Squire Boone—A Study in Historical Symbolism." *Pennsylvania History* 3 (1936): 27–40.
Sugden, John. *Blue Jacket: Warrior of the Shawnees.* Lincoln: Univ. of Nebraska Press, 2002.
Sweeney, J. Gray. *The Columbus of the Woods: Daniel Boone and the Typology of Manifest Destiny.* St. Louis: Washington Univ. Gallery of Art, 1992.
Thatcher, Benjamin Bussey. *Tales of the Indians, Being Prominent Passages of the History of the North American Natives.* Boston: Waitt & Dow, 1831.
*Thwaites, Reuben Gold. *Daniel Boone.* New York: Appleton, 1902.
———. and Louise P. Kellogg, eds. *Documentary History of Dunmore's War, 1774.* Madison, Wisc.: Wisconsin Historical Society, 1905.
———. and Louise P. Kellogg, eds. *Frontier Defense on the Upper Ohio, 1777–1778.* Madison, Wisc.: Wisconsin Historical Society, 1912.
———. and Louise P. Kellogg, eds. *The Revolution on the Upper Ohio, 1775–1777.* Madison, Wisc.: Wisconsin Historical Society, 1908.
Trabue, Daniel. *Westward into Kentucky: The Narrative of Daniel Trabue.* Edited by Chester Raymond Young. Lexington, Ky.: Univ. Press of Kentucky, 1981.
*Trumbull, John. *The Adventures of Colonel Daniel Boon . . . 1786.* Reprint, New York: Garland, 1978. First published in his newspaper in 1785.
Turner, Frederick Jackson. *The Frontier in American History.* 1920. Reprint, New York: Holt, 1962.
Van Noppen, John James, and Ina Woestemeyer Van Noppen. *Daniel Boone, Backwoodsman: The Green Woods Were His Portion.* Boone, N.C.: Appalachian Press, 1966.
Virginia. *Calendar of Virginia State Papers and Other Manuscripts: . . . Preserved in the Capitol at Richmond.* Vols. 3 and 5. Richmond, Va.: R.F. Walker, 1875–93.
Virginia Council of State. *Journals of the Council of the State of Virginia.* Richmond, Va.: Division of Purchase and Printery, 1931–.
Walker, Felix. "Narrative of an Adventure in Kentucky in the Year 1775." *DeBow's Review* 16 (February 1854): 150–56.
———. "Memoirs of a Southern Congressman Ranging the Borderlands with Daniel Boone." *Journal of American History* 1 (1907): 49–60.
Wall, James W., Flossie Martin, and Howell Boone. *The Squire, Daniel, and John Boone Families in Davie County, North Carolina.* Mocksville, N.C.: Davie County Public Library, 1982.
Waller, George M. *American Revolution in the West.* Chicago: Nelson-Hall, 1976.
Walton, John. "Ghost Writer to Daniel Boone." *American Heritage* 6 (Oct. 1955): 10–13.
———. *John Filson of Kentucke.* Lexington, Ky.: Univ. Press of Kentucky, 1956.
*Wilder, C. *Life and Adventures of Colonel Daniel Boon . . . 1823.* Reprint, New York: n.p., 1916.

Williams, William Carlos. *In the American Grain.* 1925. Reprint, New York: New Directions, 1956.

Wright, Louis B. *Culture on the Moving Frontier.* Bloomington, Ind.: Indiana Univ. Press, 1955.

Wyllie, John Cook. "Daniel Boone's Adventures in Charlottesville in 1781: Some Incidents Connected with Tarleton's Raid." *Albemarle County Historical Society* 19 (1960–1961 [issued 1963]): 5–18.

INDEX

PARTIAL GENEALOGY OF
The Boone Family
prepared with the assistance
of Louis R. Boone

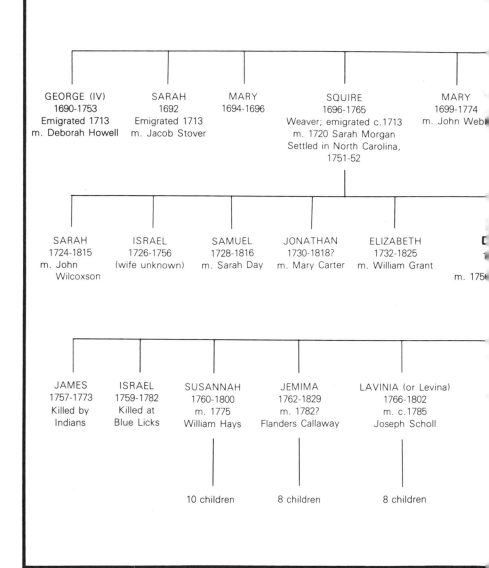

GEORGE (IV)
1690-1753
Emigrated 1713
m. Deborah Howell

SARAH
1692
Emigrated 1713
m. Jacob Stover

MARY
1694-1696

SQUIRE
1696-1765
Weaver; emigrated c.1713
m. 1720 Sarah Morgan
Settled in North Carolina,
1751-52

MARY
1699-1774
m. John Webb

SARAH
1724-1815
m. John
Wilcoxson

ISRAEL
1726-1756
(wife unknown)

SAMUEL
1728-1816
m. Sarah Day

JONATHAN
1730-1818?
m. Mary Carter

ELIZABETH
1732-1825
m. William Grant

m. 1756

JAMES
1757-1773
Killed by
Indians

ISRAEL
1759-1782
Killed at
Blue Licks

SUSANNAH
1760-1800
m. 1775
William Hays

JEMIMA
1762-1829
m. 1782?
Flanders Callaway

LAVINIA (or Levina)
1766-1802
m. c.1785
Joseph Scholl

10 children

8 children

8 children